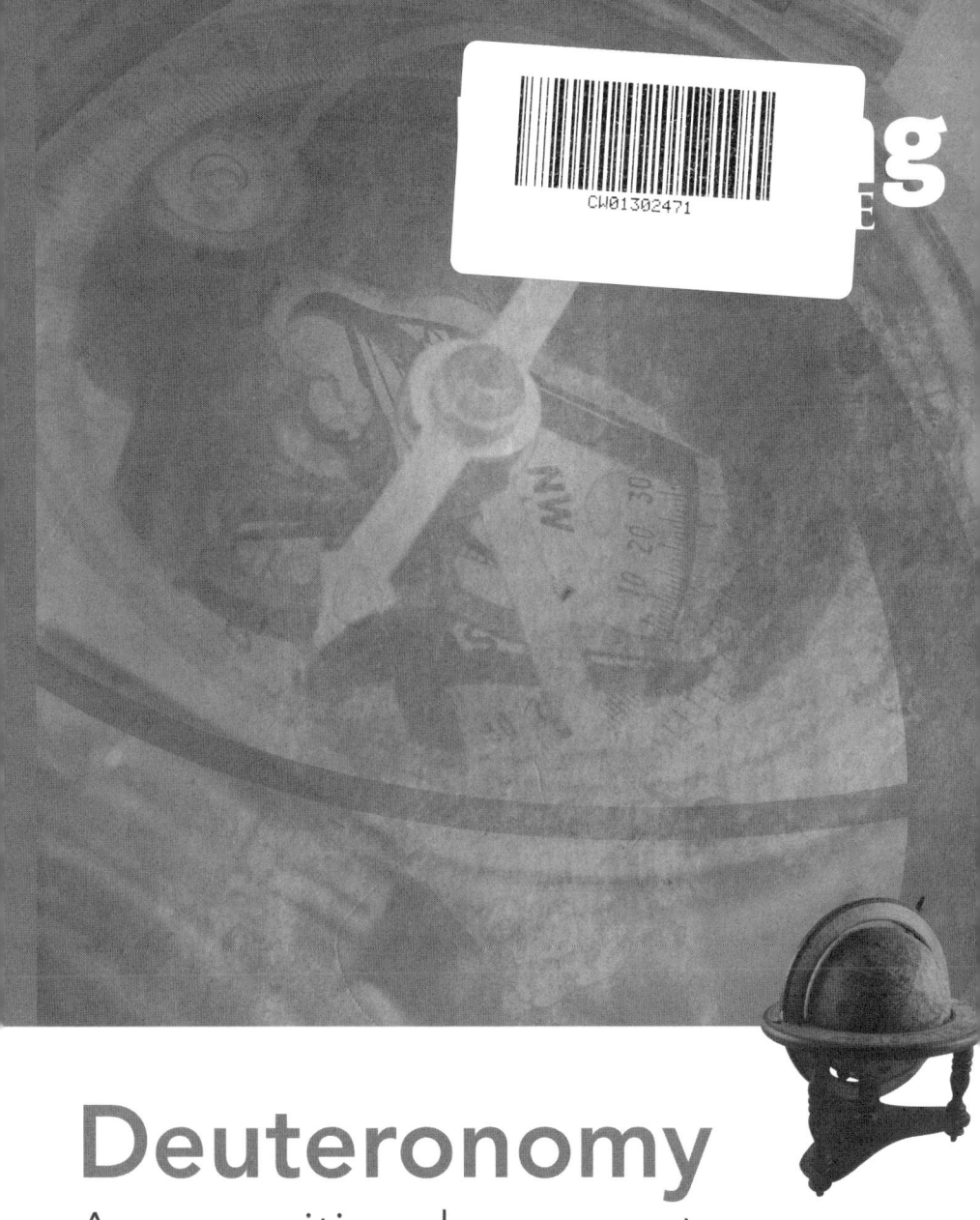

Deuteronomy
An expositional commentary

Paul E Brown

DayOne

© Day One Publications 2008
First printed 2008

ISBN 978–1–84625–112–2

Unless otherwise indicated, Scripture quotations are from **The Holy Bible, English Standard Version** (**ESV**), copyright © 2001 by Crossway Bibles, a division of Good News Publishers. Used by permission. All rights reserved.

British Library Cataloguing in Publication Data available

Published by Day One Publications
Ryelands Road, Leominster, HR6 8NZ
☎ 01568 613 740 FAX 01568 611 473
email—sales@dayone.co.uk
web site—www.dayone.co.uk
North America—email—usasales@dayone.co.uk

All rights reserved
No part of this publication may be reproduced, or stored in a retrieval system, or transmitted, in any form or by any means, mechanical, electronic, photocopying, recording or otherwise, without the prior permission of Day One Publications.

Cover design by Wayne McMaster
Printed by Gutenberg Press, Malta

Appreciations

Paul Brown reliably steers the reader through the often-alien landscape of Deuteronomy with clarity and level-headedness. His application to the Christian life, in the reformed tradition of exegesis, is judicious, never fanciful, and pastorally helpful. There is material here to aid both private study and Bible teaching.

Dr David Green, Lecturer in Hebrew, London Theological Seminary

We are familiar with the importance of Deuteronomy in providing an understanding of the covenantal unity of the whole Bible, but the message of the book is also pastoral and evangelistic, close to the very heartbeat of the Scriptures. Deuteronomy is to the Old Testament what the book of Romans is to the New Testament. It deals with many of the central themes that rise up in the remainder of the Bible. To understand the Psalms, Writings and Prophets you must come to grips with Deuteronomy. To know God's greatness, his grace, redemption and love we need to study the mighty sermons of Moses in this book.

Paul Brown is our inspiring guide in this commentary. He gives us access to these chapters, unerringly selecting the focus of the chief sermons, verses, paragraphs and chapters, showing their relevance for New Covenantal living. The commentary is concise, and yet it deals in some depth with key themes and topics. Charles Haddon Spurgeon in his summary of the best commentaries on the books of the Bible was saddened at the paucity of those on Deuteronomy. He muttered, 'So few expositions have been written upon Deuteronomy alone the reader would do well to use the commentaries upon the Pentateuch and the whole Old Testament.' He could commend Calvin ('everything that Calvin wrote by way of exposition is priceless') and one other commentary by a man named Cumming, and his three epithets on that work sweetly apply to Paul Brown's book: 'Pretty, popular and profitable.' May many be helped by it to know and adore the God of Deuteronomy, Moses' great Lord.

Rev. Geoff Thomas, pastor of Alfred Place Baptist Church, Aberystwyth and internationally-known author and preacher

Dedication

Dedication

To the congregation of Dunstable Baptist Church, who first heard in sermon form most of the exposition found here.

Acknowledgements

I am grateful to Dr David Green, who read the whole manuscript, for his helpful comments and suggestions; also to Suzanne Mitchell of Day One for her editorial work; and to my wife, Mary, for her constant support and encouragement.

William Tyndale on Deuteronomy

This is a book worthy to be read in day and night and never to be out of hands. For it is the most excellent of all the books of Moses. It is easy also and light and a very pure gospel that is to wete [know], a preaching of faith and love: deducing the love to God out of faith, and the love of a man's neighbour out of the love of God. Herein also thou mayst learn right meditation or contemplation, which is nothing else save the calling to mind and a repeating in the heart of the glorious and wonderful deeds of God, and of his terrible handling of his enemies and merciful entreating of them that come when he calleth them, which thing this book doeth and almost nothing else.

(The first paragraph of William Tyndale's Prologue to his translation of Deuteronomy.)

Contents

INTRODUCTION **10**

SECTION 1: INTRODUCTORY: MOSES RECOUNTS THE STORY OF ISRAEL IN THE WILDERNESS (1:1–4:43) **13**

1 ISRAEL REFUSES TO ENTER CANAAN (1:1–46) **14**

2 ISRAEL SETS OUT FOR CANAAN AGAIN (2:1–37) **22**

3 CONSOLIDATING THE GAINS (3:1–29) **29**

4 LAWS FOR THE LAND (4:1–14) **35**

5 LIVING BEFORE THE LIVING GOD (4:15–43) **41**

SECTION 2: MOSES GIVES ISRAEL LAWS AND INSTRUCTIONS (4:44–26:19) **48**

6 THE LAW SUMMARIZED IN THE TEN COMMANDMENTS (4:44–5:21) **49**

7 CONTINUATION OF THE TEN COMMANDMENTS (5:16–33) **58**

8 THE HEART OF THE LAW: LOVE FOR GOD (6:1–25) **66**

9 CHOSEN TO BE DISTINCTIVE (7:1–26) **74**

10 BLESS THE LORD—AND TAKE CARE! (8:1–20) **82**

11 A STUBBORN PEOPLE CHOSEN BY GRACE (9:1–12) **89**

12 A REBELLIOUS PEOPLE SPARED BY GRACE (9:13–10:11) **94**

13 WHAT THE LORD REQUIRES (10:12–11:7) **101**

14 LIVING IN DEPENDENCE UPON GOD (11:8–32) **106**

15 THE PLACE WHERE GOD CHOOSES TO PUT HIS NAME (12:1–32) **111**

16 HOLD FAST TO THE LORD (13:1–18) **119**

17 LIVE AS HOLY SONS OF GOD (14:1–29) **124**

18 CARE IN THE COMMUNITY (15:1–23) **129**

6 Exploring Deuteronomy

Contents

- **19** THREE APPOINTED FEASTS (16:1–17) **136**
- **20** THE GOVERNING AUTHORITIES (16:18–17:20) **142**
- **21** THE APPOINTED MINISTERS (18:1–22) **148**
- **22** REMOVING EVIL FROM THE LAND (19:1–21) **152**
- **23** WAR AND PEACE (20:1–20) **157**
- **24** PROTECTION IN THE LAND (21:1–23) **163**
- **25** LAWS FOR THE GOOD OF SOCIETY AND LAWS UPHOLDING MARRIAGE (22:1–30) **168**
- **26** THE ASSEMBLY, THE CAMP, AND OTHERS (23:1–25) **176**
- **27** LAWS AND PRINCIPLES FOR A GODLY LIFE (24:1–22) **181**
- **28** DOING JUSTLY (25:1–19) **187**
- **29** THANKSGIVING AND COVENANT PROMISES (26:1–19) **191**

SECTION 3: CURSES FOR DISOBEDIENCE, BLESSINGS FOR OBEDIENCE (27:1–30:20) 195

- **30** STONES, MOUNTAINS AND CURSES (27:1–26) **196**
- **31** THE BLESSINGS OF OBEDIENCE (28:1–14) **202**
- **32** THE CONSEQUENCES OF DISOBEDIENCE (28:15–68) **207**
- **33** COVENANT RENEWAL IN MOAB (29:1–29) **213**
- **34** A MATTER OF LIFE OR DEATH (30.1–20) **220**

SECTION 4: MOSES SUCCEEDED BY JOSHUA (31:1–34:12) 226

- **35** MOSES LOOKS TO THE FUTURE (31:1–29) **227**
- **36** THE SONG OF MOSES (31:30–32:52) **234**
- **37** THE LAST WORDS OF MOSES (33:1–29) **240**

Contents

38 THE DEATH OF MOSES (34:1–12) **245**

SELECT BIBLIOGRAPHY

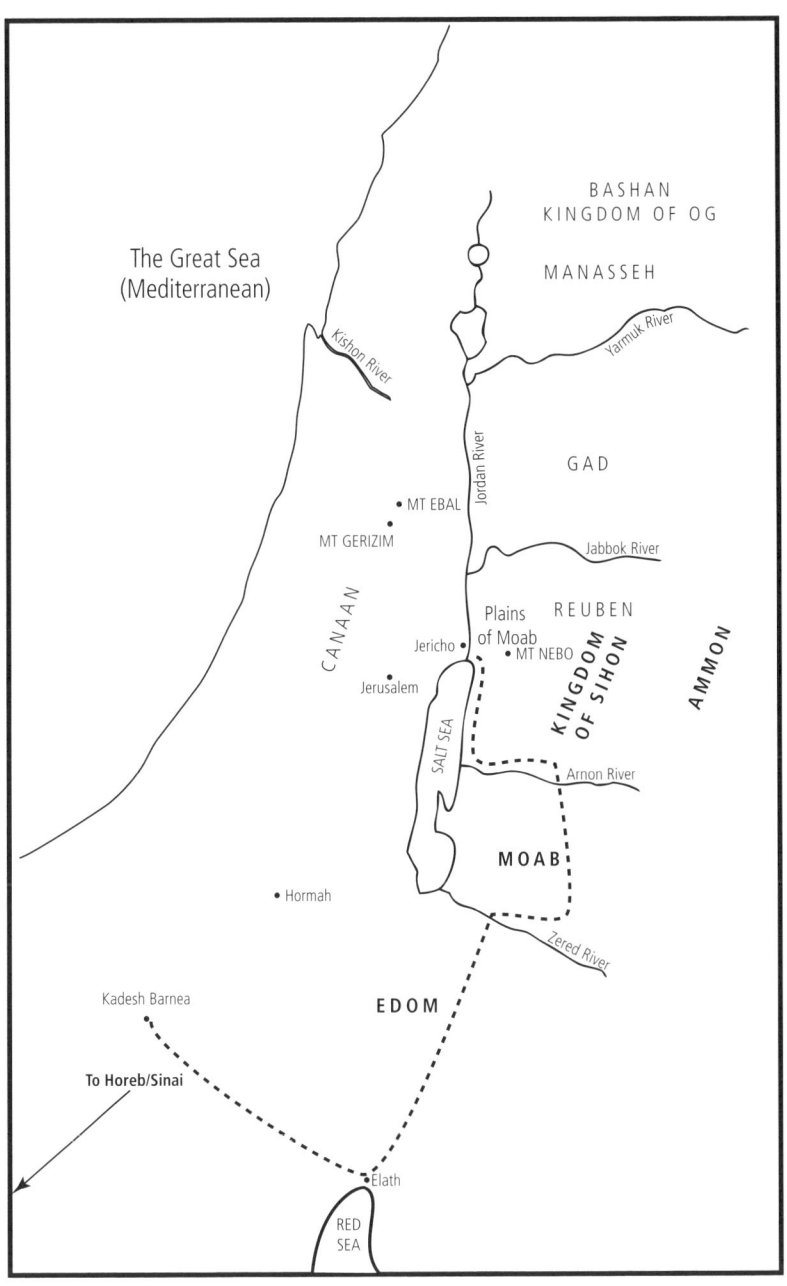

Exploring Deuteronomy 9

Introduction

This book has a threefold purpose: to encourage the reading of Deuteronomy; to give some help in understanding it, especially to those not very familiar with its pages; and to stimulate further prayerful thought about all it says. I have tried to face problems and to attempt answers. I have also tried to show the relevance of the instructions given to Israel to the present day. Though there are obvious differences between those times and today and care needs to be taken in application, there is great wisdom to be found in the book. Here are basic principles for godly living, for good behaviour and social relationships.

After wandering for thirty-eight years in the wilderness of Sinai because of their disobedience to the LORD, the Israelites had reached the northern end of the Dead Sea, where they camped in the plains of Moab. On the last part of their journey they had travelled north from the branch of the Red Sea known as the Gulf of Aqaba, going around Edom and Moab to their present position. They had already captured the region of Gilead on the east side of the northern Dead Sea and Jordan, and this territory had been given to Reuben and Gad and part of the tribe of Manasseh. The time had now come for Israel to cross the Jordan into Canaan proper and to begin the conquest of the promised land.

Deuteronomy consists mainly of two addresses given by Moses in the plains of Moab. The first of these runs from 1:1 to 4:40, and the second is introduced in 4:44, begins in 5:1 and runs to 28:68. Chapters 29 to 33 are very closely linked to what has gone before, and the final chapter records the death of Moses. Moses encourages the people to obey the LORD by crossing the Jordan and entering the land, unlike on the previous occasion when they stood on the edge of Canaan (Numbers 13–14). He sets before them the law with instructions for living in the land, promising blessing for obedience but warning against disobedience.

Deuteronomy means 'second law'. The name comes from the Greek

10 Exploring Deuteronomy

translation of the Old Testament (known as the Septuagint, LXX for short) where at 17:18 'a copy of this law' was rendered 'second law'. As a title it is not inapt, in that in this book we find Moses repeating the Ten Commandments to a new generation. In the Hebrew Old Testament the title is simply 'these are the words', which is the opening phrase.

Deuteronomy is arguably the key book in the Old Testament. It sets out the covenant relationship between the LORD and Israel.[1] This relationship is based on the love of the LORD who chose Israel to be his own treasured possession. At the heart of the response that Israel is to make is love for the LORD its God, a love which is to express itself in keeping his commandments and holding fast to him. In so doing Israel will be a witness to the nations of the greatness and goodness of the LORD, showing that his commands are wise and right.

In what we call the historical books of the Old Testament (the Hebrew Bible calls them the 'Former Prophets'), Israel's conduct and fortunes are measured against the standards set out in Deuteronomy. In the reign of Josiah the 'Book of the Law' was discovered in the temple; this was probably Deuteronomy, though it could be the whole Pentateuch (i.e. the first five books, known collectively as 'the Law'). This led to reform, though it was only partial and short lived. The rebukes of the prophets and their calls to repentance were also based on Israel's departure from the ways of God as revealed in Deuteronomy.

Deuteronomy also completes the first five books of the Bible, as well as completing the life and ministry of Moses, who wrote them. Moses had an amazing ministry, yet because he acted precipitately he, like Israel, spent forty years in the desert before he was called to lead the nation out of Egypt. Then, towards the end of the journey, he publicly dishonoured the LORD before the people and so was not permitted to enter the land. His deep sorrow at this is a sub-plot in Deuteronomy.

Though we look primarily to Leviticus to understand the regulations concerning the priesthood and sacrifices, Deuteronomy, with the Ten

Introduction

Commandments at its heart, sets out the laws and instructions for Israel to live as God's people in the land he is going to give them. Some writers see each of the Ten Commandments expounded throughout these chapters. This is certainly so in a general way, but some parts of the legislative material are not easy to fit into any pattern.

Deuteronomy is attributed to Moses within the book itself (31:24) and elsewhere in the Old Testament (e.g. 1 Kings 2:3; Ezra 3:2). We find the same in the New Testament (e.g. Matthew 19:7–8; Acts 3:22; Romans 10:19). As Merrill says, 'There can be no doubt that the prophets, Jesus, and the apostles concurred with the witness of Deuteronomy about its authorship.'[2] It is likely that in a few places small additions were made under the guidance of the Holy Spirit, particularly the account of Moses' death in the last chapter.

Deuteronomy is part of God's Word; it is a book for all time and, though addressed to Israel in the first place, for all peoples. In its emphasis on the grace of God, the covenant relationship between God and his people, and love for God as the true response to that grace, it is always up to date and relevant. As it speaks of the brotherhood of God's people, the laws that God has given and the joy of worship, it has timely truths for the church today. Though Israel's future failure shadows its pages and the death of Moses reminds us that the greatest of men have their faults, it points forward to a greater than Moses and the ultimate fulfilment of its promises in 'a land that is fairer than day'.

Notes

1 For more about the covenant background of Deuteronomy see **John Currid**, 'Introductory matters', *Deuteronomy* (Darlington: Evangelical Press, 2006), p. 13.
2 **Eugene Merrill,** *Deuteronomy* (The New American Commentary) (Nashville, TN: Broadman and Holman Publishers, 1994), p. 22.

Section 1:

Introductory: Moses recounts the story of Israel in the wilderness (1:1–4:43)

Chapter 1

Israel refuses to enter Canaan (1:1–46)

Moses speaks to the people of Israel, who are assembled on the eastern side of the river Jordan, in sight of the land of promise. He begins by reminding them of the last time the nation stood on its borders, for the same opportunity that then faced their fathers, and the same possibility of refusal, now faces them.

Location, location, location (vv. 1–8)

The first verse carefully locates where the people of Israel are at this time, also described in the last verse of Numbers (36:13) as 'in the plains of Moab by the Jordan at Jericho' (see also Deuteronomy 1:5). The point is that God had brought them back to the border of the land of Canaan. This was a place of opportunity, of promise and of decision. There are occasions in life like that, turning points that need to be faced with faith and wisdom. Perhaps even more important is to remember that every day we are faced with decisions that, though small in themselves, actually mould character and shape our lives.

The second verse speaks of a second location, Kadesh-barnea. It was here that the command of God came through Moses the first time to go up and take possession of the land of Canaan (vv. 19–21). It was also here that Israel remained for many days before setting off on their long years of wandering (v. 46; 2:1). It is the distance from Horeb which is significant: eleven days' journey through a great and terrifying wilderness (v. 19). A mere eleven days was turned into thirty-eight years because of Israel's disobedience! How much of life can be wasted when God is disobeyed!

The third location is the land of Canaan itself. Verse 5 again locates the

Israel refuses to enter Canaan (1:1–46)

children of Israel east of Jordan in the land of Moab, and here Moses begins his words, in this verse described as 'this law'. The Hebrew word translated 'law' here is *torah*, the authoritative commands of God (v. 3b). In verse 6 Moses is going back in time to what God had said to Israel at Horeb. So verse 8 is what God spoke to Israel when they first came to the edge of Canaan: 'See, I have set the land before you. Go in and take possession of the land that the LORD swore to your fathers … to give to them and to their offspring after them.'

God had kept the word he had given to Abraham (Genesis 12:1,7; 13:14–17; 15:7,13–21; 17:8). But had Israel made God's promise void by their refusal to enter the land? No: 'If we are faithless, he remains faithful—for he cannot deny himself' (2 Timothy 2:13). The present generation of Israelites were witnesses to this. As children and young people they had stood on the border of Canaan, and now here they were again, with the land of promise before them and a second opportunity to enter. In spite of the sins and failures of his people, God's promises are sure, and in his time every one of them will be fulfilled. This leads straight into the next section.

The God who keeps his promises (vv. 9–18)

The opening three verses of this section continue the same theme. God had not only promised Abraham that his descendants would inherit the land, he promised also to multiply their number (Genesis 12:2; 13:16; 15:5; 17:1–8). There is a clear reference here in verse 10 to Genesis 15:5: 'You are today as numerous as the stars of heaven.' Moses looks forward to God multiplying the descendants of Abraham even more, 'a thousand times' more. The fulfilment of this is seen in the inclusion of believers from the nations into 'the covenants of promise' (Ephesians 2:11–22).

But while Moses rejoiced in the fulfilment of God's promise, it created a problem for him, especially as there was not always perfect harmony among the covenant people: 'How can I bear by myself the weight and burden of you and your strife?' (v. 12). When God increases the numbers in

Chapter 1

churches it also creates problems for a pastor or elders, who become stretched beyond their capacity to cope (Acts 6:1–6). In Moses' case the answer was to choose 'wise, understanding, and experienced men' (v. 13), some, it appears, to act as military leaders and others as judges. Notice that the latter were to 'judge righteously', and that they were to treat the 'alien', or immigrant, in the same way they would a brother. 'The judgement is God's' (v. 17) means that they were to judge by the divine standard of impartiality, as in God's sight.

This is almost certainly the occasion that is also recorded in Exodus 18:13–27. Exodus 18:5 indicates that the chapter is out of its chronological place, for Jethro only joined Moses once Israel was 'encamped at the mountain of God' (see 19:1–2). Deuteronomy refers to the same time (compare Deuteronomy 1:9 and 1:19) and the wording is very similar. In Exodus, Moses describes how Jethro spoke to him about the burden of judging Israel by himself. In Deuteronomy, he records how he spoke to the people, putting into operation Jethro's advice. A good leader is willing to listen to advice—even from his father-in-law! It is probable that this section indicates that such a delegation of authority was to continue in Israel.

In Acts 6, referred to above, the answer to the growth of the church at Jerusalem was very similar. In this case men were appointed to care for the concerns of the widows, leaving the apostles free to devote themselves to prayer and the ministry of the Word. When churches grow considerably—and we must pray that they will—and when problems increase—and they usually do, though we hope that they won't—it becomes necessary to ensure that leaders are not overburdened and that wise and spiritual people are appointed to meet the needs.

Faith or sight? (vv. 19–25)

When the Israelites reached Kadesh-barnea, Moses gave the people a very clear instruction: 'You have come to the hill country of the Amorites,

Israel refuses to enter Canaan (1:1–46)

which the LORD our God is giving us. See, the LORD your God has set the land before you. Go up, take possession, as the LORD, the God of your fathers, has told you. Do not fear or be dismayed' (vv. 20–21). Then the people asked that men might be sent before them to explore the land, which seemed a good idea to Moses (vv. 22–23). This raises two questions.

The first is that in Numbers 13:1–2 we read, 'The LORD spoke to Moses, saying, "Send men to spy out the land of Canaan, which I am giving to the people of Israel. From each tribe of their fathers you shall send a man, every one a chief among them."' How do we fit these two accounts together? The best explanation seems to be this: the people first came to Moses with their request, which Moses thought was good. Then either Moses felt he ought to ask the LORD about it and did so, or else God spoke to him confirming what he had already decided to do.

The second question is to ask whether this was actually the right thing for Israel to do. Or we might put it like this: Why did the people ask for spies to be sent out? The command was clear enough; ought they not to have obeyed it in faith? There are several indications that this was unbelief, that they did not want to commit themselves until they had seen what they were in for. First there was the command with its attendant 'Do not fear'. Was there fear behind their desire for the land and its cities to be explored first?

Then there is the fact that they said, 'Let us send men before us.' Throughout their journey so far they had gone at the commandment of God without spying out the land before them: 'All the congregation of the people of Israel moved on from the wilderness of Sin by stages, according to the commandment of the LORD' (Exodus 17:1). It was the LORD who indicated when they were to move, and it was he who went before them in the pillar of cloud: 'Throughout all their journeys, whenever the cloud was taken up from over the tabernacle, the people of Israel would set out. But if the cloud was not taken up, then they did not set out till the day that it was taken up' (Exodus 40:36–37). Notice the contrast in Deuteronomy 1

Chapter 1

between verse 22, 'Let us send men before us', and verses 30–33: 'The LORD your God who goes before you ... Yet in spite of this word you did not believe the LORD your God, who went before you in the way to seek you out a place to pitch your tents, in fire by night and in the cloud by day, to show you by what way you should go.'

This is probably why Moses included verses 9 to 18. The downside of appointing heads of the tribes to help Moses was that, as the representatives of the people, instead of simply acknowledging God's will and supporting Moses by urging the people to obey, they relayed the desire of the people for spies to go into Canaan first. While it is right to receive advice and to listen to what people say, this must never be put before a clear command from God.[1]

If this is a correct understanding of the situation, why did God confirm what the people and Moses thought was good? This is not the only place where God confirmed what people already wanted to do. We have the example of Balaam (Numbers 22:12; 18–21), and it is recorded of the wilderness generation of Israelites that 'he gave them what they asked, but sent a wasting disease among them' (Psalm 106:15). If your mind is made up, God will sometimes allow you to go ahead, but, as with Israel, you will have to bear the consequences. But we must remember that we are talking about clear commands of God. These are found in Scripture. In other circumstances it is right to consider all the possibilities and options.

Unbelief wins (vv. 26–33)

In spite of the fact that the land was obviously a good land (v. 25; Numbers 13:27; 14:6–8), the people 'rebelled against the command of the LORD your God'. Moses spells out how serious the past failure had been. It was rebellion against their God. More than that, they grumbled against God, not merely doubting his love but actually saying that he hated them (v. 27). Before we blame them too harshly, though, we ought to remember that when the future seems dark, and there are difficulties and struggles ahead

Israel refuses to enter Canaan (1:1–46)

which seem likely to overwhelm us, we too can doubt God's love and are tempted to blame him for our circumstances. Our hearts are inclined to melt (v. 28) when the odds seem stacked against us.

Their unbelief, however, was wholly unjustified. These people had had ample evidence of God's grace towards them (vv. 30–31). God had delivered them from Egypt with great displays of his power; then it was as if God had lifted them up and carried them through the wilderness. He had guided them by the fire and cloud (Exodus 13:21–22). He provided them with bread each day, and quail (Exodus 16). Water gushed from the rock to supply their need for drink (Exodus 17:1–7), and God gave them victory over the Amalekites (Exodus 17:8–13). Yet even when Moses reminded them of these things, unbelief won the day. Never underestimate the power and possibility of unbelief.

Back to the future (vv. 34–40)

God had a good land and a glorious future for Israel, but for the time being they had to turn their back to it and return towards the Red Sea (v. 40). Not one of that evil generation would enter the land other than Caleb and Joshua, the spies who had brought back a good report. It cannot have been easy for those two to stand out against the other ten spies, but they did, and God honoured them for it.

We must remember that Moses is recounting what took place thirty-eight years earlier; this is why he then refers to something that happened well after the rebellion at Kadesh-barnea (v. 37; Numbers 20:10–13). At the time of the rebellion everyone would have assumed that Moses would lead the people into the land. But he allowed the people's carping and grumbling to get to him and did not uphold the LORD as holy before their eyes (Numbers 20:12). As a result, he was forbidden to enter the land, something which he felt very deeply (Deuteronomy 3:23–29). His sadness and submission run as sub-themes through this book. The point he is making is this: if this present generation of Israelites disobeys God, let them not think that God will let them into the land either. God's promise will be fulfilled eventually, but only by those who obey him.

In verse 39 Moses refers to the way the disobedient generation said that if they went into the land, their children would become 'a prey', or 'victims' (NKJV). These children were the generation now facing the opportunity of going into the land. But in a real sense they had been victims—of their fathers' folly. It cannot have been much fun growing up during Israel's wilderness wanderings. Direct disobedience to God's commands usually hurts more than simply the person who is at fault. The consequences of disobedience are often shared by others, especially by those in the family.

Up to the top of the hill—and down again (vv. 41–46)

When the people heard that they were to wander until all the generation over twenty years old had died, they changed their mind and determined that they would go up into the land after all. But it was too late. God wants those who obey him gladly and freely, who act in faith because they know his command is right and good, and who trust him for his help. The Israelites decided to go up simply because they hoped that this would avert the verdict that God had passed on them. This was not repentance, it was recklessness; they 'thought it easy to go up into the hill country' (v. 41).

Moses warned them that the LORD had said, 'I am not in your midst' (v. 42). So by actually going up to attack the Amorites, the Israelites were compounding their sin; they 'presumptuously went up into the hill country' (v. 43). After their failure, they returned and wept before the LORD, but he did not listen to them. Tears without repentance flow from the eyes but not from the heart.

This chapter sets the scene for the whole book. It is an extended appeal by Moses to the generation of Israelites before him not to repeat the sins of the past, but rather to grasp the moment and go forward in faith in their faithful God. Human beings seem constantly to repeat the foolish disobedience of previous generations. Can we learn from the past? Can

Israel refuses to enter Canaan (1:1–46)

today's churches learn from the past? The call is to obedience in faith to what God commands us to do.

Study questions
1. What lessons can be learnt from the example of Caleb and Joshua?
2. What does this chapter tell us about Moses as a man and as a leader?
3. How can we evaluate what has happened to us in the past so as to learn lessons for the future?

Note

[1] For this understanding of the passage see **Millar,** *Now Choose Life: Theology and Ethics in Deuteronomy* (New Studies in Biblical Theology) (Leicester: Apollos, 1998), p. 70.

Chapter 2

Israel sets out for Canaan again (2:1–37)

Moses recounts the way in which God brought the people to the border of Canaan by a different route and to a different place from the first occasion. This time they came from the south via Ezion-geber and northwards on the eastern side of the Dead Sea.

Grace and judgement (vv. 1–8a)
Moses disposes of the wilderness wanderings in two sentences (v. 1). The time had come for the people to turn again (compare v. 1, 'Then we turned …'; v.3, 'Turn northward …'; and v. 8b, 'And we turned …'). They were headed for the promised land once more. There is a certain irony between verse 3, 'You have been travelling around this mountain country long enough', and verse 8, 'So we went on'. Travelling is not necessarily progress. In this chapter there is now purpose and progress, as there should always be for God's people.

Moses does not explain all that happened between the Israelites and Edom, the people of Esau. More is recorded in Numbers 20:14–21. The details of the way they went are not absolutely clear. Edom would not let them go directly through its territory; it seems they had to skirt around it to the south, for they went northwards from Ezion-geber, which was on the coast of what is now known as the Gulf of Aqaba.

Note that the Israelites were to look upon the Edomites as 'brothers', related as they were through Jacob and Esau. They were also to be very careful, as they could easily appear to be a threat to the Edomites. What is particularly important is that God told Israel he would not give them any portion of Mount Seir because he had given it to Esau's descendants. This

Israel sets out for Canaan again (2:1–37)

was an encouragement to the Israelites. If God had given that land to Esau, and ensured that his people had it, would he not do the same for them if they obeyed him and went forward into Canaan? We have an even greater reason to rely on God. If he cares for sparrows, how much more will he care for those for whom he sent his Son to die, in order to redeem them to himself (Luke 12:6–7)?

Although those years of wandering were a judgement from God upon a disobedient generation, the grace of God was also seen. By his grace the generation growing up were different from their fathers (see Jeremiah 2:2–3a), and God blessed them. He blessed the work of their hands so that they had money to pay for food and water (vv. 6–7a). God's eye was upon them throughout their perilous journey; he was with them; and, though the way was hard, they lacked nothing (v. 7b). God has not promised that the path of believers will be an easy one, but he knows our way and goes with us. Faith needs to grasp this, and derive hope and confidence from it.

Obeying each step of the way (vv. 8b–15)

As Moses goes back over the recent past he stresses how they have been obeying God's commands. Although we can also see this in verses 1 to 8, it is particularly noticeable here in verse 13: '"Now rise up and go over the brook Zered." So we went over the brook Zered.' The repetition of words emphasizes the exact manner in which Israel obeyed God's command. The same obedience is seen in the fact that Israel made no attempt to harass the Moabites or Ammonites (see vv. 9,19). The Zered River was the southern border of Moab.

Once again, Israel was told that God had given another people the land in which they lived, this time the descendants of Lot, the Moabites (and, in vv. 16–25, the Ammonites). Both these groups of people overcame foes who were especially tall, just as Israel would have to. This reinforces the encouragement that Israel was to take from the example of the Edomites, but there is also a deeper principle at work here. God is Lord over all

Chapter 2

nations. Where a people lives and what happens to a nation are not haphazard things, matters of chance and accident. As Paul explained at Athens, 'He made from one man every nation of mankind to live on all the face of the earth, having determined allotted periods and the boundaries of their dwelling place' (Acts 17:26). It was God's purpose that Israel should settle in Canaan, so in his time that was sure to take place. The same is true today. Where we live is not a matter of chance but of God's purpose, and part of that purpose is that we should be his witnesses and serve in the place where he has put us.

These three nations, Edom, Moab and Ammon, were all related to Abraham. It is for this reason that God particularly blessed them. This is covered by the scope of the promise to Abraham in Genesis 12: 'I will bless you and make your name great, so that you will be a blessing. I will bless those who bless you, and him who dishonours you I will curse, and in you all the families of the earth shall be blessed' (vv. 2–3). There is here an anticipation, or foreshadowing, of the spiritual blessing to come to the nations through the coming of Jesus Christ and the preaching of the gospel.

Verses 10 to 12 form a parenthesis describing the peoples who originally lived in Moab and also Edom, here called Seir. This was written some time later—see the last part of verse 12—to help a later generation who would not have known the information given here. A similar parenthesis occurs in verses 20 to 23. These and other additions (such as chapter 34, which records the death of Moses and includes the words 'there has not arisen a prophet since in Israel like Moses') were written to make the book complete. This was all under the guidance of the Holy Spirit.

Thirty-eight years (v. 14) is a long time, more than half a lifetime (Psalm 90:10) and considerably more than half a working lifetime. It was a long time to trudge through the desert, while the older generation of men died off. That itself was a tragic thing. The dead bodies of those who died had to be buried en route. No cemetery, no place where grieving relatives could

Israel sets out for Canaan again (2:1–37)

stop and mourn, or revisit and remember. God's hand was against them (v. 15). Direct disobedience to a clear command of God is a fearful thing, and the consequences of sin may have to be borne for a long time.

Not a day too late (vv. 16–25)

As soon as all the men of war had perished, the LORD said, 'Today you are to cross the border of Moab.' God was right on time. Not a day was lost. Israel had been brought right up to the Arnon valley, the northern edge of Moab. When the last funeral had been conducted, they crossed over into the first piece of territory that was to become theirs.

In crossing the river Arnon they were going into the territory of Sihon the Amorite, the Amorites being one of the seven Canaanite tribes that they were to dispossess (see 7:1). But to the east lay the land occupied by the Ammonites, so the warning of verse 19 was an important one. The Caphtorim, referred to in verse 23, were the Philistines, who came from Crete (Caphtor). They were not one of the original Canaanite tribes, but later, of course, became a thorn in Israel's side.

The command to enter and take possession comes in verses 24–25. Note the words, 'I have given into *your* hand …' (emphasis added). God had given land to Esau, Moab and Ammon, and now Sihon and his land had been given into Israel's hand. It was time for them to rise up and go over the Arnon in faith. But this was going to involve battle, so a special promise was given in verse 25. God would go before them and put a dread and fear of the Israelites upon their enemies. Rahab bore witness to this in Joshua 2:9–11. In her case it led to her hiding the spies sent out by Joshua and the deliverance of her family. For the rest of the people of Jericho—and Canaan—they feared, but it did not lead to their submission to Israel or their seeking mercy from them and their God. Fear of death and judgement does not always have a beneficial effect.

There are times when the Lord seems especially to go with his people. Revivals are times when many sense the presence of God in public worship

Chapter 2

and the preaching of the gospel. They are times when there is great fear, as people realize there is a living God to whom they are accountable, but that fear is turned into greater joy through believing in Jesus Christ. There is no simple answer to the question as to why God's presence is realized particularly at certain times, but certainly, when the churches are obedient to him and go forward in faith, crying out to him for his presence, that presence is more likely to be known.

The beginning of victory (vv. 26–37)

This passage shows the strategy that was followed. Rather than Israel attacking Sihon, Moses sent messengers to him with words of peace, giving him an opportunity to let the Israelites pass through his land on the way to the Jordan in order to cross over into Canaan proper (see also Numbers 21:21–30). Sihon did not respond to this gesture. The LORD hardened Sihon's spirit in judgement. The time had come for him and his people to receive the punishment for their evil ways. As a result, Sihon came out to fight against the Israelites.

This meant that, instead of Israel taking the offensive, they had to respond to the attack of the Amorites. Thus they were thrust into battle without having to make a decision themselves. After Israel had been thrown in at the deep end in this way, 'the LORD our God gave him [Sihon] over to us, and we defeated him and his sons and all his people. And we captured all his cities at that time' (vv. 33–34a). So the Israelites, without having had to take the initiative, found themselves victorious at the very outset of the campaign. And victorious not only in a single battle: 'From Aroer, which is on the edge of the Valley of the Arnon, and from the city that is in the valley, as far as Gilead, there was not a city too high for us. The LORD our God gave all into our hands' (v. 36). Such a comprehensive conquest would give them great confidence about crossing the Jordan. This was surely why God brought them by this roundabout route to the land of Canaan itself. God knew what he was doing; and as Moses

26 Exploring Deuteronomy

Israel sets out for Canaan again (2:1–37)

recounted all that had happened, the people could see that they had every reason to go forward in faith.

There is one matter which demands special attention. The second half of verse 34 reads, '[We] devoted to destruction every city, men, women, and children. We left no survivors.' This seems hideous. Nor was this the only occasion when destruction on such a scale took place: the same happened when Israel fought with Og, king of Bashan, another Amorite kingdom (3:6). And more than that, this was to be standard procedure when Israel went into Canaan (7:2). God himself commanded it, yet it seems like genocide and ethnic cleansing. How are we to understand this? It is impossible to give detailed consideration here, but note the following points:

- Messengers had been sent with words of peace (v. 26), and 20:10–18 shows that this was to be standard procedure, giving enemies an opportunity to come to terms (we shall consider this later). It was only if peace was rejected that the destruction spoken of here would take place. In other cases, women and children would be spared; the treatment of the Canaanite tribes was exceptional because of their grievous sins.
- Israel was here carrying out the judgement of God upon these people for their sins. This had nothing to do with ethnicity: it was a moral and spiritual matter. At the time when Sodom and Gomorrah were destroyed (Genesis 19), these tribes were spared because '[their] iniquity ... [was] not yet complete' (Genesis 15:16). These peoples had had Abraham, the friend of God, living among them for many years, yet they continued in a paganism that provoked God by its evil, involving gross immorality, sacred prostitution and child sacrifice, and barbaric cruelty. There were 400 years in which these tribes could have turned from their evil ways, yet instead they continued until they were ripe for judgement. Even though their hearts failed when they heard of what Israel had done (Joshua 2:9–11), and they had the example of Rahab and her family who were spared, no others submitted to Israel or pleaded for

Chapter 2

mercy from the LORD, except the Gibeonites who went about it deceitfully (Joshua 9).
- God chose to use Israel as his instrument of judgement in this case. This sets no precedent for any other nation to act in the same way. It may be that God chose to use warfare as the method of judgement, rather than flood or volcanic eruption, for example, because the Canaanite tribes were themselves particularly cruel and vicious (see 1 Samuel 15:33).
- Chapter 7 makes it clear that part of the reason for this was to preserve the holiness of Israel (see 7:2b–6). We have here a clash between a virulent paganism and the nation chosen by God to be his witness among the nations (see 4:6–8). It was essential for Israel to be different and holy to the LORD. The tragedy was that Israel actually fell far short of its calling.
- In practical terms, the judgement of the Canaanites is a foreshadowing and warning of the final day of judgement. We also see the importance of God's people maintaining their distinctiveness as those who are holy to him.

Study questions

1. What does this chapter reveal about God's sovereignty over all things?
2. What does it show us about God's grace?
3. Are wasted years totally wasted? Can you see God's grace at work in them, and lessons to be learned from them?

Chapter 3

Consolidating the gains (3:1–29)

Moses continues recounting recent events. Bashan had also been conquered, meaning that Israel had taken all the east bank of Jordan, from the Arnon valley in the south to Mount Hermon in the north. This area had been settled by the Reubenites, the Gadites and half the tribe of Manasseh. Moses also speaks about himself. These great works of the LORD made him long to cross the Jordan himself, but this was not to be. Joshua would lead Israel into Canaan.

The defeat of Og, king of Bashan (vv. 1–11)

After taking the territory of Sihon, Israel continued north towards Bashan. Once again it appears that the initiative in battle was taken by Israel's enemies: 'And Og the king of Bashan came out against us, he and all his people, to battle at Edrei' (v. 1). Moses encouraged the Israelites with God's promise that he had also given these people into their hand, and that he would give them the victory just as he had done over Sihon. We take heart from victories, and from our experience of the presence and help of God. As the hymn says, 'Each victory will help you some other to win.'

The territory won by this second campaign was considerable in size, stretching as it did as far north as Mount Hermon. Moreover, the strength of its cities is also noted: 'All these were cities fortified with high walls, gates, and bars ...' (v. 5). A lesser victory prepared the people for tackling a stronger foe. Faith tested and proved is emboldened to trust God when a more serious challenge is faced. Notice also how this description of the cities recalls what the Israelites had said thirty-eight years earlier when the spies came back from viewing the land: 'The cities are great and fortified

Chapter 3

up to heaven' (1:28; compare Numbers 13:28). Having conquered Bashan, the Israelites could take heart when they came to cross over the Jordan and enter Canaan.

Not only were the cities of Bashan strong and fortified, but its king was also a very formidable figure (v. 11). He was one of the remnants of the giants, and his bed was made of iron, just over four metres long and nearly two metres wide. It was the sight of giants like this which had also filled the hearts of the spies with fear: 'And besides, we have seen the sons of the Anakim there' (1:28). In all these things we see the goodness of the LORD, leading his people on from strength to strength, preparing them and encouraging them for what lay ahead in Canaan. This is how God deals with us in our lives.

Two and a half tribes settle east of Jordan (vv. 12–17)

A considerable area of land with towns and villages, fields and livestock now belonged to Israel. This passage tells us how Moses divided it up and gave it to the tribes of Reuben and Gad, and half the tribe of Manasseh. Numbers 32 tells how Reuben and Gad came to Moses to ask for the land that became theirs, but that is not important for what Moses has to say to the people here. Machir (v. 15) was the son of Manasseh, and it was his clan that captured Gilead (Numbers 32:39–40). Jair, who took the region of Argob (v. 14), was Machir's great-grandson (1 Chronicles 2:21–22). Manasseh was a larger tribe than the other two, with over 50,000 men, though four other tribes were larger still, with Judah having over 75,000 men (see Numbers 26). Reuben had the southernmost area, from the Arnon river to just north of the Dead Sea. Gad had the middle section, with Manasseh in the north (see Joshua 13:8–33).

The division of the land by Moses, the God-appointed leader, and later by Joshua, was very important. The possibility of conflict between the tribes was very real, and it was essential for each tribe to realize that it had been given its territory by God. Each had a responsibility to clear the land

Consolidating the gains (3:1–29)

of remaining enemies, and then to settle and cultivate it for the good of their own people and for the welfare of the nation as a whole. Regrettably, there is often discord among Christians, both within churches and between churches. Unity and co-operation are often sadly missing, as is also a sense of the importance of the witness of the whole people of God.

Helping your brothers (vv. 18–22)

The practical importance of the good of the whole nation comes out immediately in this section. Initially, Moses was very angry when Reuben and Gad approached him about settling in the land they had just conquered. He thought this meant that they were not willing to go over the Jordan and take part in the conquest of Canaan. They assured him, however, that they would settle their wives and children in the fortified cities east of the Jordan and then cross over to help in the conquest, and that they would not return home until Israel had gained its inheritance (Numbers 32:6–19). In this passage Moses commands them to act as they have said they will.

Significantly, Moses calls the nine and a half tribes 'your brothers' (vv. 18,20). They are to recognize their kinship with the rest of Israel. They are all descendants of Abraham, Isaac and Jacob. They all belong to the people chosen by God, redeemed from out of Egypt and constituted God's people by covenant, a covenant initiated by God to which their fathers had given allegiance (Exodus 19:8; 24:1–8). Their unity is to be a practical matter; they are to act as brothers and stand shoulder to shoulder with the other tribes until the LORD gives rest to them also (v. 20).

At the same time as this Moses also spoke to Joshua, for it was he who was to lead Israel into the land. He needed to draw encouragement from all that he had seen. What God has done not once but twice he can do again and again. Joshua, one of the two spies who had brought back a good report of the land all those years ago, knew the hard time Moses had sometimes faced as leader. He knew how awkward and rebellious Israel

Chapter 3

could be. Just as Moses urged the two and a half tribes to help their brothers, so he helped his brother, Joshua. This may not have been easy for him. It is not always easy to encourage and reassure the one who is going to take your place. Moses does not show any resentment; rather he speaks as a true servant of God: 'You shall not fear them, for it is the LORD your God who fights for you' (v. 22).

The sorrow and submission of Moses (vv. 23–29)

Perhaps it was speaking to Joshua as he had just done that filled Moses' heart with a great yearning to go into the land and see the great works which the LORD would then do—note the phrase 'at that time' (v. 23). Moses felt that they were on the verge of great things, and he longed to be able to see God's greatness and his mighty hand demonstrated in an even more wonderful way. So he came before God and pleaded with him. We can understand just how he felt, but he had to learn submission to God's will. It was a hard lesson, and one that we all have to learn, though not necessarily in similar circumstances to those of Moses.

God did not change his mind; his words were conclusive, putting an end to further pleas on Moses' part: 'Enough from you; do not speak to me of this matter again' (v. 26). When God's will is absolutely clear and we submit to it, it brings a sense of peace and closure into our hearts, even though it might put an end to hopes we have entertained. We must be careful in our thinking about this because Moses was in a special position and God spoke personally and directly to him. Nevertheless, once we are sure that some matter is scriptural and that a particular course of action has to be followed, then we can see that this is God's will. It is also the case that God's will appears evident by the ways in which things work out, and there is peace in accepting that.

It is not quite clear whether verse 26 means that God was angry with Moses for asking to go over and see the land, or whether this is a reference to God's anger on the occasion when Moses and Aaron dishonoured God

Consolidating the gains (3:1–29)

before the people (Numbers 20:10–13). What is clear is that it was 'because of you', that is, the people. If this refers to the original event, it means that Moses was excluded because as leader he had set an example of petulance with Israel that dishonoured God. God could not overlook such a serious sin in a man in Moses' position. If, however, it refers to the time when Moses prayed, it means that God could not go back on his word and allow Moses into the land. How could he do that when he had kept his word so as not to allow in any of the older Israelite generation? God has to maintain his consistency.

However, Moses was permitted to view the land (v. 27). He would see all the land; he would be assured that God would keep his promise. This was God's land and God would bring his people into it. After all, what did it really matter that as an old man of 120 he did not enter it himself? He had fulfilled the task God had given him to do. He had brought Israel to their land and his work was now finished.

Although Moses had already encouraged Joshua, the LORD told him to do so again. Moses knew that Israel would be in good hands. The responsibility that he was laying down would be taken up by Joshua, so while he had opportunity, Moses had to encourage and strengthen Joshua. The future was assured: 'He shall go over at the head of this people, and he shall put them in possession of the land that you shall see' (v. 28). It is easy for Christians to wonder what the future holds. It is easy to become discouraged and wonder where all the leaders have gone, and why there are not the godly men and women we knew when we were young! It is better by far to encourage those who are serving the Lord and those who are taking up positions of responsibility, and to remember that the cause is his and that he will certainly bring his own purposes to pass.

Study questions
1. What principles for co-operative action both within the local church and between churches can you find in verses 18 to 22?

Chapter 3

2. How long should we go on praying that God would change our circumstances, and what appears to be his will? Consider also 2 Corinthians 12:7–10.

3. Why was Moses' sin so serious?

Chapter 4

Laws for the land (4:1–14)

Moses now turns to introduce the 'statutes and the rules' which God has given to govern the life of Israel in the land they are to go and possess. He reminds them of the solemnity of that day at Horeb when God gave them the Ten Commandments.

You held fast to the LORD, go on doing so (vv. 1–4)
Obedience is not just a matter of one occasion, crossing the Jordan and going into the land of promise. How are the people of Israel to live when they are in the land? At this point Moses is going to teach them God's statutes and rules. Already as God's people they have to keep his commandments. Now, in the rest of this book, there is going to be a reminder and amplification of the commandments they have already received, and an adaptation for their new situation in Canaan. If they keep these commandments, they will live. This generation are all alive today (v. 4) because, when their fathers disobeyed, they had held fast to the LORD their God. The clear implication is that they need to continue to hold fast to him, and keep his word.

Keeping God's commandments means receiving them for what they are. They are not Moses' ideas, they are part of God's word. For this reason the people must neither add to them, nor take away from them. There is a temptation to do both. In practical terms at least, there were often times in Israel's history when they took away from the commandments by disobedience. And at the time when Jesus was in the world, the Pharisees had added considerably to the commandments. Adding to God's commandments is as bad as taking away from them, for it implies that God has been remiss and has not given sufficient instruction to his people. This warning, given in verse 2, is repeated in 12:32; see also Proverbs 30:6 and Revelation 22:18–19.

Chapter 4

This generation of Israelites were witnesses of the disobedience of their fathers at Kadesh-barnea, and of the resultant judgement of God that had unfolded before their eyes during the thirty-eight years of wandering. And, although they had seen victory over Sihon and Og, they had also seen God's judgement again at Baal-Peor (Numbers 25). At that place Israel began to take part in idolatry through contact with Moabite women, though the Midianites were also involved (Numbers 25:16–18; ch. 31). This was at the instigation of Balaam (Revelation 2:14). All the men who took part in worshipping Baal on that occasion had been destroyed. This was a necessary warning, in case the encouragement from their victories should make them careless and complacent. They needed to hold fast in obedience. Warnings are as necessary for us as words of encouragement; complacency and taking God's blessing for granted are attitudes that we can fall into all too easily.

Living in the sight of the nations (vv. 5–8)

In the middle of verse 6 comes this phrase: 'in the sight of the peoples'. This tells us that Israel in Canaan will be surrounded by pagan nations, who will observe the people's life and behaviour. This will include not only larger nations like Egypt and Assyria, but also Syria, Moab, Ammon and Edom. Important trade routes passed through Canaan, so caravans of merchants would travel along them with their goods. In Ezekiel 26:2, Jerusalem is called 'the gate of the peoples', which seems to suggest that people from many lands called there on their way to different destinations.

The implication of this is that God is going to put Israel in a place where they will be a witness for him. The statutes and rules that God has given to Israel are not simply for their benefit alone. As they live in the way God tells them to, they will show to the peoples around the blessing of being a nation that trusts and obeys the LORD. Here is a God whose commands are wise and good, who makes those who live by them wise and understanding. We should realize that this was part of the calling of Israel. It was not chosen to

Laws for the land (4:1–14)

keep the blessings of God to itself, but to show to the world around the holiness and goodness of its God; to demonstrate that it was a nation who had a living God near at hand, one who acts when his people call upon him. This is true also of the church of Jesus Christ. It is a city set on a hill, to give light to all around. Its members are to let their light shine before men and women, so that they will be brought to give glory to our Father in heaven.

If the people of Israel do this, then those around them will look upon them as a 'great nation'; indeed they will be a 'great nation'. This cannot mean in terms of numbers of people (7:7), nor of the strength of their army, but rather in the cohesiveness of the nation, arising from their obedience to all the ways of God. They are to be a people marked by social justice and high standards of conduct, leading to prosperity under God's blessing. The peoples around them will also call them 'wise and understanding' because of their wisdom which arises from receiving, considering and living out the commandments of God. Israel needed to realize its high calling, just as the Christian church needs to do today. Churches should be communities marked by love and unity, compassion and a wholehearted embracing of the whole Word of God. God's Word makes us 'wise and understanding'.

However, it is not simply the fact that Israel had statutes and rules from God that mattered; even more important was the fact that their God was near to them, ready to respond 'whenever we call upon him'. Obedience and living according to God's instructions would not happen apart from the presence and active enabling of God; they were to take place within a relationship with God in which the people called upon him and received his help. Moses himself knew this very well, for the people had often benefited from his intercession for them. The life of God's people is always envisaged as a life lived in dependence upon him and in fellowship with him. It is sadly all too easy for us today to forget that we have the Lord our God so near to us, whenever we call upon him.

Moses put this final challenge to the people: 'What great nation is there, that has statutes and laws so righteous as all this law that I set before you

Chapter 4

today?' God's law is righteous. It is right for his people and enables them to live aright before God. It is a good law, given by God's goodness, so that the people will live good lives. It would be perverse to think that God's law is in any way unnecessarily restrictive, or that it is harmful or against the best interests of his people. As the apostle Paul was later to say, 'The law is holy, and the commandment is holy and righteous and good' (Romans 7:12).

A never-to-be-forgotten day (vv. 9–14)

At this point Moses reminds the people—or at least, the older generation among them—of the occasion when God first gave his law to them. What took place at Horeb (called Mount Sinai in Exodus 19) when God came down upon the mountain and spoke 'out of the midst of the fire' (v. 12) was of crucial significance for Israel then, and for future days when they had settled in the land. What the people saw and experienced on that occasion was never to be forgotten; it was to be taught to each new generation—'your children and your children's children' (v. 9).

On that day the people 'stood before the LORD [their] God' (v. 10). They were there to hear his words, and to learn to fear him all the days of their lives. They stood at the foot of the mountain 'while the mountain burned with fire to the heart of heaven, wrapped in darkness, cloud, and gloom' (v. 11). It was an overwhelming experience, awe-inspiring, and calculated to remain forever imprinted upon their memories. Their God was a consuming fire, far above them, hidden from them, separate from them; a God of justice whose law was holy, who demanded obedience. Yet, for all his greatness, he had chosen them in grace. He had made them his own; and his laws were for their good, and would promote their welfare and lead to his blessing. They were to fear him with the fear of awe and reverence, for his grace and goodness ought never to lead them to presumption, carelessness or irresponsibility. To be recipients of his loving care demanded a wholehearted response of faithfulness and obedience. If we

Laws for the land (4:1–14)

are believers, we are 'their children' in a spiritual sense, and this is our God and our Father. We have not come to the mount that may be touched (Hebrews 12:18), but God has spoken to us from heaven through his Son, and we need to 'offer to [him] acceptable worship, with reverence and awe' (Hebrews 12:28).

There are three more strands to pick up and examine in these verses. Firstly, there is this note in verse 12: 'You heard the sound of words, but saw no form; there was only a voice.' This prepares for the next paragraph, which emphasizes the fact that, as God did not reveal himself by any form, Israel must not fashion any form intended to represent him. It also throws the emphasis on God's words. The LORD is not a God who is seen: he is heard. He has a voice and speaks, and his people are to live by his words. This, of course, contrasted with the ideas of the nations around them. They had gods which they represented by images, but which did not speak; they had no message. It also contrasts with the ideas of many people today, who have little time for revealed words but fashion a god of their own liking by their own thinking.

Secondly, we have here the first occurrence of 'covenant' in this book. The idea of covenant is central to the whole book. Israel was a nation in covenant with God, a covenant made unilaterally by God in grace, in which the nation became God's people and he pledged himself as its God. But the covenant imposed obligations upon Israel. In general terms, this was love for God issuing in faithfulness to the covenant. In detail, it meant keeping his commandments, at the heart of which lie the Ten Commandments (v. 13). These commandments were written by God on two tablets of stone, indicating their permanence and thus the continuing covenant obligation for Israel.

Thirdly, God also gave Moses 'statues and rules' at that time, presumably Exodus 21–23 in particular. These rules looked forward to the settlement of the people in the land that God had destined for them. Implied in these commandments was the promise that the people would

Chapter 4

enter into and dwell in Canaan. This was both an encouragement to Moses' hearers to cross the Jordan, and a reminder that they were to observe all that God had told them, in order to ensure their continuance in the land.

Study questions

1. Consider further the command in verse 2, particularly in view of the fact that it is often said that the Old Testament historical books are written from a Deuteronomistic point of view, i.e. that they assess the lives of Israel's kings and the state of the nation in the light of Deuteronomy. Consider the command also in the light of the prophets' calls to repentance and renewed obedience to its laws. What application does verse 2 have for today?

2. What is the significance of Deuteronomy 4:1–14 for the mission of Israel and for the church?

3. Why are we as we are if the Lord our God is so near to us whenever we call upon him?

Chapter 5

Living before the living God (4:15–43)

In this passage Moses warns the people of Israel against making any image for themselves, or worshipping sun, moon or stars. They have seen that the LORD who delivered them is unique in his power and greatness, so they must keep his commands. A short narrative section recounts how Moses set apart three cities of refuge.

Do not try to make the invisible visible (vv. 15–24)
Moses has already reminded the people of Israel of one of the features of their experience at Mount Sinai: 'You heard the sound of words, but saw no form; there was only a voice' (v. 12). Here he proceeds to the practical application: 'Since you saw no form on the day that the LORD spoke to you at Horeb out of the midst of the fire, beware lest you act corruptly by making a carved image for yourselves, in the form of any figure' (vv. 15–16).

The people saw no form of God; they heard his voice, but there was nothing to see that they could identify with God himself. He is an invisible God, for he is spirit (John 4:24). Nothing in creation can represent him because he is the Creator of it all. He is greater, above all that he has made, and to try to represent him by something he created is to bring him down to the level of that which he has made. Unlike all the nations around it, Israel was to be entirely different in its beliefs and worship. It had one God, the true and living LORD, who, being above all, could not be seen, but who had to be worshipped according to his word.

If the people lifted up their eyes above the creatures to be found on earth and saw over them the sun, moon and stars, they were not to think of these

Chapter 5

as powers or gods and bow down to them. These, too, had been created by God and allotted to all the peoples for light and warmth, to mark off day and night, and to divide up the seasons and the years. They are our servants, but to worship them makes us their servants. Those who follow astrology can only act when the stars are right. They are in bondage to the right forecast—perhaps even the right newspaper!

Israel's God had brought them out of Egypt. Perhaps the reference in verse 20 is not only to the 'iron furnace' of suffering they had endured; they had been brought right out of a pagan environment and had now become 'a people of his own inheritance'. Life in Egypt, with its many gods and images of those gods, was over. Everything was different now. Their worship had to reflect the reality of what their God was like. They owed their deliverance to him, and it was he who was forming them into a nation that would live in the land he was giving them. For this reason they had to listen to him and faithfully worship him. So, too, must we, who have been delivered from a greater bondage and brought into an even more privileged position (see 1 Peter 2:9–10).

Moses cannot refrain from again referring to his own experience (v. 21). The Lord was angry with him and therefore he is not going to enter the good land. You can sense the sorrow he feels in verse 22. He recognizes the certainty of what God has said: 'I *must* die in this land; I *must not* go over …' (emphasis added). They will go over, but let them take care. God is not to be trifled with, and if they turn to idolatry, they can expect to bear the consequences, just as he has had to bear the consequences for his failure to honour God.

The point is that Israel is now in covenant with the Lord (v. 23). He made it with them, but they accepted its terms (Exodus 19:8). So if they forget the covenant and break its terms, God will punish them: 'You only have I known of all the families of the earth; therefore I will punish you for all your iniquities' (Amos 3:2). God is a jealous God; idolatry and the worship of created beings arouse his jealousy. He loves Israel. That is why

Living before the living God (4:15–43)

he chose them (v.37; 7:7), and why he delivered them and made them his own. Later, in the prophets, God would use the picture of husband and wife to speak of his relationship to Israel (e.g. Jeremiah 3:1). The same idea of outraged love at unfaithfulness is implicit in the term 'jealous' (Deuteronomy 4:24). Modern Christians need to remember that the writer to the Hebrews says, '*Our* God is a consuming fire' (Hebrews 12:29, emphasis added). It is because God is love that disobedience and sin are so serious. Love spurned, or toyed with and taken for granted, provokes a just and holy response.

From idolatry to idolatry (vv. 25–31)

Moses now looks into the future and warns the people of what they can expect if they turn to idolatry. When they have 'grown old in the land', they may forget the goodness of God in the past and the commands he has given them. The implication is that, not only must the present generation go forward across the Jordan in faith and keep themselves from all trace of idolatry, they must also warn their children seriously, doing what they can to ensure that future generations remain faithful. There is always a duty resting on parents and church leaders to teach and warn the rising generation.

That Moses is deadly serious is shown by the way he speaks: 'I call heaven and earth to witness against you today' (v. 26). Though they will enter God's land at this time, if a future generation turns to making a carved image or doing evil in God's eyes, they will not continue in the land. A disobedient people will be turned out, destroyed as a nation, and scattered with very few of them left (vv. 26–27). There, dispersed among pagan nations, they will learn what it is really like to serve gods of wood and stone, gods that cannot see, hear, eat or smell. If they want idolatry they will have it, with all its despair. They will have gods that can neither hear nor help, and they will get caught up in all the desperate ways that people use to try to get such gods on their side.

Chapter 5

But that will not be the end of the matter. The LORD God is a merciful God (v. 31). Moses does not simply say that, in such circumstances, if the remnant of Israel calls upon God, he will hear. Rather he says this: 'But from there you will seek the LORD your God and you will find him, if you search after him with all your heart and with all your soul' (v. 29). As the next verse explains, the very tribulation the people will endure, and all the things that will come upon them in those days, will impel them to turn back to the LORD and obey his voice. If God punishes them for their covenant-breaking, he will still not forget the covenant; the chastisement itself will bring them to seek after him again.

Truly God is a merciful God, one who sent his own Son for sinners. The promise of God stands throughout the centuries: those who search after him with all their heart and soul will find him. It stands true even for those who have abandoned the faith and gone off, like the prodigal son, into a far country with all its attractions and apparent pleasures (Luke 15:11–24). If in trouble they return to the Lord, they will receive the same heart-thrilling welcome that the prodigal found.

No other God (vv. 32–40)

In this last section of Moses' first address to the people he asks them to reflect on what God has done and to consider that there is no other god who has ever been heard to act in such a way. The LORD is God—there is no other—and his mighty acts show what a God he is.

Moses reminds them that their God spoke out of the fire to Israel; he took them for himself and delivered them by his mighty hand and outstretched arm. We do well to ask ourselves whether there is any other God who is even spoken of as giving his own beloved Son to redeem sinful people for himself by death on a cross. The very idea is breathtaking, and full of mystery and grace. Yet this is what the God who delivered Israel went on to do in fulfilment of his covenant purpose. We should never be ashamed of this; rather we should glory in it. It is supremely in this way that

Living before the living God (4:15–43)

God has defined himself. In the cross we see both the justice of God that needed to be satisfied, and the overwhelming love of God himself, in the person of the Son, paying the price that secures forgiveness and full salvation for all who believe. There is no other God than this one.

In Israel's experience, too, justice and mercy were combined. Horeb manifested the justice of the God who gave his commands. Yet Israel stood before the mountain only because of God's love, choice and deliverance. In verses 37 and 38 we can bring together the words '[he] brought you out' and 'to bring you in'. This fits in directly with Moses' concern. God did not bring Israel out of Egypt to leave them in the wilderness, but rather to give them the land which he had designated as their inheritance. On the day in which Moses addressed them they stood on the very edge of that land. Therefore, they needed to go forward in obedience and faith to take the inheritance that God was giving to them. There is a sense in which God's people are always on the march, always going forward. Is this true of us? Is it true of our church?

Moses' final application comes in verse 40. Keeping God's statutes and his commandments included going forward when he told them to, but primarily referred to keeping the commandments received at Horeb, both the Ten Commandments and the subsequent instructions contained in the rest of Exodus, in Leviticus and in Numbers. The God who spoke these commands was their sovereign LORD, and he was to be obeyed. We naturally understand 'that it may go well with you and with your children after you' as referring to God's blessing upon an obedient people. It is clearly not wrong to understand it in that way. Yet there is probably also the thought that God's commands are just what his people need; they are suited to them and are given for their good. To do what was commanded by their good God, who made them and saved them, was sure to mean that it would go well with them. That's why God gave them the commands he did.

We can say the same about the final phrase: 'that you may prolong your

Chapter 5

days in the land that the LORD your God is giving you for all time'. God's commands were intended to result in a long continuance in the land. If they obeyed, their own relationships would be strong; they would be a cohesive nation caring for one another. They would be able to stand together against their enemies; there would be no internal strife or civil war. Children would be brought up well, family life would flourish, the poor and needy would be provided for, work would be satisfying and life would have the LORD at its centre. Things would go well in the land.

It is worth considering this a little further, for many people have a sneaking suspicion that God's commands are somewhat arbitrary and unduly restrictive. Those who are not Christians often seem to feel that progress, freedom and joy come from breaking them rather than keeping them. Even some Christians seem to take the view that God's commands are rather burdensome, but that obeying them is worth it because God rewards those who keep them. All this is far from the truth. God's commands are good for us all and lead to a happy life and a wholesome society. It is true that we find it difficult to keep them, but that is because of our sinfulness. The ways of God are pleasantness and peace.

Cities of refuge east of the Jordan (vv. 41–43)

The setting apart of cities of refuge in the territory east of the Jordan shows that Moses recognized that Israel was already beginning to settle into the general area. This act further reinforced the fact that the time had come for Israel to enter into its inheritance. Some already were claiming part of the land the LORD had given to them in battle; it remained for the rest of the tribes to cross over the Jordan and enter into their full inheritance. The very act of Moses appointing these cities was a strong signal to the people to go across the Jordan in faith to take up their inheritance. Moreover, he was setting the Israelites an example of obedience; the LORD had commanded him to do this (Numbers 35:14).

We are likely to find the emphasis on the cities of refuge rather strange

Living before the living God (4:15–43)

(see Numbers 35:9–29; Joshua 20). What we have here is a provision both of justice and of mercy. The details are set out in Numbers 35. At that time, if a murder was committed, a member of the dead person's family—the avenger of blood—was responsible for executing justice on the murderer by putting him or her to death. But the family, and the avenger of blood, might well not distinguish between murder and unintentional killing, so cities were set apart in the various regions. In the case of an unintentional killing, the person responsible could go to the nearest city of refuge and find sanctuary there. The case could be considered (Numbers 35:24) and if no murder had been committed, the person would remain in the city of refuge until the death of the high priest. After that, he or she could return home. Justice would be done, the avenger of blood would be kept from becoming a murderer, and time would be given for the whole incident to be seen in proportion. This act of setting apart cities of refuge, close to the beginning of Deuteronomy, shows the importance of justice, a thread that runs through all the legislative material in this book.

Study questions

1. Search out as many reasons as you can as to why God has commanded us not to make any visible representation of himself.
2. Why might Israel have begun to forget God once they were settled in the land? What factors might tend to make us forget God?
3. What truths about God set Christianity apart from all other religions?

Section 2:

Moses gives Israel laws and instructions (4:44–26:19)

Chapter 6

The law summarized in the Ten Commandments (4:44–5:21)

Moses begins a long address by setting out the Ten Commandments before the people. He reminds them of their response to hearing the voice of God, and of the words that God gave him to speak to them.

The setting for the second giving of the law (4:44–49)

This passage acts as an introduction to the law that Moses is going to give to the people and that is set down in the next twenty-two chapters. In verse 44 this is called 'the law', emphasizing its unity and also implying its divine authority. In the next verse we read of 'the testimonies, the statutes, and the rules'. There is probably no great distinction between these words; they simply indicate the variety of instructions that were given to Israel to direct and enrich their lives as a community and as individuals.

In describing the setting in which these laws were given, the first phrase used is 'when they came out of Egypt'. The focus first of all is on the fact that they have been delivered from slavery. The LORD had done this, and he had brought them out to make them his own, to fashion them as a nation and settle them in the land he had promised. Now Moses, God's spokesman and representative, would give them the law for their obedience as his people in his land. From verse 46, attention switches to the victories the LORD has already granted them over Sihon and Og. The whole area now under Israelite control and already being settled by the Reubenites, Gadites and half the tribe of Manasseh is indicated. This is 'beyond the Jordan', showing

Chapter 6

that there is a territory across the Jordan that needs to be taken and settled, and where God's writ must run. All that God has done shows that he is their sovereign LORD, and that it is their duty and blessing to keep his commandments. Similarly, our service and obedience derive their impetus and motivation from his great mercies towards us.

The setting of the first giving of the law (5:1–5)

Moses' second address to the people takes up where the first left off, at Horeb with the giving of the Ten Commandments. The first verse begins Moses' address after he has called the people together. These statues and rules will not be rehearsed among them second hand; Moses will speak them in the hearing of everyone. They are to learn them and take care to do them.

Then, in the next four verses, Moses reminds them of what took place at Horeb. In particular, he reminds them that it was with those listening to him now that God had entered into a covenant. While it is true that God had made a covenant with their fathers, 'this covenant' was specifically made in the lifetime of those who are now the older generation standing before Moses. They heard the voice of the LORD speaking to them out of the fire, they witnessed the fire that surrounded the mountain, they feared when they realized the holiness and justice of the LORD. They, then, must take to heart his words, keep them faithfully and teach the rising generation to live in the same obedience. In all this, two emphases underlie what Moses says. Firstly, it is God's grace and love that have brought Israel to where they stand. They owe everything to him. But, secondly, the grace and love are God's, and God is great, holy and just. He is not man, or even man writ large. He is Lord of all, majestic, clothed in clouds and fire, glorious, the Creator before whom human creatures feel overwhelmed and utterly out of their depth, sinful and unworthy. These two emphases run throughout the whole Bible and need to be held together in our understanding and worship.

The law summarized in the Ten Commandments (4:44–5:21)

The Ten Commandments repeated (vv. 6–21)

We can sense these two emphases in the opening words of the Ten Commandments. 'I am the LORD your God' is a declaration of his greatness; he is God. Yet even here, 'your God' emphasizes the covenant relationship in which he stands with Israel. 'Who brought you out of the land of Egypt, out of the house of slavery' shows his mercy to Israel, and their indebtedness to him. These commandments are commandments for a redeemed people. They were never intended as a way of salvation, nor were they spoken to the world in general. They were specifically given to the redeemed, covenant people of God and summarize the behaviour that the LORD expected from those whom he had made his own. The grateful response of those who have been delivered by his grace is to live according to his law.

This raises the question of what relevance the Ten Commandments have to Christian believers (and, indeed, to unbelievers, but we will touch on that later). There has been unnecessary polarization in answering this, with different groups approaching the question from different angles and intending to guard against different perceived dangers. Quite clearly the first commandment, 'You shall have no other gods before me', is valid for Christians. In the early centuries after Christ this was very important because the Roman emperor was considered a god. Christians died rather than say, 'Caesar is Lord.' It is also self-evident that 'You shall not steal' is binding upon Christians. In fact, only a fairly casual examination will show that all but the fourth command, 'Observe the Sabbath day, to keep it holy', must be binding upon Christians; Christians are not justified by obeying the law, but they have not been set free to break it subsequently. But if nine are clearly binding, it becomes very difficult to treat one differently. The Ten Commandments have a unity (4:13), and they surely either stand or fall together.

There are other considerations that strengthen this understanding. It is often said that the rest of Moses' address consists of an exposition and

Chapter 6

application of these commandments. This may be going beyond the evidence, but the commandments certainly seem to form the bedrock on which the rest of the rules and instructions are based. Indeed, just as Deuteronomy underlies the message of the prophets, with their exposure of disobedience and calls for repentance, so do the Ten Commandments. Moreover, this is also the case in the New Testament. It is the law that exposes sin (Romans 3:20), and these commandments form a fundamental summary of the law. In the first place it is the law that brings the knowledge of sin to unbelievers, but it also functions in the same way in believers. We all fail and fall, and these commandments and their implications are one of the means the Holy Spirit uses to make us aware of our sins and lead us to repentance and renewed obedience.

It is true that these commandments have to be looked at in the light of the coming of Jesus Christ and all that he did. This certainly means that we look beyond the outward application of the words to the attitudes and motives in our hearts. Jesus taught us this in the Sermon on the Mount (Matthew 5:21–48, but especially vv. 21–32, where he applies the commandments 'You shall not murder' and 'You shall not commit adultery'). It also includes enlarging the scope of the commandments so that they apply beyond the boundaries of the land of Israel. This is what Paul does with the fifth command in Ephesians 6:3, when he quotes the promise attached to the command in this way: 'that it may go well with you and that you may live long in the land' (compare with Deuteronomy 5:16). He omits the final words 'that the LORD your God is giving you', thereby making the promise applicable to Christians living far away from the land of Israel itself. The Sabbath command has also generally been understood to have been modified in a similar way, so that it now applies to the first day of the week, the day of resurrection, the Lord's Day.

If it is through the law that unbelievers are taught the knowledge of their sin, then the law is binding upon them and highly relevant to them. In Romans 2:14–15, Paul speaks of the Gentiles, who do not have the written

The law summarized in the Ten Commandments (4:44–5:21)

law, having 'the work of the law … written on their hearts'. This must be the same law in essence, even though it is imperfectly written on their hearts, or, we might say, does not perfectly inform their consciences. Does this mean that the laws of a land today ought to be based on these commandments? In a democracy, the law will by and large depend on the consensus of the people. What is most significant is that virtually all societies have laws that reflect commandments six to nine. In the nature of the case, commandments five and ten are unsuitable for enshrining in legislation, while the first four clearly reflect on the covenant status of Israel. Now that God's people are constituted from many different nations, it is not the responsibility of secular rulers to enforce laws that directly concern the honour and worship of God.

The first commandment is fundamental. The LORD is Israel's God and he does not permit his people to acknowledge any other. This is not simply because of all that he has done for Israel, but because there is no other (4:35). To turn to other gods, of whatever sort, is to turn from the real God to what is not God, from the living God to supposed entities that do not exist and can do nothing. This God has not left himself without witness (see Psalm 19; Acts 14:17), and everyone ought to acknowledge and submit to him.

The second commandment turns from the subject of acknowledging other gods to the ways in which God is brought down to the level of created things by the use of images to represent him. God is invisible; he is over and above his creation and cannot be pictured by anything in it. His creative works bear witness to his existence and his transcendence, his Word tells us all we need to know about him, and his character shines out supremely in his Son Jesus Christ. To desire anything further is sinful impertinence; more than that, it is wilful folly and shows a darkened heart (Romans 1:18–25). Once people begin to think of God in terms of created things, their understanding of God is deformed, and often becomes more and more so. The more they lose touch with the real God, the more their worship

Chapter 6

becomes debased and the need for careful obedience becomes undermined.

This commandment was given against the background of idolatry in which images were used as instruments of worship. The command explicitly says, 'You shall not bow down to them or serve them.' Though the use of images and statues can be said to focus the thoughts of the worshippers upon the deity, almost inevitably people begin to feel that in some way the god, or his spirit, is located in or with the image. So they act as if that were true, bowing towards, praying towards or walking quietly past the image. But God will have none of this. The only worship which is acceptable with him is 'in spirit and truth' (John 4:23–24).

Two cautions and one encouragement are attached to this command. Firstly, God is a jealous God. His love is stirred into jealousy by unfaithfulness. Secondly, as a result, upon those who hate him he visits their own iniquity. Fathers who hate God generally bring their children up to do the same, so a cycle of hatred and punishment is set up which may last for several generations. This seems to be mitigated by the way it is limited to the third or fourth generation. Perhaps this indicates that God periodically sends prophets to his people to recall them to their allegiance to him, and grants them repentance and renewal.

The encouragement is a powerful one. God shows steadfast love to those who love him, evidenced by their keeping of his commandments. We are probably to understand this as applying to thousands of generations, as the ESV margin note suggests. In other words, God's steadfast love never wanes or fails towards those who love him.

The third commandment is not primarily about speech; in fact, it is probably not about speech at all, except by implication. It is about God's reputation, God's name. Israel is not to behave in such a way as to tarnish that reputation; rather the nation is to act in ways that enhance it. This goes to the heart of Israel's calling to be God's people in a pagan world. As such the nation is to honour God in its corporate life, and in the personal lives of those who belong to it, as most of the commandments make clear.

The law summarized in the Ten Commandments (4:44–5:21)

This certainly means that no one in Israel was to use God's name in a curse as if it had magic power, but it went far beyond that. By love for God and obedience to him, by placing worship at the centre of its national life, Israel was to reflect the character of the LORD to the world round about. This is the calling of God's people in all ages (1 Peter 2:9).

Not surprisingly, a warning is also attached to this command. Regrettably, in his day Paul was able to write about many of his countrymen as follows: 'For, as it is written, "The name of God is blasphemed among the Gentiles because of you"' (Romans 2:24; see also Isaiah 52:5; Ezekiel 36:22). It is a tragedy when the same is true of those who bear the name 'Christian'.

The fourth commandment is the longest of the commandments, as is also the case in the Exodus account. There are some differences between the two accounts, but there is nothing contradictory between them. The Sabbath is the day of rest, which is what the word means. When we read the phrase 'to keep it holy', the emphasis is on keeping it as a day separate from the other six, a special day, one without work. There was no religious ceremony or worship commanded for the Sabbath, though later it became a suitable day for the synagogue service because people were free to gather together. The Sabbath duty towards God was to abstain from work and use it for rest, following God's own pattern in creation (Genesis 2:1–3).

This means that the Sabbath was for the benefit of people (note Mark 2:27) and animals, and godliness consisted in using it like that. In this way it was different from the first three commands, which are all directed towards God himself. By giving this command God was establishing a rhythm for human life: six days work, one day rest. Just as at creation God had established the rhythm of day and night and the seasons (Genesis 1:14–19; 8:22), so in bringing his creative activity to a conclusion God established the seven-day week with its sequence of work and rest. The evidence seems to indicate that a seven-day week is built into the human life-clock. To suggest that this command has been abrogated by the

Chapter 6

coming of Christ ultimately means abolishing the seven-day week—a feature ever more evident in our secular society. It is also interesting to note the importance of the number seven in Scripture, which seems to derive from the fact that the seventh day is the day blessed by God.

There is a greater emphasis here on servants and animals being allowed to rest on the Sabbath than there is in Exodus. Perhaps this reflects the fact that, once Israel has settled in Canaan, there will be greater pressure to work on the land at certain times of the year. The temptation might be for the Israelites to rest, and for foreign servants to be made to carry on working. But both servants and animals need rest and a change; note the last words of verse fourteen: 'that your male servant and your female servant *may rest as well as you*' (emphasis added).

The words 'You shall remember that you were a slave in the land of Egypt' seem to function in two ways. Firstly, they give a reason for the people to ensure that their servants enjoyed a Sabbath rest. The implication is that the Israelites knew what it was like to labour without any respite day after day, and their servants were not to be treated in that way. But the words also provide a reason for God giving the commandment, and therefore for the people to keep it. No longer is Pharaoh, with all his cruelty, their sovereign. The LORD is their sovereign now, and his rule is a beneficent one. They would demonstrate this by their obedience to this command. In doing so, their pattern of life would be different from those of others. They had a different God; they were a different people, living in a different way.

It is a matter of deep regret that when the Jews, much later in their history, began to emphasize law-keeping, they fastened particularly on this command. By the time of Jesus, the command to keep the Sabbath had been elaborated with all sorts of extra-biblical rules and an attitude which concentrated on rigidly obeying the letter of the law. Jesus frequently clashed with the Pharisees over Sabbath observance (e.g. Matthew 12:1–14). In resting on the Lord's Day, Christians need to keep in mind the

The law summarized in the Ten Commandments (4:44–5:21)

example and teaching of Christ. It is his day, and he is Lord of the Sabbath (Mark 2:28). His Word and Spirit will guide us in its use.

These first four commandments provide the theological basis for the other six and the motivation for keeping them. It is because the LORD is the God he is, and because he had done what he had for Israel, that they were to keep his commands; and in doing so they would display his nature, and show the wisdom and relevance of his commands to all human beings.

Study questions

1. What attitude do you find in the New Testament to the Ten Commandments?
2. What is it about the first four commandments that makes them so important?
3. How should those who preach and teach use the Ten Commandments?

Chapter 7

Continuation of the Ten Commandments (5:16–33)

The last six commandments (vv. 16–21)

The fifth commandment is different from the rest in being framed positively: 'Honour your father and your mother' rather than 'You shall not murder'. Ostensibly the previous command is also positive: 'Observe the Sabbath day, to keep it holy.' However, observing the Sabbath means 'On it you shall not do any work', so that commandment is fundamentally the same as the rest. It has often been pointed out that the negative form of the commandments implies a positive duty. 'You shall have no other gods before me' means 'You shall acknowledge and worship me as God, and not turn to any other in addition or as a substitute.' The same is true for all the commandments. Nevertheless, it is striking that the fifth command is framed in this way, and it serves to emphasize its importance.

Its importance is also underlined by the fact that Moses adds: 'as the LORD your God commanded you'. This, of course, is simply a reference back to the giving of the command by God at Horeb. But God gave all ten commandments at Horeb, so it suggests either that Israel had been in danger of neglecting this particular one, or that this command had a special significance for the nation as it went into the promised land. Quite clearly the latter was the case (though the former may also have been true), not only because of the reference to the land at the end of the command, but also because Moses here enlarges on the Exodus version. 'That your days may be long in the land that the LORD your God is giving you' becomes 'that your days may be long, and that it may go well with you in the land that the LORD your God is giving you'.

Continuation of the Ten Commandments (5:16–33)

The purpose, or promise, is not likely to mean simply that God would bless Israel if this command were kept; God would bless Israel if all his commandments were kept. It must mean that there is some relationship between obeying this particular command and a long period of prosperity in the land. Israel was a nation of families. They were all descended from Abraham. Their tribes were descended from the sons of Jacob, and the families were grouped into clans within the tribes. So the family in Israel was not an isolated unit in which its members took refuge from society around, as it can easily become today; it was what linked everyone together. So, honouring father and mother meant a stable family life, which in turn meant stability within the nation. The family should still fulfil this function of preparing children for good relationships in the wider world, and the fifth commandment is of crucial importance for this purpose.

The command includes both father and mother. This suggests it is not about just recognizing authority but respecting persons and appreciating what they do. Such attitudes are clearly necessary for things to 'go well' in a country. This is a reminder that the command is not about outward action but an inner attitude that will express itself in both speech and actions. Similarly, the tenth commandment is about the inner life, the desires that mould and motivate action. As Jesus taught in Matthew 5:21–32, although the other commands are expressed in terms of action, they also forbid the inner passions from which wrong actions spring.

The word 'murder' in 'You shall not murder' has a footnote in the ESV indicating that 'the Hebrew word also covers causing human death through carelessness or negligence'. There is no exact equivalent word for this in the English language. The AV's 'Thou shalt not kill' is even less exact. The precise meaning has to be ascertained by comparison with other teaching in Exodus to Deuteronomy. In a world of hatred and violence, this commandment has always been an important one. It does not, in itself, prohibit war or the death penalty, but it condemns many wars that have been fought. The preservation of life is a theme that recurs in Deuteronomy and this commandment undergirds it. In a day when anger is sometimes approved as a natural way to let off steam, we do well to remember Jesus' words about rage and contempt for a brother, as recorded in Matthew 5:22. While there is such a thing as righteous anger, uncontrolled rage is a terrible thing and has led to appalling deeds.

The seventh commandment forbids adultery. Its obvious purpose is to protect the marriage relationship, and this is seen in other parts of Deuteronomy (22:13–30; 24:1–5; 25:5–10; 27:20–23) as well as in earlier instructions (Exodus 21:7–11; 22:16–17; Leviticus 18; 20:10–21; Numbers 5:11–31). As it stands, it simply commands complete faithfulness in marriage. It is possible by extension to see it applying to fornication before marriage, but this itself is to be understood in the interests of marriage. Sexual intercourse belongs within marriage; indeed, the union of man and woman as one flesh is part of what marriage is. The Bible is fully realistic in speaking of the sinful situations that obtain in the world, but it is also clear that marriage and sexual union belong together. This is the principle that the seventh commandment protects. It is not popular today, but when you see the damage done by unfaithfulness and irresponsible sex, in terms of broken relationships, abortions, mixed-up children and single mothers unable to cope, you realize the wisdom of God's command. Currid comments, with Matthew 5:27–28 in mind, 'The body may commit the act, but the heart has given it birth.'[1]

The eighth commandment forbids stealing, that is, taking what belongs to another as if it were your own. At least two other principles lie behind this. Firstly, in Israel each clan and family had its own inheritance and this was inalienable. Although, through poverty, a family might sell its land temporarily, at the time of jubilee it all had to be returned to its inheritors (consider the instructions in Leviticus 25). The land was actually God's (Leviticus 25:23), and his people lived as sojourners in it. He owned it, and so they had no right to buy or sell what was his. Secondly, goods and possessions should be the fruits of work. This is implicit in the Sabbath

Continuation of the Ten Commandments (5:16–33)

command: 'Six days you shall labour and do all your work' (v. 13), which itself depends on God's pattern of work and rest in Genesis 1–2:3. In Genesis 2:15–17 man was to tend the garden and eat of its produce, while in Genesis 3:17–19 work became labour and toil as a result of man's disobedience. In any society, however, not everyone is able to work and the work of some is in the interests of others, so Deuteronomy emphasizes the importance of provision being made for widows, orphans, immigrants and the Levites (see, for example, 10:18–19; 14:27–29).

This command, then, is not based on a right to own private property, although the legitimacy of private property is implied. It is based on following God's pattern, and obeying him as his people. Generous giving to the needy is simply doing what God does and is itself a preventative to stealing (see Proverbs 30:7–9). Stealing is a denial of brotherliness or neighbourliness. It treats the other person as if he or she didn't count. It is disruptive of society and brings suspicion and fear into a community. It should not simply be assessed in monetary terms, because its effects are far more extensive than that. Not least are its effects on the person who steals. He or she becomes increasingly alienated from others, unproductive and lazy, and self-respect is undermined.

What is interesting about the ninth commandment is its explicit reference to 'your neighbour'. This command is not about an abstract principle—truth-telling—but about the harm that can be done to another by bearing a false witness about him or her. In view of this reference (and also the similar reference to 'your neighbour' in the next commandment), it is right to see the three previous commands as concerned with the good of 'the neighbour', 'the other person'. Murder and violence obviously harm 'the other'. Adultery harms 'the other': both the wronged spouse and the other party involved. Stealing harms 'the other', as earlier comments have tried to demonstrate.

The overriding concern here, then, is love for a neighbour. All slander and gossip is condemned by this command. So, for that matter, is relating

Chapter 7

what is true when it does nothing more than injure the reputation of another: 'Hatred stirs up strife, but love covers all offences' (Proverbs 10:12). This does not mean that we should overlook the seriousness of speaking what is false. God is a God of truth, who never lies (Titus 1:2), and Jesus taught us that our 'Yes' should mean 'Yes', and our 'No', 'No' (Matthew 5:37). But there is all the difference in the world between speaking the truth in love, and speaking it without love.

This is not the time to consider those places in the Bible where it appears that lying is condoned (as, for example, in the case of Rahab and the spies in Joshua 2). There are some exceptional situations in life—particularly in time of war—when it is difficult to believe that simple truth-telling is right. In some cases it might well mean the death of innocent people, the neighbour whom you are to love. In extreme circumstances, the preservation of life must take precedence over speaking the truth.

As already noted, the final command directs attention to inner desires: 'You shall not covet.' Here in Deuteronomy, the order of things that might be coveted is listed slightly different from that given in Exodus, and 'field' is also included. The emphasis is very practical; each phrase prohibits the coveting of something belonging to a neighbour. It is clear that this prohibition underlies the previous four commands as well: Ahab had Naboth judicially murdered because he coveted his vineyard (1 Kings 21); David coveted Uriah's wife, Bathsheba, and committed adultery with her (2 Samuel 11); once Naboth was dead the way was open for Ahab to steal the vineyard which he had desired; the way in which Naboth was killed involved false witness being given against him.

To covet means to have a strong desire that longs to be satisfied. This commandment is also couched in terms of love for a neighbour. It is not wrong to desire to be married because you see someone else who is happy and fulfilled in marriage; what is wrong is lusting after someone else's wife or husband. Greed is always wrong—a desire that must be gratified is wrong—but this commandment focuses in particular on desire that harms

Continuation of the Ten Commandments (5:16–33)

the relationship with a neighbour. And the desire doesn't have to be followed by any action. Envy prevents many people from showing anything more than a bare civility—at the most—towards those who are envied. It can spoil relationships even within the home. It is a pernicious evil, and God forbids it.

Israel responds to the voice of God (vv. 22–27)

The opening verse in this section sets the Ten Commandments apart from any other instructions which would be given and gives them a special foundational significance. They were spoken directly to Israel, 'to all your assembly'. God spoke with particular solemnity 'out of the midst of the fire, the cloud, and the thick darkness'. He spoke 'with a loud voice; and he added no more'. There was no mistaking what he said, and it was particularly these commands that he wanted to give. They were written in stone for Israel, indicating that they were to be a perpetual expression of God's holy will.

Not surprisingly, the sound of the voice of God had a profound effect on the people. We might feel that they were mistaken in asking, 'Who is there of all flesh, that has heard the voice of the living God speaking out of the midst of fire as we have, and has still lived?' After all, God had spoken directly to Moses, as well as to earlier figures such as Abraham, Isaac and Jacob. However, there is no doubt that this was a unique occasion, both in the displays of God's glory and greatness (v. 24), and in the fact that he spoke to the whole nation together. The people knew that God spoke at times to special chosen individuals, who then relayed what he had said. But it was a quite different thing when he spoke to them all, from the highest to the lowest.

So the people therefore asked that God would not again speak directly to them, but follow the pattern of speaking to Moses, who would then speak God's message to them (v. 27). But what they had already experienced had had its effect upon them so that they said, 'And we will hear and do it.' We

Chapter 7

today have never heard the voice of God speaking to us, neither should we seek for such an experience nor expect it. We have God's word already written down for us. But our response should be the same: 'We will hear and do it.'

The LORD responds to the words of Israel (vv. 28–33)

Moses continues to recount what had happened at Horeb. What the people had said was right, so God would no longer speak directly to them. On this occasion there could be no doubting the sincerity of the people in their desire to hear and do what God said. But God knows the human heart, so he said, 'Oh that they had such a mind as this always, to fear me and to keep all my commandments, that it might go well with them and with their descendants forever!' (v. 29). We must not lessen the force of that 'Oh'. God earnestly desires obedience, and he desires that people will obey so that things will go well with them for ever. He takes no pleasure in the death of sinners, but instead longs for them to turn back from their evil ways and live (Ezekiel 33:11).

In verse 32 Moses has finished speaking of what happened in the past, and he turns directly to the people who are before him and addresses them. In view of what they have said in the past, and the fact that the LORD has now brought them to the edge of their inheritance, they need to be careful to obey all that he has commanded them. If they walk in his way, they will 'live long in the land that [they] shall possess' (v. 33). We, too, need to walk in his way, and the Ten Commandments provide a valuable summary of that way and a spur to obedience in our ongoing pilgrimage.

Study questions

1. In what ways do the Ten Commandments reflect the character of God himself?
2. What functions does the law, as expressed in these commandments, fulfil?

Continuation of the Ten Commandments (5:16–33)

3. How far is it possible to see a parallel between Israel as God's covenant people, committed to holiness by obeying his commands, and the church, as the new covenant people of God?

Note

1 **Currid,** *Deuteronomy*, p. 552.

Chapter 8

The heart of the law: love for God (6:1–25)

Here Moses tells the people that command that Jesus was to call 'the great and first commandment' (Matthew 22:38). Verses 4 and 5 have always been of the greatest importance to Jewish people. These verses lie at the very heart of the relationship between God and his covenant people, then and now.

Love the LORD your God (vv. 1–9)

At the end of chapter 5, Moses recounted how, at Mount Horeb, the people of Israel felt it was too great a thing for them to listen to the voice of God as they had done when he gave them the Ten Commandments. So Moses was to hear what God had to say, and he would then relay to the people all the commands and instructions that God gave. In these verses, Moses begins to do this: 'Now this is the commandment, the statutes and the rules that the LORD your God commanded me to teach you …' (v. 1).

The opening paragraph (vv. 1–3) emphasizes certain things about these commands. They are being given with a view to Israel entering the land promised to their fathers, a land flowing with milk and honey. Here are instructions for the new life awaiting Israel. Obedience is to flow out of and lead to fear of the LORD, that is, a true recognition of all that he is and an attitude of deep reverence and respect. Obedience is to be a feature of succeeding generations—'your son and your son's son' (v. 2)—and it will lead to God multiplying the nation greatly (v. 3). Obedience and blessing go hand in hand.

Verses 4 and 5 bring us to the heart of the law, indeed, the heart of the relationship between the LORD and his covenant people. First is a

66 Exploring Deuteronomy

The heart of the law: love for God (6:1–25)

declaration that Israel must hear and note: 'The LORD our God, the LORD is one.' This statement is made against the backdrop of the polytheism of the nations around Israel. Quite unlike those nations, the people of Israel have only one God; therefore their allegiance and devotion are not shared out among competing deities, but are rather to be wholly given to the LORD. This one God is their God, for he has pledged himself to them by covenant. This covenant is based on his love (7:6–8), and the only adequate response is for Israel to love God in return.

This definitive assertion of the unity of God is of the greatest importance. The LORD has no rivals; he is the self-existent One, the 'I AM WHO I AM' (Exodus 3:14), the living and true God. To love and worship any other is to turn from him to what is not God, to an idol or idols. As those who have the New Testament, we know that God is Father, Son and Holy Spirit, but the revelation of the unity of God comes before the revelation of the Trinity in Scripture (although by reading the Old Testament in the light of the New, we can see indications of the Trinity). If this were not so, it is likely that the tendency would be for people to think in terms of three Gods, or tritheism, as it is called. There is, even now, a danger of some Christians thinking in this sort of way, emphasizing or preferring one person of the Trinity before the other two. The unity of God, however, is absolutely fundamental; but it is not the unity of splendid isolation, but of interpersonal community in love.

The 'first and great' commandment, then, is this: 'You shall love the LORD your God with all your heart and with all your soul and with all your might.' As we have seen, this was to be a responsive love. Israel had every reason to love the LORD. There was much the people knew about him and about what he had done. They knew him as Creator of all things. They knew him as the God of Abraham, Isaac and Jacob. They knew him by personal experience. Many of them had seen his mighty acts: of judgement upon the Egyptians and upon those among themselves who had sinned; of deliverance in bringing them out of Egypt. They had all eaten manna day

Chapter 8

after day, and quail. They had drunk water out of the rock. Their clothes had not worn out and their sandals still protected their feet from the rocky paths they travelled. We who know of the giving and coming of the Son of God—his life, ministry, death and resurrection—and who have tasted of his grace have even greater reason to love God. It is to the shame of many of us that our love is so fitful and half-hearted.

We have seen, too, that this was to be an undivided love, and, as such, it needed to be wholehearted. It is difficult to be sure how to distinguish between 'heart' and 'soul' in this verse. In ordinary conversation in English, 'heart and soul' is simply an emphatic way of saying 'wholehearted', but the repetition of the phrase 'with all your' and the addition of 'might' may indicate some difference here. What is certain is that God should be loved with the totality of our being. The quotation of this verse in Luke 10:27 adds the word 'mind', and Matthew 22:37 has 'mind' but not 'might'. From our perspective, it is right to think of mind, emotion and will—all our powers—as united in loving God, and of loving him with all the strength that we have.

This is not the only place in Deuteronomy where the command to love God occurs. We shall meet it again in 7:9; 10:12; 11:1,13,22; 13:3; 19:9 and 30:6,16,20. It is essential to keep love for God central when we think about the laws and instructions in this book, indeed in Israel's religion as a whole. Keeping the Ten Commandments and obedience to all the other laws and instructions were intended to flow from loving God. Without love, outward obedience was nothing. Throughout the Bible, it is clear that the relationship between God and his people is intended to be one of mutual love. The Bible never contrasts law and love in the way people sometimes do today. The law informs and guides love into those ways that please God and which are beneficial to our neighbour, who was made by God. Because of indwelling sin and living in a godless world with its temptations and enticements, love needs that guidance and rejoices in it: 'Oh how I love your law! It is my meditation all the day' (Psalm 119:97).

The heart of the law: love for God (6:1–25)

Such love has a practical expression (vv. 6–9). These verses are commands, yet they are also the natural consequence of loving God. Those who love God will love what he says, and they will take his words to heart. They will treasure them up in their minds, meditate upon them and put them into practice in their lives: 'His delight is in the law of the LORD, and on his law he meditates day and night' (Psalm 1:2). Verses 8 and 9 are to be interpreted metaphorically. God's commands and words are to be ever before the eyes of his people. Their houses bear witness to their obedience to God's word and they do not change into different people when they pass through their gates and go out and about for work or business. Privately and publicly they are to live out what God says.

Just as the LORD in his love gives his words to his people, so his people who love those words are to teach them carefully to their children. As God blesses Israel with multiplication (v. 3), so the people must be careful to see that the new generation knows the ways of the LORD. This teaching is to be informal as well as structured. Many occasions will give opportunity to teach and answer questions. This obligation of spiritual education still lies on Christian parents and needs to be taken very seriously. Those who love God, and recognize the great blessing of having his Word and living by it, will take care to fulfil this responsibility.

Do not forget him (vv. 10–15)

The LORD was sure to keep his promises, so Israel would enter the good land as he had said. But that itself would bring its own temptations in due course. Although the Israelites would have to fight their way into the land, its cities, houses, fields and vineyards would be there ready for them to take over as their own. The danger was that, when they began to eat and become full, they would forget God. Every circumstance or situation, no matter that it may come as a gift from God, has temptations peculiar to it. When things go well, even under the blessing of God, watch out! As C. H.

Chapter 8

Spurgeon is reputed to have said, 'Adversity has slain its thousands, but prosperity its tens of thousands.'

But there was another danger. Israel had gone down into Egypt as a large family. As such, the people had lived apart from the Egyptians (see Genesis 46:31–47:6). They were not treated as equals by the Egyptians, who made them into slaves and had little social contact with them. The Israelites were therefore drawn together and cast in upon themselves. But once settled in the land, they would not only become aware of the sort of people who had lived there, they would also have increasing contact with the nations around them. They would get to know about their gods and their worship. They could easily feel their own difference from others, indeed the uniqueness of the religion of the LORD, so they would feel the pull of the temptation to 'go after other gods, the gods of the peoples who are around you' (v. 14).

So Moses warns against forgetting the LORD. The people would need to remember that he was the LORD their God, and that all the many good things they had received were his gifts to them. They were to 'fear' him (v. 13); perhaps 'fear' has the sense of fearing to provoke him, a fear engendered by the remembrance of his greatness and holiness which they saw at Horeb. They were to serve him, and take their oaths attesting to their truthfulness by his name. They were to remember that he is a jealous God; he loved them, and unfaithfulness would stir up anger against them. To turn to idols would risk destruction from the face of the earth. Such serious considerations should bring a caution into our lives, too. It is utter foolishness to play fast and loose with God.

Do not put him to the test (vv. 16–19)

What took place at Massah is recorded in Exodus 17:1–7. In fact, Massah means 'testing', and Moses gave it that name because the Israelites 'tested the LORD by saying, "Is the LORD among us or not?"' (Exodus 17:7). When the people arrived at this place there was no water for them to drink, and

The heart of the law: love for God (6:1–25)

they fell to grumbling against Moses and quarrelling with him, and indeed with God himself. It seems that they made supplying water a test as to whether God was with them or not. Instead of recalling all that they had already experienced, and the promises he had made to them, all they could think of was their present thirst. So they made this a test of the Lord. If he provided water, then he was with them, and they would continue to follow him; but if he didn't, then they would know he wasn't with them. What they would have actually done then is not clear, but they would no longer have trusted or followed the Lord.

Moses warns the people against repeating their behaviour at Massah. There would be hardships in capturing the land, and things would not go absolutely smoothly all the time after that, so the people were to settle it in their minds to keep God's commandments diligently and do what was right and good in his sight. It is not unusual to find people who once professed faith in Jesus Christ, but who have given up following him because at some point their prayers were not answered as they wanted. Things turned out in such a way that they felt justified in deciding that he had not passed their test. So they no longer followed him. The fact is that God may test us, but we have no right to put him to the test. Jesus himself used verse 16 to reply to the devil when he was tempted to throw himself down from the pinnacle of the temple (Matthew 4:7; Luke 4:12). As followers of Jesus Christ, we have to follow his example in this respect also.

The crucial words come at the end of this passage: 'the good land that the Lord swore to give to your fathers by thrusting out all your enemies from before you, as the Lord has promised' (vv. 18–19). God had given his word that he would thrust out their enemies and give them the land. They did not need to test whether he was going to or not; their business was to get on and obey what he had told them, relying on his promise. God has given us his promises, too (2 Peter 1:4). It is our business to rely on them and get on with what we know is right and good in his sight.

Chapter 8

Teach your son about him (vv. 20–25)

Children are naturally curious. Why do we do this? Why do we live differently from other people? Moses recognizes that, as the next generation grows, the time will come when sons will ask their parents about the meaning of God's commandments. This will give them the opportunity to recount the story of the Lord's redemptive mercy. There are three features of the reply they are to give that are particularly worthy of note. Firstly, once again the emphasis is on the fact that God brought the Israelites out of Egypt that he might bring them into the land (v. 23). Redemption from slavery in Egypt had a positive purpose: a land to be occupied and a life to be lived there for God.

Secondly, these statutes are 'for our good always' (v. 24). They are beneficial for Israel, they promote their good, things will go well with them. The phrase 'that he might preserve us alive, as we are this day' is not a reference to mere existence. Through God's commands, which are wise and good, and with his blessing, Israel will be preserved and prosper.

Thirdly, Moses points out that 'it will be righteousness for us, if we are careful to do all this commandment' (v. 25). The people of Israel will be righteous if their lives are aligned with God's will, as revealed by his commandments. Righteousness consists in obeying God, because what he commands is what is right. What he commands reflects his character, and he is righteous and good in every respect.

This section draws attention to an opportunity and a responsibility. The curiosity of children and their readiness to ask questions provide opportunities for teaching them the ways of the Lord. Parents need to seize these natural opportunities. In this lies their responsibility. Children are to be taught the story of God's redeeming love. They are to be encouraged to believe his Word, to fear and reverence him, and to walk in his ways.

The heart of the law: love for God (6:1–25)

Study questions

1. What reasons can you find in this chapter—and perhaps the earlier chapters—for loving God?
2. Why is it easy to forget God when things go well? How can we guard against this?
3. What principles does this chapter provide for the education of our children?

Chapter 9

Chosen to be distinctive (7:1–26)

When Israel enters the land there will be danger, not only in the long term: there will be the immediate danger of intermarriage with the Canaanite tribes, especially as God will only drive out these tribes little by little (v. 22). So Moses warns the people against intermarriage: they have been chosen as God's holy people and must live in obedience to him.

Make no covenant with the Canaanites (vv. 1–5)
The nations already resident in Canaan are described as 'seven nations more numerous and mightier than yourselves' (v. 1). This was why Israel needed a firm trust in God and the assurance of his ability to give them victory; by themselves they were quite incapable of capturing the land. This was also why Moses constantly urged them to go forward without fear, and encouraged them with God's promises. We must never think of them as a powerful army going in and crushing weak enemies and exterminating them. Here were a weak people, relatively few in number (v. 7) and vulnerable, going to take on cruel and vicious nations, secure in walled cities and with giants among them. This is David and Goliath in national terms. The temptation would have been to do the minimum to get a foothold in the land, and then come to some accommodation with the existing population.

The Israelites were also vulnerable in another way. Their background was one of idolatry. Abraham came out of Ur, which was a centre of the worship of the moon god, and all their lives, he, Isaac and Jacob lived among those who worshipped false gods by means of images. At Horeb

Chosen to be distinctive (7:1–26)

itself the older generation of Israelites had fallen into idolatry. Humanly speaking, the knowledge of the LORD, the true God, depended upon the feeble and fickle Israelites. The light of truth and righteousness in the world depended on them maintaining their distinctiveness.

We need to approach this opening section with these things in mind. It was God who would clear away the nations before Israel (v. 1), but in doing so he would give them over to the Israelites (v. 2). It was essential that Israel remained uninfluenced by Canaanite religion and Canaanite standards of conduct. They must not allow themselves to be drawn away from the LORD to other gods. So Moses gave a series of commands to the people. The Canaanite tribes were to be devoted to complete destruction. No covenant was to be made with them, nor were they to be shown any mercy. While any of them remained alive, there was to be no intermarriage with them. Intermarriage would be sure to result in compromise, leading eventually to the sons of Israel turning away to serve other gods (v. 4).

However, even when the Canaanites themselves were no longer a threat, their religious sites and images would still be in place. So verse 5 instructs Israel to destroy all vestiges of Canaanite religious culture so that no Israelites would begin to feel that, as they lived in the land, they ought to follow the rites that had been used in it. 'Asherim' (v. 5) were probably poles representing female deities, while 'carved images' might include images of animals as well as erotic images. Canaanite religion was basically concerned with the fertility of the land, so fertility rites had a large place within it.

To turn to the debased and idolatrous religion of the Canaanites would provoke God's anger—Israel was God's chosen people, a recipient of his grace and called to holiness. Such covenant unfaithfulness would lead to Israel being quickly destroyed. In the event, Israel did turn to idols all too soon after the settlement in the land. God did not destroy them quickly, but chastised them repeatedly through incursions by other armies until eventually they were taken away into exile in Babylon.

Chapter 9

Nevertheless, God's covenant still stood, and the remnant returned after seventy years.

The way in which we worship God both shows and moulds what we think of him. Our worship needs to be consistent with all that he has revealed about himself and what is acceptable to him.

God made a covenant with you (vv. 6–11)

The reason why Israel was to avoid intermarriage or using pagan paraphernalia in its worship is spelled out here: 'For you are a people holy to the Lord your God' (v. 6). God's grace to Israel is set out in some detail. Its origin was not anything in Israel itself. Far from being the most numerous of nations, the people of Israel were fewest of all. When Israel went into Egypt the people numbered only seventy (Genesis 46:27). Rather, the origin of God's grace was wholly to be found in God himself: 'The Lord set his love on you and chose you' (v. 7). No other reason can be given, and it is futile to try to get behind these words. Israel was 'a treasured possession' of the Lord's (v. 6), redeemed with a mighty hand from slavery (v. 8), and even at that time kept because of the oath the Lord had sworn. The people of Israel's response therefore, ought to be grateful obedience to the One who had so signally blessed them.

The Lord is a God who honours his own covenant. But this is a double-edged truth. He is a 'faithful God who keeps covenant and steadfast love with those who love him and keep his commandments', even 'to a thousand generations' (v. 9). But to covenant breakers who hate him rather than loving him and throw off his beneficent rule, covenant faithfulness means that he repays them to their face (v. 10). For this reason, the Israelites were to be careful to do his commandments, statutes and rules (v. 11).

In considering this and applying it, we have to remember that there was no promise of regeneration attached to the covenant made at Horeb, though this does not mean there were no true believers in Old Testament

Chosen to be distinctive (7:1–26)

times, or that these were not born of the Spirit. A new covenant, however, was essential (Jeremiah 31:31–34). All believers in Jesus Christ are beneficiaries of this new covenant; they have all been born again by the Spirit of God and have the law written in their hearts. Those who break covenant and turn away from God completely are apostates, who by this action demonstrate that they were never truly God's people at all (1 John 2:19). Having reason to believe we have been born again should not make us complacent; nevertheless, the strong warnings, such as we have here in verses 10 and 11, belong to the old covenant and should not leave Christians in a permanent state of uncertainty and fear. Having received such a superior redemption through Jesus Christ, we have far more incentive to loyalty and obedience. And half-heartedness and lukewarmness are correspondingly far more serious.

Covenant obedience leads to covenant blessings (vv. 12–16)

Throughout this chapter—and the book itself—a reciprocity about the covenant relationship between the LORD and Israel is highlighted. The covenant is initiated by God in his grace, but Israel is to respond by faithful obedience that, in turn, brings the covenant blessings that God has for it. In general terms, this is described as God keeping the covenant and his steadfast love (v. 12). More specifically, it means 'He will love you, bless you, and multiply you' (v. 13). This then opens out into a wonderful vista of the way in which God will prosper the people (vv. 13–15). We have already noted that Canaanite religion was primarily concerned with the fertility of the land. Here Israel is shown that this fertility actually depends upon the blessing of the LORD. Increased numbers and increased prosperity would lead to increasing contact with the peoples around, who would see what happens when the LORD is loved, honoured and obeyed. This would be a powerful witness to them.

We cannot take these words and simply apply them unthinkingly to ourselves as Christians. In general terms, it is true that those who trust and

Chapter 9

obey God will usually be healthier and more contented than they would have been had they remained in unbelief, but there are many exceptions, especially in periods of persecution. There is no promise of material prosperity and wealth for us, but these promises do serve a twofold purpose. Firstly, they are fulfilled in a spiritual sense: 'From his fulness we have all received, grace upon grace' (John 1:16). Secondly, they point forward to the time when there will be new heavens and a new earth, when God makes all things new, and sin and suffering will be gone for ever (Revelation 21:1–5). Right through the Bible, everything is moving ultimately towards this great climax when all the promises of God will reach their final and complete fulfilment.

Because God's blessing will depend on Israel's obedience, this section ends with another warning to deal thoroughly with the Canaanites, otherwise they will prove 'a snare to you' (v. 16). Some earlier commentators tended to apply this to us as ruthlessly 'slaughtering' our sins. This is not strictly a proper understanding of the passage, but it does remind us that we cannot afford to be anything but firm in removing things that we know are a snare to us.

Trust the God of the covenant (vv. 17–26)

In view of what Moses had said to the people in verse 7, 'You were the fewest of all peoples', it would not be surprising if they began to say in their hearts, 'These nations are greater than I. How can I dispossess them?' (v. 17). So Moses tells them not to be afraid of them and gives two reasons to set their fears to rest. Firstly, he says that they must remember the past evidence they have of God's delivering power. The Egyptians were far more powerful than Israel; the Israelites were but slaves with neither army nor weapons. Yet the LORD delivered them, and they had seen with their own eyes the wonders and mighty hand of their God. The first time the Israelites had stood on the borders of Canaan with the land before them, they had been afraid and had refused to go on. They may be afraid again,

Chosen to be distinctive (7:1–26)

but God will act towards the enemies that confront them now just as he acted towards the Egyptians (v. 19).

Secondly, Moses gives them the assurance of God's help (vv. 20–23). There are several elements to this assurance. There is the nature of the LORD himself, 'a great and awesome God'; and he will be in their midst (v. 21). Then God will use others to help them, and he 'will send hornets among them', which will seek out even those who have hidden themselves (v. 20). There is no agreement among commentators about the meaning of 'hornets'. Some believe it should be translated 'panic', others, 'discouragement'. Some think it should be understood literally: stinging insects would be used against those hidden away. Others think it should be interpreted metaphorically: Israel would swarm all over them like hornets or bees. Whatever the precise meaning, it is a promise of special help from the LORD.

Then a guarantee is given that God will enable them to overcome the Caananites (vv. 23–24). Their ultimate overthrow is assured. In verse 22, Moses indicates that the LORD will clear these nations away little by little. To make a sudden end of them, before Israel was ready to settle in the towns and spread out over the land, would mean an increase in wild animals, and this was something God would spare them. Centuries later, when the Assyrians captured the northern kingdom of Israel (as opposed to the southern kingdom of Judah), we read of an increase in lions in the devastated areas of the north (2 Kings 17:25–28; the fact that they were sent by the LORD does not necessarily mean that there was not also a natural reason for such an increase at that time). Israel's steady conquest of Canaan over time is indicated in verses 23 and 24 by the phrases 'until they are destroyed' and 'until you have destroyed them'. It is common for Christians to want God to do things quickly, but he has his own good reasons for taking the time he does.

This section concludes with warning. Total victory was in view, but again, the danger posed by Canaanite images after the people have been

Chapter 9

destroyed was a very real one. Carved images were to be burnt, but many of them would have been covered by silver or gold, posing a natural temptation. Theoretically, it would be possible to look on the silver or gold simply as precious metal and use it for other purposes. In practice it would be difficult for the Israelites to forget the use to which it had previously been put, or escape the feeling that it was sacred, devoted to the pagan god. It may be that they might be tempted to use these materials to make an image of the LORD himself, as seems to have been the case in Exodus 32:1–6 (note v. 5). The strong implication is that the images were to be burnt and destroyed, silver and gold and all.

It is difficult to know what 'an abominable thing' (v. 26) means, unless it is simply another reference to an image. Perhaps it refers to small figurines, or household gods. The reason for calling such things 'abominable' is that they come under the same category of that which had been devoted to destruction. This was the case, not only with the Canaanites themselves, but with all traces of their religion. No 'souvenirs' of Canaanite religion were to be kept. The Israelites were to detest everything to do with that religion and destroy it all thoroughly. If any of them did bring something devoted to destruction into their houses, they too would become devoted to destruction. This was what happened in the case of Achan (Joshua 7). When we read his story we need to remember the clear warning that Israel was given here.

As Christians we have to remember that we are called to be different. Our spirituality and worship are to be based firmly upon the self-revelation of our God. The spirit of the age and the priorities of those of other faiths and none are to be resisted in so far as they draw us away from biblical obedience and faithfulness to God.

Study questions

1. What parallels are there between the election of Israel (vv. 6–8) and the election of Christians as described in the New Testament?

Chosen to be distinctive (7:1–26)

2. What are people afraid of today? What antidotes to fear does Deuteronomy 7 supply?

Chapter 10

Bless the LORD—and take care! (8:1–20)

This chapter looks both backwards, to the years of hardship and testing in the wilderness, and forwards, to the good land to which the LORD is bringing Israel. In future days Israel must remember God's goodness to them in bringing them through the wilderness and giving them the land. To forget the LORD and turn to other gods would be tragic.

If you look carefully at this passage you will see that verses 12 to 18 are virtually a mirror image of verses 1 to 10a. This becomes clearer if we set it out in this way:

A verse 1: The land the LORD swore to give to your fathers.
B verses 2–6: Going through the wilderness.
C verses 7–10a: The good land in which you will eat and be full.
D verses 10b–11: Bless the LORD and take care not to forget him.
C verses 12–14a: Having eaten and become full in the good land.
B verses 14b–16: Going through the wilderness.
A verses 17–18: The covenant the LORD swore to your fathers.

This type of pattern, called chiasm, is quite common in the Bible. It tends to throw the emphasis on the middle section, D (vv. 10b–11), hence the title given to this chapter. In this case it also leaves verses 19 to 20 as a solemn conclusion. The repetition of ideas underlines the thrust of what Moses is saying. It is helpful to bear this in mind while going through the passage.

Hard times in the past (vv. 1–5)

In the course of urging obedience to God's commands upon the Israelites, Moses tells them to remember the whole way in which the LORD led them

82 Exploring Deuteronomy

Bless the Lord—and take care! (8:1–20)

in the wilderness. Those forty years—the first two before Israel's refusal to enter Canaan were also in the wilderness—were hard years. God did not even lead the people of Israel by the most direct route from Egypt to Canaan at the beginning. There were probably several reasons for this. They had to go through a desert region in any case, and God used this to humble and test Israel. This was then, of course, extended to forty years because of the refusal of the people to enter Canaan the first time they reached its borders.

It is likely that 'humble' in these verses means 'made you feel your weakness and dependence' (see v. 3 especially). Israel needed to learn complete dependence upon God. In Egypt, life had been predictable; every year the Nile flooded and provided fertility for food production. But in Canaan it would be different; there they would be dependent upon rain, and rainfall would in turn depend upon their obedience to God (11:10–17). So in the desert God was training them to trust him and rely on his provision. This is why 'He … let you hunger and fed you with manna, which you did not know, nor did your fathers know.' God provided for them miraculously in order to teach them to depend upon him. This provision included the fact that their clothing did not wear out, and it even extended to their feet. With all their journeying their feet might have been expected to become swollen and painful, but God preserved them from this.

Two reasons are given for God bringing them through a hard time in the wilderness. Firstly, God was testing them, to see what was in their hearts (v. 2). We have to recognize that God still tests his own people—see, for example, 1 Peter 1:6–7. Such testing does not necessarily mean that God is displeased, and we must not think that it is an unusual thing or that it indicates an uncertainty about whether we are truly members of the Lord's people. In fact, this testing indicates that we *are* his people: 'Know then in your heart that, as a man disciplines his son, the Lord your God disciplines you' (v. 5). The classic passage on such discipline is Hebrews 12:5–11.

Chapter 10

There, too, the assurance is given that discipline is an evidence of sonship, not lack of sonship: 'It is for discipline that you have to endure. God is treating you as sons. For what son is there whom his father does not discipline?' (v. 7). As saved sinners living in an evil world, God uses discipline to draw us from sin so that we may share in his holiness (v. 10). Many Christians have found that hard times have been some of the most valuable times of their lives, when they have learned dependence and grown close to the Lord.

The second reason for God bringing Israel through the wilderness comes at the end of verse 3: 'that he might make you know that man does not live by bread alone, but man lives by every word that comes from the mouth of the LORD'. The point here is not that human beings are intended to live by following what God says, true though that is, but rather that, ultimately, people live because God provides for them. In the wilderness they had to trust God and rely on him to provide in special ways because they were not able to provide for themselves, which is the usual way that God has ordained. They depended on his word to give them what they needed. As Christians we need to realize the same is true for us. In the prayer that Jesus taught us, we ask for God to give us our daily bread. However that prayer is answered, we are acknowledging that in the end, everything comes from God, and that our whole lives are lived under his overruling providence.

The good times yet to come (vv. 6–10)

Verse 6 links this section together with the first. Because God has been disciplining the Israelites, they are to keep his commandments and fear him. And they are also to do this because God is now on the verge of bringing them into the good land which he has for them. In the verses that follow there is a lyrical description of the land with its abundance of provision for the people. There they will eat and be full. It is the same God who tested and disciplined them who will bring them into this idyllic

Bless the Lord—and take care! (8:1–20)

place. They were never less than his people while in the desert, and they will not be more his people when in the land. Whatever the circumstances he brings his people to and through, he is still their God and they are his people in covenant with him. As it was for Israel then, so it is for believers now.

This description of Canaan is a reminder to us that the world God has made is a beautiful and productive place. We must never identify 'the world' in a verse like 1 John 2:15, 'Do not love the world or the things in the world', with the earth that God has created; rather it means human society under the power of the evil one (1 John 5:19). While it is true that a curse lies on the ground, it is also true that 'The earth is the Lord's and the fulness thereof' (Psalm 24:1). We can revel in the goodness of the natural world and enjoy what God has provided for us, remembering always to be thankful to him for all he has given us.

At the same time, we must remember that the blessings of the new covenant are primarily spiritual blessings. Our 'good land' consists of peace with God and fellowship with Father and with Son. Israel only knew of the Messiah in type and shadow, in prophecy and promise, and these were enigmatic and limited at the time of the Exodus. We have the New Testament, with its clear revelation of Jesus Christ, and are brought into a union with him that transcends anything possible for the Israelites. In the end, though, the 'good land' looks forward to the new heavens and new earth that we read about in 2 Peter and in the book of Revelation (2 Peter 3:8–12; Revelation 21–22). This is the final destination of the whole people of God from every age and every part of the world. The beauty of the descriptions of its perfection and glory in the book of Revelation is all that we can at present comprehend.

When Israel ate and were full, they were also to bless the Lord for the good land he had given them. They were to recognize his goodness in all that had come about for them, and express their thanks to him. This must always be our attitude, too.

Chapter 10

Never forget the LORD (vv. 11–17)

The danger for the Israelites, of course, was that they would begin to take God's blessings for granted and forget to thank him, and eventually forget that he was the one who had given those blessings. True gratitude was to be shown not simply by thanksgiving but by obedience—keeping God's commandments. As Jesus said, 'If anyone loves me, he will keep my word' (John 14:23; see also v. 21). Moses gives a necessary warning here against forgetfulness. Such forgetfulness could well come about through pride (v. 14), the heart being lifted up with the attitude expressed in verse 17: 'My power and the might of my hand have gained me this wealth.'[1] Israel had to fight its way to conquest over Canaan and settlement in the land. It would be only too easy for the Israelites to think that they had gained victory by their own strength, forgetting that it was God who had strengthened them and given them every success in battle. Such an attitude starts in the heart. It is possible to express thanks to God with the lips while the heart begins to take the credit to itself.

Not only would it be possible for the people of Israel to forget that it was God who had given them victory, this would also easily lead to their forgetting the time of testing in the wilderness. There they had been completely dependent upon God. There was no question of putting their survival through those years down to their own power and might. God gave water when there was no water; he provided manna when there was no food. He kept them safe, leading them through 'the great and terrifying wilderness, with its fiery serpents and scorpions' (v. 15). As time passes, it is all too easy to allow the memory of God's past goodness to fade. This is why God ordained feasts like Passover and Tabernacles. Every year the people were to be reminded of God's deliverance, in order to keep alive among them the memory of his goodness.

We need to note the final words of verse 16. The humbling and testing times were difficult for Israel but God had a good purpose in view. Similarly, James, in speaking of the steadfastness of Job, goes on to say,

Bless the Lord—and take care! (8:1–20)

'You have seen the purpose of the Lord, how the Lord is compassionate and merciful' (5:11). It may be that 'to do you good in the end' refers to Israel's settlement in Canaan, but it could also indicate that God was teaching them lessons in the desert which would always be valuable for them.

Always remember the Lord (vv. 18–20)

These verses round off the chapter. First there is a reminder that it is the Lord who gives Israel power to get wealth. It is true the people will have to exert themselves and fight to gain possession of Canaan. But it is also true, and vital for them to remember, that this power will come from God. Moreover, power is given to confirm the covenant. Victory over Canaan is God fulfilling his covenant promise to Israel; there is no reason at all, therefore, for the Israelites to begin to take the credit for victory to themselves. Similarly, in our Christian lives and service for the Lord, it is the power and grace of God that enables us. We, too, have no reason to lift up our hearts in pride or to congratulate ourselves on what we think are our achievements.

Finally, Moses turns to warning. The Canaanites themselves stand as a solemn warning to Israel. Why are they destined to perish? Because of their idolatry and the sinfulness of their behaviour. Israel is in a far more privileged position than they were, so if the Israelites turn to other gods and refuse to obey the voice of the Lord their God, they are more responsible, and they, too, will perish. Just as Chorazin, Bethsaida and Capernaum were more responsible than Tyre, Sidon and Sodom (Matthew 11:20–24), so those who live in countries with a Christian heritage, and who have many opportunities of hearing the gospel, have a great responsibility. Those who read this book bear a greater responsibility than the peoples of Canaan.

Chapter 10

Study questions

1. Consider the significance of Jesus' use of verse 3 (Matthew 4:4; Luke 4:4), bearing in mind its context of testing in the wilderness.
2. Why is it that good things are more likely to lead to people forgetting God than difficult experiences?
3. This passage is very carefully crafted (see the opening explanation); what might this teach us about sermons and Bible talks?

Note

1 This follows the ESV translation in the Collins edition, 2002.

Chapter 11

A stubborn people chosen by grace (9:1–12)

Moses impresses upon the Israelites the fact that victory in Canaan will only be gained because the LORD goes before them. The Canaanites will not be driven out because of Israel's righteousness, but because of their own wickedness. The Israelites, in fact, are a stubborn people, prone to rebelliousness.

This passage continues the warning note with which the last chapter concluded. It also links up with 7:6–11. In that passage, Moses told the people that the LORD did not choose them because of their great numbers—they were actually the fewest of all peoples—but simply because he loved them. Here they are reminded that God is not giving them the land because they are righteous. Quite the opposite; they have a very stubborn streak that has been only too evident in their history.

There is a general point arising from this that we ought to note. It is extremely easy to get the wrong idea about God's choice of Israel, so we must take what is said in this chapter and chapter 7 seriously. The Israelites were very poor material to be God's nation and God's servants. Their choice was by God's sovereign grace, and such victories they gained were by his power and according to his promise. It was humbling for them to realize and acknowledge this. But in this they were a pattern to the rest of the world. God sets his love on and calls *sinners* to be his people. If Israelites can become his people, then a Canaanite prostitute like Rahab can find mercy, and so can you or I. It is humbling for us, too, to look at it like this, but that is what we have to do. For Jew and Gentile, salvation is by grace—unmerited, forfeited favour—from first to last.

And there is a further truth here. It was extremely humbling for Pharaoh

Chapter 11

to acknowledge that the God worshipped by those who had been slaves to the Egyptians for years was actually the true and living God who had to be obeyed. In spite of all the evidence he was presented with, he was simply not willing to do that. Down through the centuries the Jews have been a despised nation. Anti-Semitism has been rife in Europe and beyond. Yet whoever we are, British, Arab or German, the Bible demands that we acknowledge that the Jewish nation was chosen by God to be a blessing and a light to the nations (Genesis 12:1–3; Deuteronomy 32:43 [Romans 15:10]; Isaiah 60:3). And more than that, we all have to acknowledge that the Saviour of the world was a Jew, a root out of a dry ground (Isaiah 53:2), yet the only One who is the way, the truth and the life, through whom we come to God.

A consuming fire (vv. 1–3)

This section functions in two ways. As already noted, there is warning here. The enemies confronting Israel are formidable. The only reason Israel will be able to overcome them is because God is going to go before them. This takes away all basis for future pride or boasting of their own military prowess. On the other hand, they are just on the verge of entering the land: 'You are to cross over the Jordan today' (v. 1). They need the assurance that the LORD is going with them as they confront great nations, cities fortified up to heaven, and people great and tall. Warning and encouragement go hand in hand.

Verse 3 continues to act in this twofold way: 'Know therefore …'; be assured that the LORD goes before you. 'Over' refers to crossing the Jordan. Once across the river there is no going back; they will not have burnt their bridges, for there is no bridge! But God—their God—goes over first, so they need not fear. But he goes over before them as a consuming fire. They have already seen the reality of this (5:25). If the consuming fire is on their side and goes before them, then it is their enemies who will feel its effects and be destroyed. 'Drive them out' probably refers to driving them out of

A stubborn people chosen by grace (9:1–12)

their cities and fortifications, rather than driving them out of the land.

The description of the Canaanites and their cities in the first two verses reminds us again that Israel was about to take on the most formidable of enemies. Without God's help they would be sure of overwhelming defeat and destruction.

Wicked nations (vv. 4–5)

The temptation in verse 4 is one to which sinful people are very prone. It is almost natural for us to think that if we have victories, if God blesses us or our churches, this must be because of our obedience, our righteousness. This is the secret thought that we so easily speak to our hearts. We need this passage as much as the Israelites were going to need it.

Moses makes it clear that the reason why the Canaanites are going to be destroyed is because of their wickedness, and the reason why Israel will be God's instrument is because he has chosen them for this and it is part of the word sworn to their fathers. This is not the 'goodies' driving out the 'baddies'. What happened to the Canaanites sets no precedent for 'good nations', however defined, to invade 'bad nations'. God could have punished the wickedness of the Canaanite tribes in the way he punished Sodom and Gomorrah, but he did not do so. Perhaps, as already suggested, he used warfare because they were themselves warlike.

Stubborn people (vv. 6–12)

The people of Israel, then, must certainly not think that they are going to possess the good land because of their righteousness. It is a gift, springing from God's grace. In fact, the Israelites have proved themselves to be a stubborn and rebellious people. In the Authorized Version of the Bible, the word 'stubborn' is translated 'stiff-necked'. The imagery here may come from domestic animals. Donkeys and mules could be stubborn creatures. When their owners pulled on the rope, either to get them to move or to direct them in a different direction, the animals might stiffen their necks

Exploring Deuteronomy **91**

Chapter 11

and resist the pull. A certain stubbornness can be a virtue in some circumstances, but not when it resists the word of God and refuses to be pulled away from its own ideas and agenda. Many relational problems and difficulties in churches are caused by stubbornness.

So Moses calls on the people to remember how they have provoked the LORD in the past, and he especially reminds them of what happened at Horeb—'Even at Horeb you provoked the LORD to wrath' (v. 8). The second half of verse 7 indicates that from the very day God delivered them from Egypt, they were rebellious against the LORD. That they should be rebellious at Horeb, however, after all that they had seen and heard, and the covenant commitment they themselves had made to the LORD there, was tragic. This is emphasized in a number of ways. Notice, for example, the repetition of 'forty days and forty nights' (vv. 9,11). Just a few weeks after the voice of God speaking the Ten Commandments had filled the hearts of the people with fear, they joined together in breaking the second of those commandments. Note also the repetition of 'quickly' in verse 12: 'Arise, go down quickly ... They have turned aside quickly ...'

In the next section Moses develops this theme and retells what happened at that time of rebellion. Before we move on, however, we must remember again that all this was intended to humble the Israelites and keep them from pride and a complacency that could arise from their knowledge that God had chosen them. They owed everything to God's grace and forbearance, and so do we. There is no place in the Christian life for pride and self-righteousness. Just like the Israelites, Christians have many painful memories they can recall which bring them down on their knees before God. Such memories burst our pretensions and keep us low, but also underline the marvellous grace of God and lead us to fresh amazement at his kindness and to heartfelt thanksgiving.

Study questions

1. How does this chapter, and the earlier chapters of Deuteronomy, help us

A stubborn people chosen by grace (9:1–12)

in our understanding of the present status of the state of Israel, and in our assessment of its actions?

2. What factors in church life today remind us that God's blessings and good gifts are not rewards for our own righteousness?

3. Once we recognize that God's blessing is not a necessary evidence of our righteousness, what other dangers in our thinking might we fall into?

Chapter 12

A rebellious people spared by grace (9:13–10:11)

Moses recounts from his own perspective what happened at Horeb when the Israelites made the golden calf. He tells them how he prayed earnestly and at length for the LORD to be merciful to them. The LORD listened to him, gave him the commandments again, and sent them off to resume their journey to possess the land.

The golden calf (9:13–17)

The LORD had said to Moses, 'Arise, go down quickly from here, for *your people whom you have brought from Egypt* have acted corruptly' (v. 12, emphasis added). In this whole passage and on into chapter 10 we shall see that Moses accepted the responsibility implied in the phrase 'your people'. In fact, this passage sheds a flood of light on Moses' character and his deep sense of responsibility and concern for the people of Israel. God himself recognized Moses' commitment to Israel, and this comes out in his words at the beginning of verse 14: 'Let me alone, that I may destroy them …' Even before Moses had seen what Israel had done, God knew that he would plead on their behalf.

We must not forget the point of Moses' retelling of the events recorded here. The people needed to be reminded of their stubbornness. They needed to remember how so shortly after they had accepted covenant obligations at Horeb (see Exodus 24:3–8) they broke those covenant vows by idolatry and degrading behaviour (Exodus 32). They needed to realize also that their lives had been forfeited by breaking the covenant, and that it was only through the intercession of Moses and the mercy of God that they now, thirty-eight years later, stood on the border of the land of promise.

A rebellious people spared by grace (9:13–10:11)

When they entered the land, and when, in due course, they would be able to enjoy its good things to the full, their attitude needed to be: 'Through the LORD's mercies we are not consumed, because his compassions fail not' (Lamentations 3:22, NKJV). Nor must we forget its truth in our own case. It is not our righteousness but God's grace that saves us, keeps us and will bring us safely to his better land in the end.

Moses' prayers for the people are even more striking in the light of what the LORD says at the end of verse 14: 'And I will make of you a nation mightier and greater than they.' Moses does not seem to have even hesitated when this proposal was put to him (see Exodus 32:10–14). This raises a problem that has troubled many people. Did God really intend to destroy Israel after all his promises to them and their forefathers? Did he actually intend to make a new nation descended from Moses? Did everything hang on Moses' intercession? What if he had failed or wavered? These are questions that we cannot answer fully. They arise because we are not capable of understanding the relationship between limited, responsible people and the sovereign LORD of all. But we have to acknowledge that everything did hang on Moses' intercession. The nation deserved God's judgement, but God had already put a covenant mediator in place and so things turned out exactly as he determined they should.

There is a fearful contrast in verses 15 and 16. Moses comes down from the mountain, a mountain still blazing with the fire of God. He carries the two tablets of the covenant in his hands. He looks, and there are the people; oblivious to the burning fire and the covenant they had entered, they have made a golden calf! He smashes the tablets to the ground, which break in the sight of the people, for they have broken the covenant and quickly turned aside from the way the LORD had commanded them to follow.

There could be no greater indication to the people of the seriousness of their sin, yet they do not seem to have been affected by what Moses did. Exodus 32:25–29 shows that at least some of the people continued their wild revelry until the Levites intervened with force. It is likely that we

Chapter 12

ourselves do not realize the seriousness of the idolatries of which we can be guilty, nor of the inadequate and inappropriate worship to which we may be prone.

The covenant mediator (9:18–24)

Moses, however, did appreciate how serious Israel's sin was and had heard God's threat of judgement. For forty days he fasted and lay prostrate before the LORD, until he knew that God was going to be merciful and spare the people. These forty days and nights matched the previous period of time he had spent on the mountain (see 10:10): forty days receiving the details of the tabernacle, and forty days praying for the people. This period seems to mirror the forty years Israel was to spend in the desert.

Not only did Moses realize the seriousness of Israel's sin, he was also afraid that the people had so provoked the LORD that he would destroy the nation in his 'hot displeasure' (v. 19). It is doubtful that we have much idea of the ways in which God's people offend him today. It is also probably true that few of us are anything like as earnest in prayer with God as Moses was. He had, of course, been made responsible for the people; he was the mediator of the covenant that was made at Sinai (Galatians 3:19–20). In this he points forward to Jesus Christ, the mediator of a new covenant (Hebrews 9:15), one who ever lives to make intercession for us (Hebrews 7:25). Just as the lives of the Israelites were spared through the intercession of Moses, so our lives have been spared through the mediation of Jesus Christ, and our final salvation is guaranteed by his constant presence as our High Priest at his Father's side.

Moses was concerned not only for the people in general, but also specifically for Aaron, who, under pressure from them, had made the calf of gold (Exodus 32:1–6). It must have been a terrible disappointment for Moses to find that his own brother had acted in this way. It is remarkable—and magnifies God's mercy—to remember that it was after this that God appointed Aaron to be the first high priest in Israel. Not only

A rebellious people spared by grace (9:13–10:11)

Aaron's life, but also his future usefulness depended on Moses' prayer for him. When we reach heaven, how much we shall find that was the result of earnest, faithful, believing prayer!

Tragically, what took place at Horeb was only the first in a series of rebellious acts against God on the part of Israel. At the first two places mentioned in verse 22, Moses came before God, and on the first occasion, fire that came down from the LORD was extinguished at Moses' prayer. Moses recalls these things in order to prevent Israel from rebelling again. Now was the time for them to obey God and go forward in faith.

The fervent prayer of Moses (9:25–29)

Here Moses reveals the content of his prayer for Israel. All the way through he was pleading with the LORD on the basis of what he had promised and what he had already done. God had said to Moses, 'Your people ... have acted corruptly' (v. 12). But Moses prayed, 'O Lord GOD, do not destroy *your* people and *your* heritage' (emphasis added). He reminded the LORD that he had redeemed them and brought them out of Egypt by his greatness and mighty hand. How could he then go back on what he had done? These were the descendants of Abraham, Isaac and Jacob, to whom he had given promises; how could he go back on these? He asked God not to regard the stubbornness and wickedness of the people in case the Egyptians should say that God was not able to bring them into the land that he had promised them. All these are powerful arguments. You can see how Moses concluded with almost the same words with which he began. For forty days Moses pleaded with God, and God heard and had mercy. His persistence was remarkable, and God honoured it. We must notice that at the heart of this prayer is Israel's stubbornness, wickedness and sin. Moses relates to the present generation just what the situation was, so that they would obey the LORD and not repeat the stubbornness and sin of the past.

In our praying we can, and should, use arguments based on what we know to be the truth about God's character and promises. But we must also

Chapter 12

be absolutely honest in acknowledging sin for what it is. We do not, and cannot, plead our own righteousness as a basis for God to answer our prayers. We can only confess the reality of our sins and plead his mercy. As Daniel prayed, 'We do not present our pleas before you because of our righteousness, but because of your great mercy' (Daniel 9:18).

The covenant restored (10:1–5)

When Moses broke the two tablets of stone (9:17), it symbolized the fact that Israel had broken their covenant with the LORD. So when the LORD told Moses to cut two further tablets and bring them up on the mountain, it indicated that the covenant had been restored. In spite of what Israel had done, God had responded to the pleas of Moses and was again going to give his commandments to the people. The tablets on which God would write the commandments were to be put in an ark of acacia wood, which seems to have been a temporary box—perhaps 'chest' is a better word—used during the time that Moses' tent functioned as the meeting place of God (Exodus 33:7–11). When the tabernacle was completed the two tablets were put into the ark of the covenant (Exodus 25:16; 40:20; compare Hebrews 9:1–5). This is similar to the custom of those times when kings would put copies of treaties beneath statues of the gods. What happened here reminds us—as it was intended to remind Israel—of the central importance of the Ten Commandments to Israel as a people in covenant with the LORD. Note how Moses finishes telling the Israelites about the commandments: 'And there they are, as the LORD commanded me' (v. 5).

The journey resumed (10:6–11)

The ESV puts verses 6–9 in parentheses, and it may be that they did not form part of Moses' address to the people but are included for completeness in the written book. Verse 6 provides two important pieces of information. Firstly, Israel did journey on. In God's mercy, the people were not consumed and they continued towards the land of promise. Secondly,

A rebellious people spared by grace (9:13–10:11)

Aaron's life was spared and it was not until the last months of Israel's wandering that he died (Numbers 33:38–39). In both cases, Moses' intercession proved effective. The reason why Aaron didn't enter the promised land was because of his rebellion at Meribah (Numbers 20:24), in which, of course, Moses was also implicated, and for which he also was excluded from entering Canaan. The place names here do not seem to tally with those given in Numbers 33, but we do not know enough about the area at that time to be able to give an answer as to why this is.

Verse 8 takes up the mention of the ark in the earlier verses. 'At that time' does not refer to the time of Aaron's death, but the time just after the incident of the golden calf and the subsequent erection of the tabernacle. The setting apart of the Levites is described in Numbers 1:47–54. The Levites were set apart to carry the ark of the covenant of the Lord, and this is primarily why they are mentioned here. But they had additional duties which would be particularly evident once Israel had settled in Canaan. They would settle in special cities throughout the land (see Joshua 21) as a tribe whose inheritance was the Lord himself. The phrase 'to this day' at the end of verse 8 may suggest that this section was added, under the guidance of the Holy Spirit, some time after Israel was established in the land. God not only restored the covenant with Israel, giving them his commandments again, but he also ensured that the tablets on which the commandments were written were carefully preserved through the years of travelling by a tribe set apart for this purpose.

Verse 10 brings us back to Moses' address to the people. This is not a third period of forty days, but, as the verse indicates, Moses is summarizing what happened. This leads to the last sentence in verse 10 and to the Lord's words in verse 11. Because of Moses' prayer, and the oath sworn to Israel's fathers (v. 11), the Lord said, 'Arise, go on your journey.' This whole section from 9:8 has emphasized Israel's proneness to disobedience in the past, and God's forbearance and mercy with the nation. In view of both these realities, and the fact that their journey would not be finished until

Chapter 12

they were settled in the land, the Israelites needed to look forward in faith, and arise and go over the Jordan to take the land. God's people are always on pilgrimage while they are in this world. The challenge to us is to get up and get on; to keep on until we reach the end of our journey.

Study questions
1. In what ways may we be stubborn and rebellious?
2. What has Moses to teach us about prayer?

Chapter 13

What the LORD requires (10:12–11:7)

Moses, in his address to Israel, turns from reminding them of the past to spelling out their duty in the present. It is not just a matter of crossing the Jordan in obedience to God; there is a life of loving service to God that lies before the people in the land to which they are going.

A fivefold requirement (10:12–13)

These verses make up one sentence which is framed as a question, one, though, that includes the answer. By speaking in this way, Moses elicits a response from the people, for quite clearly this is indeed what God requires. This is a covenantal requirement; being in covenant with such a God as the LORD must inevitably be expressed in these ways. These five elements form an agenda for Israel's life. All of them will be repeated and elaborated in the chapters ahead. Apart from some modification in our understanding of 'the commandments and statutes of the LORD, which I am commanding you today', each of these elements is what God requires of his covenant people today, and, indeed, what he requires from all those made in his image. This passage down to 11:1 is one of great relevance for us all.

'To fear the LORD your God' is to have that fear which is the beginning of wisdom and true knowledge (Proverbs 1:7; 9:10). It is that sense of awe, respect and reverence that arises from considering the greatness and majesty of God, as seen, for example, in verses 14, 17 and 21. It also reflects on his holiness and goodness. We rightly fear to offend such a God of holiness, who has showered us so richly with his benefits. But the text says, 'your God'. He is our God, and it is because we are in covenant with him

Exploring Deuteronomy **101**

Chapter 13

and know him, and the revelation he has made of himself, that we respect him and honour him.

'To walk in all his ways' could be understood as living according to the ways that God has laid down for us in his commands and statutes. But it may be that here the sense is rather that we are to follow his example. Look at the end of verse 17: 'the awesome God, who is not partial and takes no bribe'. Surely the implication there is that his people must be just the same. This is even clearer in the next two verses: 'He [God] executes justice for the fatherless and the widow, and loves the sojourner, giving him food and clothing. Love the sojourner, therefore, for you were sojourners in the land of Egypt.' God's goodness to the fatherless, widow and sojourner is the pattern for his people. They are to 'walk in all his ways'.

'To love him.' This requirement can never be repeated too often; this is the first and great commandment, and all the other commandments flow out of this. God has set his love on us, and we are to set our love on him.

'To serve the LORD your God with all your heart and with all your soul.' This is love in its outward expression. Heart and soul love leads to heart and soul service. Service like this is not forced or a burden; it is free, joyful and fulfilling. Those who think that service can win God's love are desperately mistaken. God loves us freely, and we are to love him in return, and freely and gladly serve him. Love serves, not as servants serve, but as lovers serve.

Love also shows itself as we 'keep the commandments and statutes of the LORD'. These commandments were given to Israel 'for your good'. They were wise commands, suited to the needs of Israel, the circumstances they were in and the times in which they lived. All God's commands are given for our good. They are to help us and guide us in our living. Life is better when we do what God says.

A multiform incentive (10:14–11:1)

Verse 14 begins with 'Behold'. It is a call to consider, to think of what God

What the Lord requires (10:12–11:7)

is like and what he has done. Knowing what God requires of us, we are now to consider why we should do it. Here are incentives to glad obedience. The first of these is the amazing love of God and his choice of those who comprise his people. Note the importance of the word 'yet' at the beginning of verse 15. The heaven of heavens belongs to the Lord, and so also does 'the earth with all that is in it' (v. 14). 'Yet the Lord set his heart in love'—what a remarkable phrase that is!—'on your fathers and chose their offspring after them, you above all peoples.' How can we ever get over the amazing truth of election: God chose us above all peoples! Who like we his praise should sing?

But there is another emphasis here. How unworthy was Israel of the love and choice of God! There might even be something of that idea in the phrase 'you above all peoples'. Fancy choosing people like you! This might almost catch the sense of the last phrase in the verse: 'as you are this day'. Certainly when we come to verse 16 this is the case: 'Circumcise therefore the foreskin of your heart, and be no longer stubborn.' Israel's rebelliousness and stubbornness have already been highlighted, for example from 9:6. God had been wonderfully gracious to Israel, and he has been wonderfully gracious to each one of us who has been called to faith in Jesus Christ. How much we ought to love him! What a debt of love and glad service we owe to him who has been so good to us!

As we have already noted, what the Lord has done for us gives us a pattern for our lives. He shows no favouritism and cannot be bribed, and his people must be the same. He acts justly to relieve orphans and widows and cares for people in need like that; and it was to be the same in Israel, and among Christians. He loves the foreigners who come to take refuge in his land, and he provides food and clothing for them. How does he do that? He does it by stirring up his people, those who love him, to love as he does and to help immigrants in their distress. Israel, of course, knew precisely the feelings of those who settle in a strange land. Because they had been sojourners, they were to show mercy to such people who came among them.

Chapter 13

Not only the choice of God and his example, but also all the great things that he has done constitute an incentive to fear him and hold fast to him (vv. 20–22). These are summed up in the reminder that there were seventy persons who went down into Egypt (see Genesis 46:27), and now the nation is as numerous as the stars of heaven. In spite of ill-treatment by the pharaohs and the rigours of the wilderness wanderings, God has delivered them and blessed them. We are sometimes despondent over the number of believers in Jesus Christ, yet the eleven disciples to whom Jesus gave his great commission have multiplied and multiplied. We know, too, that in heaven there will be a great number, which no one can number, of those redeemed by Christ, singing the praises of Father and Son (Revelation 7:9–10). What incentives we have to loving service!

The application is drawn in 11:1: 'You shall therefore love the LORD your God and keep his charge, his statutes, his rules, and his commandments always'—'therefore', that is, 'in view of all that God is and all that he has done'. And it is always love that is to the forefront.

A necessary consideration (11:2–7)

There is a further consideration. The Israelites need to remember what God has done both by way of encouragement and also by way of warning. Although all the older generation had died in the wilderness, many of the adults among the people were still able to remember the deliverance from Egypt and all that God had done for them throughout the forty years in the desert. There was a whole generation of people who were under twenty when Israel refused to enter Canaan the first time (Numbers 14:28–33), and it is to these leaders and older people that Moses is directing his words (v. 2).

The Israelites are to consider 'all the great work of the LORD that he did' (v. 7), 'his greatness, his mighty hand and his outstretched arm, his signs and deeds' (vv. 2–3). On the one hand, they must consider what the LORD did to Pharaoh and the army of Egypt, but on the other hand, what he did

What the LORD requires (10:12–11:7)

to them in the wilderness, and in particular to Dathan and Abiram, whom the earth swallowed up. Those who withstand the will and word of God experience his judgement. Israel must consider this as they face the decision to enter the land that God promised to them, and the call to remain true to the LORD and to fear and love him. God can deliver them from their enemies and give them victory. He has done so in the past. He can also humble them and chastise them, and he has done this in the past, too.

We must not think of the way God speaks here in terms of a crude 'stick and carrot' approach. Nor must we understand the Christian life in such a way. The LORD is the God of ultimate truth and ultimate right. To respond to his love is bound to result in joy, peace and blessing. To reject his love and despise his word can only bring loss and suffering to us. So to consider the discipline—or instruction (v. 2, margin)—of the LORD means to learn the lessons taught by the past.

Study questions

1. How far does 10:12–13 sum up the totality of what God requires of us? What different aspects of our lives are covered in these verses?
2. In what way does the character of God set a pattern for our living?
3. What can you see of the discipline of the Lord as you consider your own life?

Chapter 14

Living in dependence upon God (11:8–32)

The land to which Israel is going depends upon the rains for fruitfulness, but the rains depend upon the blessing of God. In that land live nations greater and mightier than Israel, so victory, too, depends upon the blessing of God. For the present and future generations of Israelites, 'trust and obey the LORD' is the watchword.

Living in an uncertain environment (vv. 8–12)

Although the Israelites had been slaves in Egypt, there had been a certain stability and predictability about life in that land. Although they had suffered great hardship, it was in the interests of the Egyptians to keep them alive, and the regular flooding of the Nile meant that they could sow their seed and irrigate it. Egypt was 'like a garden of vegetables' (v. 10). It was the unpredictable hardships of the desert that caused them to hanker after a return to Egypt (see, for example, Exodus 16:2–3). In the desert they had to depend upon the constant provision of the God who had delivered them from Egypt, and this they found hard to do. Now Moses informs them that they are going into a land where they will have to depend upon the LORD continually for the growing of their crops.

We, too, long for security; we do not like the uncertainty of life in the world as it is. We like to be in control and to have every eventuality taken care of. But we have to live in this world, and as Christians we also find that very often God brings us through times and experiences in which we are completely cast on him. Churches have to depend entirely upon him for their fruitfulness, and as individuals we have to live by faith every day.

Although from one point of view Canaan was an unpredictable

Living in dependence upon God (11:8–32)

environment, in that it depended upon the rain coming for its fertility, from another point of view it was a better environment than Egypt. This was 'a land that the LORD your God cares for. The eyes of the LORD your God are always upon it, from the beginning of the year to the end of the year' (v. 12). To live in daily direct dependence upon the God who made everything, and who controls it all, is far better than relying on the regular rising of the Nile or an apparently secure job, or investments or insurance policies. That did not mean that the Israelites were to make no provision for themselves in Canaan—they were to till the land, plant the seed, save some for the next season and so on. But their priority was to trust in God and rely on his blessing, and we are to act and trust in a similar way.

Trusting in a faithful God (vv. 13–17)

Trusting and obeying go together; the latter is the evidence of the former. But note what obeying means. As we have already seen several times, the essential command of God is to love him, and here we have it again (v. 13). It is not, 'If you are good, God will give you rain'; rather it is, 'If you love God—and this will mean that you serve him with all your heart and soul—then he will give you rain and bless you in the land.' It is the relationship with the LORD that is of supreme importance; keeping his other commands flows out of that.

This matter of relationship comes up again in the warning in verse 16: 'Take care lest your heart be deceived.' There are other gods that bid for the trust and worship of God's people. Or rather, there is an enemy, the devil, who seeks to turn people from the living God by presenting to them other gods that are no gods. The danger for Israel was to start thinking in the sorts of terms that generally prevailed in those days and to imagine that there were special gods that belonged to Canaan—territorial gods—and that these needed to be worshipped and appeased. Like Israel, we are called to be loyal to the God who has revealed himself in his word.

If Israel turned aside to other gods, then God's anger would be kindled

Chapter 14

against them and the heavens would be shut up. God cannot be trifled with, and those who owe so much to him must not play false with him. He pardons weakness that looks to him again and again in repentance and cries for strength and grace. He judges apostasy that tramples on his grace and presumes on his mercy. But for those who love and serve him there is the promise of rain, grain, wine, oil and livestock: 'You shall eat and be full' (v. 15). And there are many promises for twenty-first-century Christians, too.

Keeping God's word before your eyes (vv. 18–25)

Both for the present and the future, the Israelites needed to store up God's words in their hearts ('mine' in verse 18 refers to Moses, but all that he said to Israel came from the LORD). While the focus is obviously on God's commands at this point, these commands do not stand on their own. The people needed to keep *all* his words in mind: the revelation of his own character, his promises and warnings, everything he had made known to them. This is once again expressed in a very vivid way: as binding them on the hand and putting them as frontlets between the eyes (see Exodus 13:16 for the first occurrence of these words, where they are clearly used in a figurative way). If God's words are stored up in the mind, they will also be before the people's eyes; they will be constantly in view. This may not refer to actual memorization of God's words—in the context 'these words' comprise practically the whole of the book of Deuteronomy—but the substance is to be kept in mind. Memorization of Scripture is valuable, but there is a danger of memorizing the verses we like and passing over more challenging or humbling verses.

As in chapter 6, there is an instruction to teach the children, and this was obviously to be an ongoing responsibility. If this was faithfully done, and the word of God heeded, then Israel's days in the land would be multiplied 'as long as the heavens are above the earth' (v. 21). From verse 22, the more immediate future is in view. Notice again how doing 'this commandment'

Living in dependence upon God (11:8–32)

is described: 'loving the LORD your God, walking in all his ways, and holding fast to him' (v. 22). 'Holding fast to him' means being faithful to him in days to come, but may also have the sense of clinging to him, keeping close to him. Certainly both aspects are important for us.

If Israel obeys in this way, then God will enable them to take all the land that he has for them. We might note that God promises to 'drive out all these nations before you' (v. 23). Presumably this would be the result of God laying 'the fear of you and the dread of you on all the land' (v. 25). They would flee before Israel, and those who fled would not be exterminated; only those who resisted would suffer in that way. It was not until the days of David and Solomon that the whole of the territory described in verse 24 came to be under Israelite control. Greater faith and obedience would have seen that happen much earlier. It may well be that, if the churches today were more faithful to God and his word, and acted more boldly in faith, there would be much more numerical growth and spiritual prosperity than is the case at present.

The nations in Canaan were 'greater and mightier than yourselves' (v. 23), but that was no problem to God. Similarly, the difficulties twenty-first-century churches and Christians face are no problem to him either. Entrenched unbelief, arrogant intellectualism, socially-accepted sin, careless indifference—all can be broken down by the power of the Holy Spirit. 'For the weapons of our warfare are not of the flesh but have divine power to destroy strongholds. We destroy arguments and every lofty opinion raised against the knowledge of God, and take every thought captive to obey Christ' (2 Corinthians 10:4–5).

Looking at the options (vv. 26–32)

Moses calls on the people to look, to consider: 'See, I am setting before you today a blessing and a curse' (v. 26). The blessing would follow obedience to God's commands. The curse would follow disobedience, the turning aside from God's way and going after other gods. But this 'seeing' was not

Chapter 14

to be simply metaphorical, a 'seeing' in the mind. When the Lord brought Israel into the land, they were to set aside two mountains, one—Mount Gerizim—on which the blessing was to be set, and the other—Mount Ebal—on which the curse was to be set. These mountains were in the central area of the land on either side of a valley. Whenever the people journeyed from north to south, they would be reminded by the mountains of the blessing or the curse. Further details of this were given later by Moses in chapters 27 and 28.

The obedience that Moses was speaking about, and that the Lord looked for from his people, was not just the matter of the decision to cross the Jordan. Verse 31 seems to anticipate that, after all the exhortations of Moses, the people would go in to take possession of the land. But God looked for ongoing obedience: 'And when you possess it and live in it, you shall be careful to do all the statutes and the rules that I am setting before you today' (vv. 31–32). The Christian life is like this: daily obedience, walking in the ways of the Lord, and so experiencing his continuing blessing.

Study questions

1. In what ways can we to lay up God's words in our hearts and souls?
2. Are there things we see that might act to remind us that we may know either God's blessing or his displeasure, in the way that Mount Gerizim and Mount Ebal did for Israel?

Chapter 15

The place where God chooses to put his name (12:1–32)

How is Israel to live in the land that the LORD is going to give them? Moses now gives detailed instructions to the people, beginning with their worship of the LORD. The principle is always to do what God says.

At this point a new section in Moses' address to the people begins. Indeed, some writers make a clear break here, though the repetition of the words used in 11:32 in 12:1 shows that this is all one address and also signals that the 'statutes and rules' are now going to be set out in detail. Up to this point Moses had reminded the people of the Ten Commandments (chapter 5) and given them general exhortations to love the LORD and to go forward in faith and obedience, but now this changes. Many writers see the Ten Commandments as underlying a great deal of what Moses is now going to say. In chapter 12, we can see that the first and second commandments are being applied to the situation Israel will face in Canaan ('You shall have no other gods before me. You shall not make for yourself a carved image, or any likeness of anything that is in heaven above, or that is on the earth beneath, or that is in the water under the earth. You shall not bow down to them or serve them; for I the LORD your God am a jealous God …'). The third command, 'You shall not take the name of the LORD your God in vain', is also relevant because God's name is going to be put at the place where Israel is to go to worship him.

It is also interesting to notice the structure of this chapter. We can set it out like this:

A verse 1: Be careful to do the statutes and rules.

Chapter 15

B verses 2–4: Destroy the places of Canaanite worship and do not worship as they do.
C verses 5–7: Worship at the place where God puts his name.

C verses 8–14: Do not do what is right to you; worship where God puts his name.
D verses 15–16: Eat meat anywhere, but not with the blood.
C verses 17–19: Eat tithes and offerings where God puts his name.
D verses 20–25: Eat meat anywhere, but not with the blood.

C verses 26–28: Take holy things and vow offerings to the place where God puts his name.
B verses 29–31: Do not be ensnared by Canaanite worship or worship as they do.
A verse 32: Be careful to do exactly what Moses commands.

Two features are immediately clear from this. Firstly, there is considerable repetition, indicating the importance of what is repeated. Secondly, the importance of 'the place that the LORD your God will choose out of all your tribes to put his name and make his habitation' (v. 5) is emphasized.

The wrong and right ways to worship God (vv. 1–7)

The first detailed command concerns the way Israel is to worship God in the land. This is of crucial importance. If the attitude of the people to the LORD is wrong, then everything else is likely to be wrong. When God is appreciated for what he is and worshipped in the ways he has laid down, the foundation for lives of obedience and service is established.

Verse 2 takes up what had been commanded in 7:5. When Israel takes possession of the land, the shrines of the Canaanites and their religious objects will still be there. These are all to be completely destroyed. One reason for this is that to allow them to remain will provide a source of

The place where God chooses to put his name (12:1–32)

temptation to the Israelites. The LORD is not to be worshipped in that way, so the temptation to do so must be ruthlessly removed. At Sinai itself Israel had worshipped God under the form of a golden calf (9:13–21; Exodus 32:4–5). They must remember their weakness and tendency to disobey, and cut off the opportunity to do so again.

So where are they to worship God? God will choose out a place where he will put his name and which will be his habitation. There they must bring their sacrifices and offerings, their tithes and contributions (vv. 5–6). Although it is not explicitly stated, it is clear that it is at this place that the tabernacle will be erected. The tabernacle was the place where they met with God; the Most Holy Place was where his special presence was located, and it was at the tabernacle that the altar was found at which sacrifices were to be offered. The fact that this place was God's habitation and the place where his name was put meant that the people needed to be careful to keep all his commands and to seek his glory. His reputation depended on how they acted at and viewed the place where his name was. If their worship was a mere matter of form, if they treated it lightly and carelessly, if they mixed it with pagan elements, God's reputation would suffer, both among Israel as a whole and among the nations around. How we worship God shows what we think of him and affects his reputation.

Their worship was also an occasion of covenant reaffirmation. When a great king had made a covenant with a vassal state, there were occasions when all the people, or their representatives, would go up to the capital city and the royal palace. They would bring their tribute, their gifts and offerings. They would pledge their loyalty to the king. There would be a great feast; in the presence of the king all would eat together. This was their king who ruled over them, defended their land and provided for their welfare. They were his loyal servants. So, in a much higher and truer way, Israel was to pledge its love and loyalty to its sovereign LORD. He was present; his name was there at tabernacle or temple. His people were to gather to show their gratitude and affirm their allegiance. As Christians,

Chapter 15

too, we come to thank the Lord and say, 'We love you, Lord. We will be true to you; we give our hearts to you alone. Grant us grace to follow you and keep us faithful even in a sinful world.'

Joyful worship at the place where God puts his name (vv. 8–14)

In the previous passage, worship at the place God would choose is contrasted with the worship of the Canaanites. Here it is contrasted with Israel's current practice (vv. 8–9). It is difficult to be sure just what is meant here, as the tabernacle was in use at this time. Perhaps because the Israelite tribes were strung out while they travelled, people still continued to offer sacrifices in the way in which their fathers had done (see, for example, Genesis 13:18; 35:6–7). We must remember that individuals continued to meet with God even though they were away from the tabernacle or temple. Even in exile in Babylon they were not cut off from access to God, as the book of Daniel bears witness.

Why was God going to choose one place to put his name once Israel had settled in the land, even though some of the people were bound to be at a distance from it? One reason must be that it would buttress the unity of the nation under their God. They were one not just by virtue of descent from Abraham: they were one by God's sovereign choice and covenant. They were bound to him together as his people, and this was made visible and strengthened by the tribes coming together three times a year to worship the Lord at the place he had chosen. We live in days of rampant individualism, with Christians scattered in many different denominations and groupings. God puts us into churches because unity is important and the witness of a vibrant Christian fellowship makes a powerful impact.

But the tabernacle located in a particular place, and the temple built at Jerusalem that replaced it, bore witness to the fact that God was available and could be met here on earth. This pointed forward to Jesus Christ himself, for it is in him that we now meet with God (see John 2:18–22; 1:18). Because Jesus is now present by his Spirit, both strands in the Old

The place where God chooses to put his name (12:1–32)

Testament—that God is everywhere and can be found anywhere, and that his presence is located especially in the tabernacle/temple—come together in him. We can only come to the Father by Jesus the Way, but Jesus can be met anywhere by those who come in repentance and faith.

In this chapter there is no reference to the regular feasts. What is in view are the individual sacrifices that people or families might offer and the eating of tithes. In both cases it would have been easy for the people to offer sacrifices or to eat in the place where they lived. This was what they must not do; for these purposes they were to go to the appointed place. When they came to present sacrifices or tithes, they were to rejoice before the LORD (vv. 7,12,18). Why should this be so? The worship of God was a joyful thing because it involved God's people coming to their God. The fact that the LORD was their God and that they could come to him was all of his grace. Their joy was a response to his mercy. How unspeakably good he had been to them! The sacrifices spoke of the reality of forgiveness, and the tithes were a visible symbol of God's continuing provision. How much there was to be glad about! Doubtless the Canaanites, when they engaged in the orgiastic fertility rites that took place at their shrines, thought that they were having a good time. But Israel's joy was far deeper, purer and greater than theirs.

True worship is always a joyful thing. It is the response of a redeemed people to a gracious God. We who know that our redemption has come through the sacrifice of the Son of God himself have even greater incentive to be full of joyful thanksgivings.

There are two further things to note. Firstly, this joy was a corporate thing: 'your households' (v. 7). This is spelt out further in verses 12 and 18: sons and daughters, servants and Levites—all rejoice together. What a great thing it is to see families joyfully worshipping God together with the rest of the church, their voices uplifted in praise, their faces showing the gladness they feel. Secondly, verse 7 adds 'in all that you undertake, in which the LORD your God has blessed you'. God's redeemed people, free in

Chapter 15

the land he has given them, keeping his statutes and offering sacrifices for their sins, are blessed by him in all they undertake, so that they rejoice at all his goodness. This is never the whole story while we are in this world, yet the life of godliness is the best life of all. It is a joyful thing to live our lives before God.

Eating meat and eating the tithe (vv. 15–19)

A clear distinction is made here between animals offered in sacrifice and animals that are killed for food. The people are able to kill and eat animals for food wherever they live. But they are not to eat meat with blood; this is to be poured out on the ground. This reflects what God had said to Noah and his sons (Genesis 9:3–4). The point here seems to be that life belongs to God, and this is symbolized by blood. To lose your blood is to lose your life. By pouring out the blood, the people of Israel would be acknowledging that it was God who had given life to the animal, and that they were killing and eating because they had his permission to do so. Leviticus 17:11–12 adds another reason for abstaining from eating meat with the blood: it is by the shedding of blood, that is, by the taking of life, that atonement is made. A substitute dies in order that a sinful person might be forgiven. This significance of blood was ever to be kept before the eyes of the Israelites when they killed an animal.

But this was not to be the case with their tithes or the firstborn of their sheep or cows, which were to be dedicated to God. It comes as a surprise to see that the tithes were to be eaten by the people who brought them. Weren't they supposed to be devoted to the support of the Levites (Numbers 18:24)? On reflection, it becomes clear that it was not possible for a tenth of a year's harvest to be eaten on one occasion. It appears that when the Israelite family brought tithes and offerings to the central sanctuary, they would eat with the Levite who had come with them from their town (v. 12), reaffirming the covenant, and then all the rest of the tithe would be given to the Levites. It looks as if it might have been possible for

The place where God chooses to put his name (12:1–32)

Levites who lived away from the sanctuary to be overlooked, and there is a warning against this in verses 18 and 19. When Israel was settled in the land it could be that the Levites in Jerusalem would seem much more important than the local man in the town. Such a mistaken attitude is not unknown today.

Blood poured out, for meat and for sacrifice (vv. 20–28)

While this section repeats what has just been said, it does so in greater detail. There is an emphasis here on the freeness of the permission to eat meat: 'whenever you desire' (v. 20); 'so you may eat of it. The unclean and the clean alike may eat of it' (v. 22).

A reason is also given here for pouring the blood on the ground: 'For the blood is the life, and you shall not eat the life with the flesh' (v. 23). This corresponds with Genesis 9:4 referred to above, and the reference to sacrifice in verse 27, with its particular emphasis on the blood, recalls Leviticus 17:11–12. Even the flesh of animals sacrificed could be eaten, but the blood was poured out, showing that the life had been taken. The animal had died as a substitute for one—or more—who had sinned.

An incentive is given for obeying God's commands at this point: 'that all may go well with you and with your children after you, when you do what is right in the sight of the LORD' (v. 25; compare v. 28). Things go well when we do what pleases God. Note also that verse 26 speaks of 'the holy things that are due from you'. Certain obligations lie on those who are God's people.

Do not follow the ways of the Canaanites (vv. 29–32)

The chapter draws to a conclusion on a note of warning. The temptation is spelled out: 'Take care that you be not ensnared to follow [the Canaanites] and that you do not inquire about their gods, saying, "How did these nations serve their gods?—that I may do the same"' (v. 30). The danger of taking our cue for the worship of God from the actions of people who are

Chapter 15

not believers in him is constant. Think of where such a procedure may lead to in the end: 'For they even burn their sons and their daughters in the fire to their gods' (v. 31).

The right way is to be careful to do everything that God commands, neither adding to nor subtracting from what he has revealed. How this principle works out in new-covenant days following the coming, death and resurrection of Jesus Christ may be subject to debate. But the principle itself should not be.

Study questions

1. What are the main principles of worship revealed in this chapter? How far are they relevant for Christians in worship today?

2. Study what the Scriptures tell us about tithing. See especially Leviticus 27:30–33; Numbers 18:21–32; Deuteronomy 14:22–29; Matthew 23:23.

3. Should Christians rejoice before God in worship? In what ways should this express itself?

Chapter 16

Hold fast to the LORD (13:1–18)

In the previous chapter the Israelites were warned against the influence of Canaanite religion turning them from obedience to the LORD. But there could be dangers nearer to home, and here Moses warns about these.

The prophet or dreamer of dreams (vv. 1–5)

The first danger is that of a prophet who may give a sign or wonder and tell the people to go after other gods and serve them. A 'dreamer of dreams' is simply a person who bases his message upon dreams which he has had. There is no real distinction between 'prophet' and 'dreamer'. 'Dreams' probably includes visions. While the LORD sometimes revealed his will through these means, not everyone who dreamed a dream or saw a vision, or claimed to do so, was a true prophet of his.

We must notice that the test was the content of the message. Any message which contradicted what God had already revealed about himself and urged the people to turn to new gods could not be right. The fact that a prophet might give a sign or wonder that came to pass counted for nothing if the nature of the message turned them away from God. We should notice the ominous words 'arises among you' (v. 1). What is envisaged is not someone coming from outside of Israel, but one of their own people. Whoever he was and however well respected, and whatever he claimed or did, if he gave a message that turned people from the LORD, it was to be utterly rejected. Such a message could not be right.

That a warning like this was necessary is shown only too clearly by Israel's subsequent history. At times false prophets abounded so that the

Chapter 16

true prophets of the LORD seemed like voices crying in the wilderness. Jeremiah was to say, 'Concerning the prophets: My heart is broken within me; all my bones shake ... Both prophet and priest are ungodly' (Jeremiah 23:9,11). And Ezekiel was told, 'Son of man, prophesy against the prophets of Israel, who are prophesying, and say to those who prophesy from their own hearts: "Hear the word of the LORD!" Thus says the Lord GOD, Woe to the foolish prophets who follow their own spirit, and have seen nothing!' (Ezekiel 13:2–3).

We need to remember, too, that Jesus Christ gave strong warnings along the same lines: 'Then if anyone says to you, "Look, here is the Christ!" or "There he is!" do not believe it. For false christs and false prophets will arise and perform great signs and wonders, so as to lead astray, if possible, even the elect. See, I have told you beforehand' (Matthew 24:23–25). Christians today are to beware of false prophets (Matthew 7:15), just as Israel was commanded in the past.

How can it be that such prophets can perform signs and wonders? We are not told, and more than one explanation is possible. What we are told is that when this happens, God is testing the loyalty of his people. Notice how it is put: 'The LORD your God is testing you, to know whether you love the LORD your God with all your heart and with all your soul' (v. 3). Once again we see that, above all else, it is wholehearted love that God desires. Those who love God will certainly not want to be drawn to other gods. Incidentally, here we are shown a test for prophets whose message is more subtle than a blunt 'Let us go after other gods'. If those who love God find that their hearts are being almost imperceptibly drawn away from their devotion to God by a message that seems right on the surface, they will know that such a message cannot be from God. The tendency of all true prophets and messengers of the LORD is to encourage God's people to 'hold fast to him' (v. 4).

Such a prophet or dreamer was to be put to death (v. 5). That seems extreme to us and a contradiction of religious freedom. We have to remember that it is an apostate Israelite who is in view—one who has abandoned the living God. Here is a redeemed member of the covenant people teaching 'rebellion against the LORD your God' (v. 5). He is a traitor both to God and to his own people. The LORD 'brought you out of the land of Egypt and redeemed you out of the house of slavery', and here is someone who is who is trying 'to make you leave the way in which the LORD your God commanded you to walk'. Israel owed everything to the mercy of God, and to seek to turn the people from him was diabolical ingratitude and treachery. Moreover, there was God's reputation among the nations to consider (4:6–8). Israel was God's representative in a sinful world. The light of truth was only to be found among its people. How serious it was, then, for someone to try to quench that light and keep the world in darkness.

We ought to reflect on what a serious matter it is for people to be turned away from the only God and the only way of salvation. Jesus said, 'Whoever causes one of these little ones who believe in me to sin, it would be better for him to have a great millstone fastened around his neck and to be drowned in the depth of the sea' (Matthew 18:6). To be responsible for leading souls into hell is a most terrible thing.

The close relative or friend (vv. 6–11)

The next danger is a most poignant and painful one. Suppose one of your closest relatives—brother, son, daughter or the wife you love—or your closest friend speaks to you secretly, as friend to friend, to entice you after other gods; what then? Such a suggestion would be made on the basis of the intimacy enjoyed. It would not be a public thing at all. Here indeed is a test of love for God. Who comes first: the Lord who redeemed you or one of your dearest earthly friends or relatives? Not for nothing did Jesus say, 'Whoever loves father or mother more than me is not worthy of me, and whoever loves son or daughter more than me is not worthy of me' (Matthew 10:37).

Chapter 16

One thing that believers need to make unconverted relatives and friends understand, with love and sensitivity, is this: there is no question of their trying to turn them away from their Saviour. Believers will debate and discuss, will listen to doubts and difficulties, especially from those who are also professing Christians or who appear to be sincerely seeking. But if there is a direct inducement to be unfaithful to the Lord, that is not to be heard or contemplated.

But in Israel it went beyond that. Such an invitation to covenant unfaithfulness could not be overlooked: 'nor shall you conceal him' (v. 8). The punishment had to be carried out and the person to whom the enticement was made, and who therefore revealed what had been said, was to cast the first stone. This would be a very sobering responsibility and would serve to reduce any likelihood of a false accusation. But this was not a personal execution, but a community one: 'and afterward the hand of all the people' (v. 9). Presumably, if someone reported a relative or friend, who denied the charge absolutely, the community, perhaps with guidance from the priest (17:8–13), would have to decide who was telling the truth, and might on occasion come down against the person who made the accusation.

Once again the seriousness of the situation is brought out: 'because he sought to draw you away from the Lord your God, who brought you out of the land of Egypt, out of the house of slavery' (v. 10). The extremity of the punishment, however, served not only to remove the source of temptation, but also to act as a deterrent: 'And all Israel shall hear and fear and never again do any such wickedness as this among you' (v. 11). Yet this was not a matter of an out-of-proportion punishment for the sake of deterrence; rather everything was intended to show just how serious apostasy, and enticement to apostasy, was. What an abuse of love and friendship, to use the intimacy they bring to try to turn someone away from the Lord!

The apostate city (vv. 12–18)

Here is a third possibility: a city that listens to 'worthless fellows' and has

Hold fast to the Lord (13:1–18)

been drawn away to other gods. If a report of such a thing came to the notice of the wider community, it had to be investigated thoroughly, and only when it was 'true and certain that such an abomination has been done among you' (v. 14) was any action to be taken. In this case the inhabitants of the city were to be put to the sword, and the whole city and all that belonged to it burnt as an offering to the Lord. Here the fate of the Canaanites would fall on an Israelite city if it followed the example of the previous inhabitants of the land. Again we have to recognize the seriousness of the situation envisaged. This could easily be the beginning of a wholesale turning from the Lord. Israel had to maintain its faithfulness in spite of all the threats and inducements that might draw it away from the only true God. And so must we.

Study questions

1. Consider what this chapter—and other similar passages in the Bible—tells us about false prophets. What are the marks by which they can be detected? How can churches guard against their influence?

2. What other passages tell us about God's testing? (See, for example, 8:1–5.) What benefits does testing bring?

3. How can we help fellow believers who are in danger of being drawn away from wholehearted trust and love for God?

Chapter 17

Live as holy sons of God (14:1–29)

This chapter, like chapter 13, is related to chapter 12. If chapter 13 gives a strong warning against being led away from allegiance to the LORD, this chapter elaborates on 12:15–19. Israel can eat meat, but not the meat of every creature. The people are to offer tithes to God, but more needs to be said about that, too.

It does not seem possible to discern an overall theme in this chapter. Nevertheless, there are links between its various parts. For example, there is a lot about eating here, in verses 22–29 as well as in the earlier verses. 'So, whether you eat or drink, or whatever you do, do all to the glory of God' (1 Corinthians 10:31). Verse 1 has something to say about the body, about what is done to it, while eating is about what we put into it. 'Do you not know that your bodies are members of Christ?' (1 Corinthians 6:15), so how we treat our bodies is important.

Appreciate what God has done for you (vv. 1–2)

'You are the sons of the LORD your God' (v. 1). All that the Bible has to say about the conduct of God's people hinges on this truth. Deuteronomy is about how the sons of God should conduct themselves. As sons (compare Exodus 4:22–23), the people of Israel are holy to the LORD (v. 2). The nation has been separated from the other nations by God's choice and covenant, so its life is to be different, reflecting its status and the holiness of the God who made it his own. Israel is God's 'treasured possession' and is to appreciate that fact and demonstrate it in its life. This is not simply to be demonstrated in its national life, but also in the life of every individual: 'You are the *sons* of the LORD.' It is worth noting how often the phrase 'the

Live as holy sons of God (14:1–29)

LORD your God' occurs in Deuteronomy; ten times in this chapter alone. Again and again Israel is reminded of its privileged position and, by implication, of the responsibility that brings.

Being sons of God, 'You shall not cut yourselves or make any baldness on your foreheads for the dead' (v. 1). The reference here is to pagan practices. 'Cutting yourselves' is reminiscent of 1 Kings 18:28 and the actions of the prophets of Baal: 'And they cried aloud and cut themselves after their custom with swords and lances, until the blood gushed out upon them' (see also Jeremiah 16:6). The latter also was presumably a pagan practice (Isaiah 15:2), but it looks as if in spite of this prohibition it became common in Israel in later days (Isaiah 22:12; Ezekiel 7:18; Amos 8:10). This prohibition may well have been intended to maintain the integrity of the body.

Christian people, too, are the elect of God and have been adopted as sons. We, too, are to be holy to the Lord. This involves our appearance, our treatment of the body that God has given us, which has been bought with a price and is a temple for the Holy Spirit (1 Corinthians 6:19–20), and the way in which we mourn. We ought not to harm or disfigure our own bodies or dress them inappropriately. When Christians mourn they do not do so as those who have no hope (1 Thessalonians 4:13). Their sense of loss, real though it is, is mitigated by the assurance that to be away from the body is to be at home with the Lord Jesus (2 Corinthians 5:8), and that is far better (Philippians 1:23). We are sons; let us live like sons.

Avoid all that is detestable to him (vv. 3–21)

Israel is not to eat 'any abomination', that is, anything that God declares detestable. Some animals, fish, birds and other flying creatures can be eaten, but there are others that are prohibited. Those that cannot be eaten are to be considered unclean, and in at least one case the carcass must not even be touched (v. 8). Why was this so? What was the difference between the clean and unclean creatures?

Chapter 17

Two suggestions are quite popular. The first is that the unclean animals and other creatures were those that were considered sacred by other religions or that figured in some way in the practices of pagan religions. Currid cites some evidence to back this up.[1] The second is that there was a hygienic reason. The unclean animals were animals that could be harmful; they could have harmful parasites or their flesh could have a measure of toxicity. There seems to be more evidence for this, and it has been worked out in great detail. The unclean birds, also, are all scavengers or carnivorous. But if this was the reason, it is more than surprising that the New Testament makes it clear that all meats are now clean (Mark 7:18–19).

It is much more likely that we should look at this from a different viewpoint. This was an exercise of God's sovereign lordship over Israel. He chose them for himself out of all other nations. This was not because they were better or larger than any other group of people; it was his sovereign choice. Just as he chose them out of the nations, so he also chose out of all the animals, fish and birds what they should eat. In both cases Israel had to bow to his sovereign will. In fact, the way they ate reflected their position. They were different by God's choice, and so they ate differently from others, demonstrating that they were a nation separated to the LORD and obeying his will. The same is true for Christian believers today; we are separated to God to live lives of holiness and moral purity. We may not always be able to see clearly the reasons why God gives us the commands he does, but we obey him because we know he commands what is right and what is for our good.

It was not only a matter of kinds of creatures. Israel was not to 'eat anything that … died naturally' (v. 21). This was not because there was anything wrong with such meat itself, but because it had not been killed in a way that recognized God's lordship over all life, as we saw when looking at chapter 12. Foreigners, whether resident or passing through the land, could eat such meat, but not Israel. They were 'a people holy to the LORD'.

Live as holy sons of God (14:1–29)

It is interesting to note that resident foreigners were not compelled to live like Israelites: 'The sojourner who is within your towns ... he may eat it.'

Finally, at the end of verse 21 we read, 'You shall not boil a young goat in its mother's milk.' This was probably a practice that took place among the Canaanites. This prohibition comes several times in the law and it is difficult to account for it unless there was some likelihood of Israel acting in this way. Why was it prohibited? Perhaps because there is something deeply offensive about it; a mother's milk was intended for the growth and health of her young, whereas in this case it would be used to prepare the young to be eaten by a predator. This seems a gross misuse of milk. It is unnatural and callous.

This chapter indicates that killing and eating meat was something that required the permission of God. The fact that life was taken had to be acknowledged by pouring out the lifeblood in recognition of God as the Creator. Moreover, unnatural and cruel practice was outlawed. All this indicates that animal life must be treated with respect. While meat can be eaten, animals are not the playthings of humans and are not to be treated with cruelty or indifference to suffering. They are God's creatures.

Acknowledge his goodness towards you (vv. 22–29)

A tenth of all the grain, wine and olive oil, and the firstborn of sheep and cattle, were to be offered to the LORD in grateful acknowledgement that he was the giver of them all. Normally these tithes were to be taken and eaten in the place where God had put his name. Clearly, however, for those who lived a long way from the location of the tabernacle—and later the temple—this would prove to be very onerous. So provision was made here for the tithes to be sold and for the money to be brought up to the sanctuary instead. Then the money could be spent in purchasing what was necessary for the covenant meal, and the family would rejoice before the LORD.

At the end of every three years a quite different procedure was adopted. The tithes were not to be taken up to the central sanctuary; rather they

Chapter 17

were to be kept in store within the towns and used for those who had no land of their own. Presumably it was anticipated that these supplies would be sufficient for the next three years. The people who would benefit were those who were dependent on God: the Levite, the sojourner, the fatherless and the widow. God provided for them through his people. The tithes were set apart for God, but used in each town for those whose situation meant they had no breadwinner or land to cultivate. As they did this, God would bless the nation in all that they did. This points to the way in which Christians ought to care for one another, especially those who have fallen on hard times.

Study questions

1. In what ways may we be in danger of abusing our bodies today?
2. From what we have seen about tithing from this chapter and chapter 12, what principles can we isolate which may also help us in our giving?
3. We, too, are sons of the Lord our God; consider four or five applications of this truth to our lives and conduct.

Note

1 Currid, *Deuteronomy*, p. 559.

Chapter 18

Care in the community (15:1–23)

The last verses of chapter 14 spoke of providing for those in Israel who had special need: sojourners, orphans and widows. This chapter makes provision for Israelites who become impoverished for some reason. It emphasizes the sense of belonging together that should characterize God's people, and the generosity that should be shown to those who fall into need. Application is easy to see, but not so easy, perhaps, to put into practice.

Making poverty history (vv. 1–6)

There is some disagreement about the precise meaning of the provision we find in these verses. The simplest understanding is that every seven years—each week of years—all debts were to be waived. This does not mean that if debts were still outstanding after any period of seven years they were to be forgiven, but that in the Sabbath year, when the fields were left fallow (Leviticus 25:1–7), all debtors were to be fully released from their obligation to repay what they owed. Part of the reason for this may be that in that year, because the fields were left and people used either what they had left over from previous harvests or what the land produced of itself, there was little opportunity for people to earn extra to pay off debts anyway.

The main reasons for acting so generously are twofold. Firstly, in Israel all were brothers, so thought for others was in order. Such generosity did not need, however, be extended to a foreigner. In any case, a foreigner would not be under the same obligation to let his land lie fallow and would be in a better position to repay his debt. Secondly, 'The LORD will bless you

Chapter 18

in the land that the LORD your God is giving you', and such blessing was to be shared; it did not originate in human labour and thriftiness, but in the goodness of God. Both of these considerations should carry a great deal of weight with Christian people. We are debtors to God and can show our appreciation of his mercies by showing generosity to brothers and sisters in Christ.

A problem arises when we consider what we are told in verse 4, 'But there will be no poor among you', and what we find further on in verse 11, 'For there will never cease to be poor in the land'. There is a tension here between the ideal and the real, a tension we will find elsewhere. The promise of God's blessing is given in the rest of verse 4, but verse 5 attaches a condition: 'if only you will strictly obey the voice of the LORD your God, being careful to do all this commandment that I command you today'. The fact is that sinful humans, even though they are God's redeemed people, are never fully obedient to his commandment. Sadly, while poverty can be greatly reduced, 'You always have the poor with you' (Matthew 26:11). There will always be need for caring and providing for the poor.

In Acts 4:34 we have an almost exact repetition of the beginning of Deuteronomy 15:4: 'There was not a needy person among them', that is, among the early Christian believers. But the very next chapter recounts the sad and tragic behaviour of Ananias and Sapphira. Sin spoils everything, and we shall never be free of sin until we are in that better land where all God's promises reach their final and complete fulfilment. Meanwhile, we have to live with the tension between what ought to be and what is. In fact, some of the instructions given in Deuteronomy are based on the fact that there will always be a shortfall from the ideal. We shall see this clearly when we come to chapter 24 and its opening instruction about divorce, for example. For the moment we note that there was a partial fulfilment of verses 4 to 6 at times, particularly during the reign of Solomon, as 1 Kings 4:20–21,24–25 makes clear. Christians have no promise of material prosperity, but under the reign of the greater than Solomon, King Jesus,

Care in the community (15:1–23)

they have spiritual riches that more than compensate, although not in the fulness that will be theirs one day.

Lending to the poor (vv. 7–11)

But if every seven years debts had to be released, didn't that mean that some might be rather reluctant to lend to those in need? It did, and so this section warns against such hard-heartedness; verses 7 and 8 deal with this in general terms, while in verse 9 another consideration is added. If the seventh year is approaching, the chances are that the lender will not get his money back, but he is warned that he must still act generously. Heart, hand and eye are important. There is a warning against hardening the heart (v. 7): there is to be no unworthy thought in the heart (v. 9); rather it should be ungrudging (v. 10). The hand must not be shut (v. 7); rather it is to be open to lend a poor brother sufficient for his need (v. 9). Indeed, verse 11 says, 'You shall open wide your hand to your brother, to the needy and to the poor, in your land.' The eye is not to look grudgingly on the poor brother as the seventh year draws near (v. 9). Heart, hand and eye must be united in providing for those in need.

Several motives are given to spur the Israelites to this caring attitude. First is the fact that the land is one that God gives to them (v. 7). Prosperity in the land comes from the good gift of God, and his people must follow his example and give freely (v. 10). Another motive is that God promises his blessing to those who give generously (v. 10). No one will be the loser for lending to one of God's people in need. A further consideration is that there will always be those who need help (v. 11). There will never be a time when poverty is completely abolished, so Israel must realize there is a constant demand for nurturing a caring spirit. One final motive arises from the reality of what hardening the heart means. It means that the poor brother will 'cry to the Lord against you, and you [will] be guilty of sin' (v. 9). Caring for the needy is not an option; it is a sin to harden the heart against them.

Chapter 18

Here is a general principle for us as Christians: have a generous heart. And here is a specific application: care for those who belong to the household of faith. 'So then, as we have opportunity, let us do good to everyone, and especially to those who are of the household of faith' (Galatians 6:10). This does not mean being naïve or taken in by plausible liars. Nor should we encourage people to take on debts they can't afford, or always help people who act irresponsibly, especially if they have been warned. But we believers in the West are rich Christians in a world of poverty, and many of God's people are in real need. The righteous 'is ever lending generously' (Psalm 37:26) and 'God loves a cheerful giver' (2 Corinthians 9:7).

The debtor-slave (vv. 12–18)

In Victorian Britain, if a person fell into debt he or she was put into prison, which was not much help when it came to paying off the debt. In Israel, those who got into debt could sell themselves into slavery, though this was perhaps more like being 'in service' than in the sort of slavery we usually envisage. A person 'in service' would live in the home of the family he or she served and would be provided with food and a wage, though this was often not very much. The idea in Israel, presumably, was that the money from the sale could be used to pay off the debt. The enslaved person then served for six years, a man probably working in the fields while a woman's work would be more in the house. They would be provided with food during that time. When the seventh year arrived the slave was released and set free. But—and this is what this passage is all about—the slaves were not to be sent away empty-handed (v. 13). Their masters were to treat them generously, providing for them from out of the flock, and giving flour and wine (v. 14). This would help to set them back on their feet.

This generosity was to be proportionate to the way God had blessed the households during the period of service (v. 14). And the Israelites were never to forget that they had been slaves in Egypt. God had redeemed them,

Care in the community (15:1-23)

and their own experience and God's mercy to them were to determine their attitude towards their own slaves. Of course, the prosperity of someone with such slaves depended in part on the hard work of those slaves, so it was only right for them to share in the blessing of God upon what had been done. This seems to underlie verse 14 and perhaps also verse 18. Acting in this way was not to seem burdensome. Masters should remember that if they had had to hire servants and pay them wages, it would have cost them twice as much (v. 18). Moreover, those who showed such generosity would know the blessing of the LORD in all they did.

But the passage envisages that some slaves might be treated so well that they had no desire to leave those they had been serving. Such slaves had learnt to love their masters and those of the household, and they saw that they were well off with them, so they said, 'I will not go out from you' (v. 16). In such cases the slaves would have their ears pierced as a sign that they were now perpetually in the service of the family. This possibility shows the sort of attitude that the Israelites needed to have towards those of their own nation who served them. They were to treat their slaves in such a way as would lead them to love those they served. This is a high ideal indeed. There is no direct application, but the implications for our relationships with those in need and who fall on hard times, and for employers and all in authority, are very clear.

The firstborn male of herd and flock (vv. 19-23)

The origin of this command goes back to the time of the Exodus and the tenth plague, when God struck all the firstborn in Egypt, both firstborn sons and the firstborn of livestock (Exodus 12:29-32). As a result, all the firstborn males in Israel, having been spared, were to be consecrated to the LORD (Exodus 13:1-2). This section in Deuteronomy is probably a transitional one leading into instructions concerning the observance of the Passover at the beginning of the next chapter. But it is also linked to some of the themes seen already in chapter 15. Recognition of God's goodness

Chapter 18

would lead not only to generosity towards fellow Israelites, but also to dedicating to him the firstborn of herd and flock. And just as it required faith in God to act generously, so, too, did it require faith to devote the firstborn. It meant giving to God first and trusting that other animals would be born later. It is not so difficult to give to God once we have already received what we are guaranteed, but to give the very first things we receive and trust there will be more to follow is quite a different matter. We need to remember that, with our salaries and pensions that come regularly, we are in a very privileged position compared with most people in history and with multitudes in other parts of the world. Does our giving to the Lord reflect this?

Israelites could easily have been tempted to use the firstborn ox before it was sacrificed to God, or to shear the wool of the firstborn sheep. After all, this could be done while they were waiting for the time when they went up to the 'place that the Lord will choose' (v. 20); but it was not to happen. The family did benefit from the animals, however, as after the sacrifice by the priests and the pouring out of the blood, they would eat the meat. Having devoted their animals to God, he gave them back to them to eat and enjoy as a pledge of his goodness and a reminder that he provided everything.

There was another stipulation. If the firstborn was blemished it was not fit to be sacrificed to the Lord (v. 21). It still appears, though, that it was not to be kept or used. So it was eaten in their towns (as opposed to being taken up to the temple); only its blood was not to be eaten but poured out. It also appears that this was sufficient to fulfil the dedication of the firstborn; there is no mention of taking the next one to be born up to the place where God put his name. It simply meant that no blemished animal was suitable for sacrifice.

Study questions
1. What does the New Testament have to say about giving to the needy?

Care in the community (15:1–23)

2. Are there principles here that ought to be applied in any country that seeks to be just and to care for its citizens?

3. Should we put aside what we intend to give regularly to the Lord before we do anything else with our money?

Chapter 19

Three appointed feasts (16:1–17)

Among the feasts given to Israel, three were of special significance (see Exodus 23:14–19 and Leviticus 23, and compare Numbers 28–29). These three were Passover, Weeks and Booths. Here Moses instructs Israel that all the males must go each year to the place the LORD will choose in order to celebrate these feasts.

The Feast of Passover, or Unleavened Bread, was pre-eminently a feast of remembrance: 'that all the days of your life you may remember the day when you came out of the land of Egypt' (v. 3). The Israelites were to look back and remember their redemption, God in his grace delivering them from the bondage of Egypt. The other two feasts can be called feasts of rejoicing: 'You shall rejoice before the LORD your God' (vv. 11,14). The rejoicing was in the goodness of God who provided the harvest for them in the land to which he had brought them and which he had given them. There is a clear parallel here to the church of Jesus Christ. Having been redeemed by his precious blood, we enjoy God's goodness and are to rejoice in all the blessings that we receive. We look back with thankfulness, and we can also look forward in hope and with anticipation.

The Feast of Passover (vv. 1–8)

The basic instructions for keeping the Passover are found first of all in Exodus 12:1–28, 43–51 and 13:3–10. What is to be particularly noted in this passage in Deuteronomy is that the Passover, along with the other feasts, was to be celebrated 'at the place that the LORD your God will choose' (v. 6). None of these feasts was to be celebrated in the towns where the people lived, but at the place where the tabernacle, or temple, was situated. This

Three appointed feasts (16:1–17)

was very important once Israel was settled in the land. The danger was that its unity as the people of God might be damaged, but the visit of all the men three times a year would maintain and strengthen that unity. It was not that women were forbidden to go up for the feasts, but there would be many occasions when it would not be possible for them to do so. We remember that the Lord Jesus instituted the Lord's Supper during the Passover meal, and the Supper also serves to remind us of our unity with all believers (1 Corinthians 10:17).

The month of Abib (v. 1) became the first month of the year for the Israelites on the occasion of the Exodus (Exodus 12:2). On the tenth day of the month the lamb was chosen; it was eaten on the fourteenth day, and the seven days of unleavened bread continued until the twenty-first. The Israelites did not begin their year by making resolutions, but by remembering that great day when the LORD redeemed them from bondage and brought them out of Egypt by his mighty arm. When a person comes to Jesus Christ in repentance and faith, and is redeemed from his or her sins by his sacrifice, it is the beginning, not just of a new year, but of a new life. That is something worth remembering very frequently and with great thankfulness.

In order to help the Israelites remember something of the affliction they suffered in Egypt, the Feast of Unleavened Bread was to be part of the Passover celebration. By remembering the hard bondage of those many years, they would appreciate even more what God had done for them. It can be all too easy for Christians to forget what it was like before their conversion. It is true that not all are saved out of a life of bondage and frustration—with some, life had been comparatively easy, and conviction of sin and conversion to Jesus Christ came very close together. But for all that, we were then lost and sinful, heading for the judgement and condemnation of God; now we are God's adopted children, destined for a better country than Canaan, that is, a heavenly one.

At Passover a lamb or goat was to be offered in sacrifice (v. 2). This was

Chapter 19

then to be cooked and eaten at sunset. All of it was to be consumed; what was not eaten was to be burned. In the first Passover, the blood of the lamb was put on the lintels and doorposts of the house so that the destroying angel would pass over the house, and those in it sheltered under the blood that had been shed (Exodus 12). Keeping the Passover reminded Israel of that historic event, and they appreciated once again the fact that God had appointed sacrifice as the means for their redemption. All this reminds us that Christ, the Lamb of God, our Passover (1 Corinthians 5:7), has been sacrificed for us, and we are redeemed by his blood. All the benefits of forgiveness, adoption and pilgrimage towards our heavenly homeland come through receiving Christ, making him ours by a living faith that is itself created in our hearts by the Holy Spirit. All this is eloquently set forth in the Lord's Supper, our memorial of Jesus' saving work for us until he comes.

The Feast of Weeks (vv. 9–12)

In Exodus 23:16 this feast is also called the Feast of Harvest, which celebrated the firstfruits of the full harvest yet to come. In verse 19 of that chapter it says, 'The best of the firstfruits of your ground you shall bring into the house of the Lord your God.' Another name, of course, is Pentecost, as it came fifty days after the Passover ('Pentecost' is from the Greek word for fifty). Leviticus 23:15–22 gives a longer description of this feast, mentioning the fifty days, and Numbers 28:26–31 records the offerings to be given on that occasion.

Returning to Deuteronomy 16:9–12, we notice that the offering the people were to bring is called 'a freewill offering' (v. 10), that is, it was a joyful, heartfelt expression of thankfulness for God's goodness. This was to be given 'as the Lord your God blesses you'. In other words, it was in proportion to the harvest that God had given. Both of these ideas are taken up in the New Testament. In 1 Corinthians 16:2 Paul indicates that giving is to be in proportion to how a person prospers. In 2 Corinthians 8 and 9, the thought of giving generously, according to the joyful desire of the heart, is

Three appointed feasts (16:1–17)

expressed. In 8:3 Paul writes, 'For they gave according to their means, as I can testify, and beyond their means, of their own free will.'[1]

It was, of course, also an act of faith to give the firstfruits back to God. By doing so, Israel was affirming its assurance that God would go on to give the full harvest that was needed. So there was also a sense of anticipation. The firstfruits were but a token of a greater harvest yet to come. In the course of time, harvest became a metaphor for spiritual blessing, as we see in Psalm 126, especially verse 6: 'He who goes out weeping, bearing the seed for sowing, shall come home with shouts of joy, bringing his sheaves with him.' In the New Testament, harvest is used as a metaphor for bringing people to Jesus Christ, as in Matthew 9:35–38; John 4:35–38; and 1 Corinthians 3:6–9. This gives a special significance to the day of Pentecost recorded in Acts 2. Peter preached and the harvest of those who believed in Jesus Christ was about three thousand souls. This first reaping gives great encouragement for the full harvest yet to be brought in.

In what way were the people to rejoice before God? It is not explicitly mentioned, but because those who rejoiced included not only family members and servants but also the Levite, the sojourner, the fatherless and the widow, the implication seems to be that the firstfruits, having been dedicated to God, were at least in part eaten and shared out among those in need. This fits in with the law on tithes (14:22–29) and the provisions for the priests and Levites (18:1–8 and ch. 26). Those who give to God never lose out as a result.

There is a final note in verse 12 telling the people they were never to forget that they were slaves in Egypt. They needed to remember that they were what they were because of God's grace and redemption. They were not to take present prosperity for granted, but were to observe the feasts that would remind them, every time they celebrated them, what they owed to the LORD. The Lord's Supper fulfils the same function for Christians. Every time we celebrate it, we are reminded that we are sinners who owe everything to the gracious mercy of Jesus, who died for us.

Chapter 19

The Feast of Booths (vv. 13–17)

Many will be more acquainted with this as the Feast of Tabernacles. It takes its name from the fact that Israel in the wilderness lived in tents (Leviticus 23:33–44, especially verses 42–43). Leviticus 23:40 speaks of the people taking 'branches of palm trees and boughs of leafy trees and willows of the brook', which seems to indicate that the booths that the Israelites were to live in for seven days were made from these materials. Exodus 23:16 also calls this the Feast of Ingathering, and says it was to take place 'at the end of the year, when you gather in from the field the fruit of your labour'. So this was also a harvest festival, celebrating the final harvest when it was all safely brought in. 'At the end of the year' means the end of the civil/agricultural year. Israel actually had two calendars. It was the religious year that began with Passover.

It is the final harvest that is particularly noticed in Deuteronomy 16: 'when you have gathered in the produce from your threshing floor and your winepress' (v. 13). This accounts for the note of rejoicing here, in which, again, those in special need would share (v. 14). In this feast, the people of Israel acknowledged the goodness of God towards them. Good harvests would come 'because the LORD your God will bless you in all your produce and in all the work of your hands'. It would be in contemplating this 'that you will be altogether joyful' (v. 15). There can surely be no doubt that we, too, should be 'altogether joyful' as we think of God's goodness to us, and that this note of joy should generally characterize our times of worship.

But, as with the previous feast, there is an implied warning note. For forty years Israel lived in tents. Instead of entering the promised land at the first opportunity, the people had wandered in the desert for thirty-eight years longer than necessary. Blessing, and the joy that follows, comes from obeying God. Taking him for granted, and taking his good gifts for granted, will soon lead to trouble.

If, as we saw with the Feast of Weeks, it is right to look beyond the

Three appointed feasts (16:1–17)

material harvest to the spiritual harvest that the New Testament speaks about, the Feast of Booths takes on a special significance. It is a reminder that the anticipation arising from the firstfruits on the day of Pentecost will be fulfilled with the great gathering-in of the elect of God from every nation and every part of the world. This will be the day when 'many will come from east and west and recline at table with Abraham, Isaac, and Jacob in the kingdom of heaven' (Matthew 8:11; see also Matthew 13:36–43; Mark 4:29; Revelation 14:14–16). What a day that will be! What praise and rejoicing for all who are brought into the heavenly barn! Then truly the whole church of God will be altogether joyful (Revelation 7:9–17).

Verses 16 and 17 repeat the instruction that all the males were to go up to the place that God would choose three times a year for these feasts. And they were not to 'appear before the LORD empty-handed'. God's blessing always demands an appropriate response.

Study questions

1. What can we learn about the Lord's Supper from the Passover?
2. How far is it legitimate to see the second two feasts in terms of a spiritual harvest?
3. Should joyfulness characterize all our services? What should a balanced service be like?

Note

1 This follows the ESV translation in the Collins edition, 2002.

Chapter 20

The governing authorities (16:18–17:20)

Once Israel has settled in the land, it will need those in authority to keep order, decide disputes and judge criminal cases. This section covers the appointment of judges and officers in each town; what to do in cases that are too difficult to be settled locally; and the appointment of the king whom the LORD will choose.

Earlier on we saw that the Ten Commandments appear to underlie many of the laws and instructions given in Deuteronomy. It is the fifth commandment, or rather, an extension of that commandment, which is in view here. That commandment established the authority of parents in the home, for there was to be order and discipline in each home, although, of course, carried out with loving care. But Israel had grown to be a nation, and it was no longer under the harsh authority of the Egyptians. Once settled in the land there would need to be those who exercised authority so that order could be established and maintained, quarrels and disputes sorted out and penalties imposed where necessary. So judges and officers were to be appointed locally, and in due course a king, too, would be chosen by God. Notice how the last words of 16:20 and 17:20 mirror the last part of the fifth commandment (5:16).

Judges to exercise authority (16:18–20)

In each town, judges and officers were to be appointed. The officers, or officials, were probably not dissimilar to policemen in some of their functions. Possibly they would ensure that people came to the judges, and also that judgments were carried out. These judges and officers were local men, hence they were respected in their communities, but they also had a

The governing authorities (16:18–17:20)

wide knowledge of the people for whom they gave judgment. They were not, it appears, under any direct external authority, but had to judge according to the law that Moses was giving.

The importance of justice is stressed: 'Justice, and only justice, you shall follow' (v. 20). But the negatives are spelled out, too: no perverting justice, no showing favouritism, no accepting of bribes. The dangers of bribery are spelled out. All that the judges and officers did would take place in 'the land that the LORD your God is giving you' (vv. 18,20). This means that they were answerable to him. He would see how they acted and hold them responsible for what they did. We live in days when the importance of justice needs to be stressed again, and not just at official level. Christians, in particular, ought to be concerned for justice, for we serve a God of justice: 'The Rock, his work is perfect, for all his ways are justice. A God of faithfulness and without iniquity, just and upright is he' (32:4). And we need to remember that God will judge us also—not for our sins, which have been pardoned, but for our works, of what sort they are (1 Corinthians 3:13–15).

The penalty for throwing off authority (16:21–17:7)

At first sight these verses seem to be a digression from the main theme. Looking at the whole passage you would expect the section commencing at 17:8 to come immediately after 16:20. Why these verses, then? In Israel, everything depended upon the recognition that the LORD was their covenant sovereign. Once the Israelites turned away from him, their whole national life would be undermined. They were his people, chosen to show his glory by doing his will, and so they must obey his law. Any signs of a weakening of allegiance to him, therefore, were danger signals, and outright rejection of him and of his authority was treachery.

So this section begins in verse 21 by forbidding any mixing of pagan practices with the worship of the LORD. An Asherah was a pole set up in pagan shrines, as was the pillar (v. 22). In 17:1, what is forbidden is any

Chapter 20

slackness in devotion to the LORD, seen in disregarding or disobeying his commands concerning sacrifice. It is with seemingly innocuous compromises, and deviations from God's revealed will, that spiritual unfaithfulness usually begins. Notice the emphasis on 'the LORD your God'. Wonderfully privileged as the people of Israel were, they needed to show their appreciation and gratitude by close obedience to him.

The great danger of dallying with pagan practices was that this might eventually lead to a turning away entirely from the LORD to some other god. Verses 2 to 7 deal with such covenant treason. The penalty for outright idolatry was death. It was the most serious sin of all, breaking the first commandment, and sinning against the grace they had experienced and the light they had been given. It undermined everything else; once that support was knocked away, the entire ethical foundation of Israel's national life would come crashing to the ground. No longer would right and wrong be defined by their Creator and Redeemer; it would be defined by the way of the world, by inner feelings and by personal preference. This is largely the state of the world today. We do not expect idolatry to be punished by death by the civil authorities now, but the penalty remains: 'The wages of sin is death' (Romans 6:23).

The process described here is instructive. First of all there would be a rumour or report of idolatry having taken place (v. 4). This was followed up by diligent enquiry to determine the accuracy of what had been heard. When it had been ascertained that the report was true and certain—clearly it was the judges who would decide this—then, and only then, the penalty would be carried out. In order for the report to be confirmed, there had to be at least two witnesses (three were presumably better) to testify to what had taken place. The evidence of one witness was inadequate and no one was to be put to death on the evidence of a single person. This laid down a precedent, not simply for idolatry, but for all cases where the penalty was death.

In such a serious matter there needed to be as near to certainty as it was

The governing authorities (16:18–17:20)

possible to get. It must have been the case that sometimes there were not two witnesses to some capital crime, which meant the guilty person would have gone free; better that than an innocent person lose his or her life. As a further safeguard, the witnesses were to begin the process of stoning (v. 7); they had to be certain enough of the guilt of the accused to be prepared to do this. Then all the people of the town were to join in; this was a community execution—the people were involved in rejecting the sin and carrying out the penalty. In this way they were purging the evil from their midst (v. 7).

The principle of two or three witnesses is repeated in the New Testament (Matthew 18:16; 2 Corinthians 13:1; 1 Timothy 5:19), as is also the principle of community action in church discipline (Matthew 18:17; 1 Corinthians 5:4–5). For unfaithfulness to God, the penalty is exclusion from the church, and 1 Corinthians 5:5 makes clear both the seriousness of this in spiritual terms and its ultimate remedial intent.

Authority exercised with wisdom (17:8–13)

Although 16:18–20 speaks of justice being administered locally, there could be cases of real complexity that the local judges felt inadequate to decide. When this arose, the local judges were to 'go up to the place that the LORD your God will choose' (17:8). The instruction, 'You shall do according to what they declare to you *from that place that the LORD will choose*' (v. 10, emphasis added), and the reference to 'the priest who stands to minister there before the LORD your God' (v. 12) indicate that this really meant bringing the case before God himself. A greater-than-human wisdom was needed.

The judge (vv. 9,12) appears to be a supreme judge appointed for the purpose of hearing these difficult cases (compare Exodus 18:13–27, especially vv. 22,26). It appears that he would act in conjunction with the priests, as he would have access to the LORD through them. While ultimately the decision would be from the LORD, the priests and judge

Chapter 20

would gain experience from dealing with the cases referred to them, and would also apply the instruction and principles they found in Deuteronomy and the rest of the Pentateuch. This suggests a combination of wisdom, experience and guidance from God in reaching decisions. It is in a similar way that decisions are to be reached in church life, for Christ has promised his presence and power when his people meet for decision (Matthew 18:20; 1 Corinthians 5:4).

In this case the decision given was final (v. 11), and because it came from God, anyone who refused to accept the verdict pronounced by the priest or the judge was to die (v. 12). Part of the purpose of this was to act as a deterrent (v. 13); to refuse a decision that came with the authority of the LORD was another act of covenant unfaithfulness that would set a precedent in rebelliousness. We know, however, that it was not long before unfaithfulness became endemic in Israel (Judges 2:11–15), and priests were themselves implicated in this (1 Samuel 2:12–17). In such a situation a king was needed (Judges 21:25), which leads straight on to the next section.

The king and his authority (17:14–20)

This section looks ahead to the time when the Israelites, settled in the land that God would give them, would see the nations around them and decide they needed a king, just as the nations had. We see this in 1 Samuel 8:5. Their motive in wanting to be like the nations was wrong, but their instinct that a king would be good for them was right. What they needed was a king chosen by the LORD their God, one who would rule in subservience to the LORD as his and their Sovereign. So they could set up as king the one chosen by God; and he was always to be a brother, part of the family of Israel under God (v. 15).

Then follow a number of instructions for the king. Notice the repetition of the words 'for himself'. He was not to acquire many horses for himself, or many wives for himself, or excessive silver and gold for himself, but he was to write a copy of this law in a book for himself (v. 18). He was not to

The governing authorities (16:18–17:20)

be a king who was out for his own aggrandisement, nor one who would lead the people back to Egypt (v. 16); rather he was to be one who feared the LORD and lived and ruled by his word. 'This law' (v. 18) means not just this short section but the whole of Deuteronomy.

All the kings of Israel, however great, were failures; none measured up to the picture of kingship here. But there is one king who does: Jesus Christ. One of us as human, of the people of Israel and the tribe of Judah, he humbled himself, giving himself to death for his people and fulfilling all his Father's will. Here is a King worth having; a King worth serving.

Study questions
1. What can we learn from these verses about authority and justice?
2. How is 17:14–20 fulfilled in Jesus Christ?
3. What can we learn from this passage about capital punishment?

Chapter 21

The appointed ministers (18:1–22)

In this chapter, instructions are given concerning those who engage in spiritual ministry: the priests, Levites and prophets. At the same time, a warning is given against all the many types of pagan 'ministers' who profess to give guidance from the gods.

The priests and Levites (vv. 1–8)

The previous section, from 16:18 to 17:20, considered what we would call the secular authorities: judges, officers and the king. This chapter deals with those set apart and called to minister in the religious, or spiritual, sphere. In Israel, of course, both groups were to be under the rule of their covenant LORD and were to be instructed by his word. In these verses the main concern is the provision that was to be made for the support of priests and Levites. General provision for the Levites has already been mentioned in 14:22–29, especially verses 27 to 29 (see also 16:9–12). But the present section appears to deal with two specific cases. Firstly, the priests, who, of course, were all Levites, being descendants of Aaron, were concentrated where the tabernacle was, and later would be concentrated in the place where God would put his name: Jerusalem. This was the place of sacrifice, and as God's servants and those who officiated in offering sacrifice, they were to have a share in what was offered (vv. 3–4). There seem to be several principles here. Those whom God chooses to minister in his name will be provided for by him, generally through his own people. Moreover, their support comes directly from the ministry in which they are engaged. Paul applies these principles to the gospel ministry in 1 Corinthians 9:3–14.

The Levites who were not priests were to be spread out through the land

The appointed ministers (18:1–22)

in cities specially set apart for them (Numbers 35:1–8; compare Joshua 21). But, secondly, a Levite might have a desire in his heart to live and serve in 'the place that the LORD will choose', in which case he was to be treated like all the other Levites there and have equal portions with them. The ESV does not seem to catch the sense adequately when it translates part of verse 6 as 'and he may come when he desires'; the NIV has 'in all earnestness' and the NKJV, 'with all the desire of his mind'. Here is a man who wants to be near to God, serving him at the place where he has put his name. Do we long to be closer to him? Are we eager for his service?

The practices of the nations (vv. 9–14)

At first sight, these verses seem to cover a quite different subject, unrelated to the previous section and similar to other warnings in this book against following the evil behaviour of pagan nations—that's how it appears to start off in verse 10. But once you read on, you realize that behind the idolatry and sins of these nations were those who gave them guidance: fortune tellers, sorcerers, charmers, mediums, wizards and necromancers. Trying to get information and guidance from the dead, from spirits, or by the use of magic are the abominations forbidden here. Even the burning of a child as an offering probably comes into the same category, for this was thought to propitiate a god and get him on your side and so give favourable guidance. God was going to drive out these nations before the people of Israel to prevent them from learning their ways. The LORD does not allow his people to use these means that were so popular among the superstitious nations in Canaan.

Why were all these things disallowed? Because none of them was necessary, and to use them was to deny what God had provided and would provide for his people. God chooses the people who will guide and lead his people. He chose Moses, and he chose the tribe of Levi to make known what he had revealed and to attend to the sacrificial worship of the tabernacle and temple. He had already given his word through Moses,

Chapter 21

which would all be written down, and he would choose his own prophets to make known his will in days to come. To turn to these other sorts of people or try to find guidance apart from him was to throw off his covenant authority. They were his people; he would take care of them and let them know all they needed to know. To turn to these illegitimate means would be to despise his word and reject what he had provided. And it is just the same today. Christians have a heavenly Father who loves them, who has given them his word and guides them constantly in his providence. What more do we need?

The prophet like Moses (vv. 15–22)

The connection between these verses and the previous section is obvious. There will be no need for any Israelite to turn to fortune tellers or mediums, for God is going to raise up a prophet like Moses; he will be the one to listen to. This tells us first that Moses was a prophet. God spoke to him 'mouth to mouth' (Numbers 12:6–8), that is, God put his own word into Moses' mouth so that what Moses spoke was exactly what God wanted him to say. God did this because when he spoke to the people directly at Horeb, his voice was overwhelming to the people. So, instead of speaking directly, he used Moses as his mouthpiece. The prophet that God would raise up 'from among their brothers' (v. 18) is the Lord Jesus Christ (Acts 3:22–23). He is the Word made flesh (John 1:14): he speaks with a human voice, but with all the authority of God. In all this we see the great condescension of God towards us in our frailty and unworthiness.

There is an implication in all this that is spelt out in these verses. If this prophet speaks 'all that I command him' (v. 18), then 'it is to him you shall listen' (v. 15). And if anyone refuses to listen, then 'I myself will require it of him (v. 19). God's final word has been 'in these last days ... spoken to us by his Son' (Hebrews 1:2). We bring guilt upon ourselves if we fail to take what he says seriously.

Though this is a prophecy that clearly found its ultimate fulfilment in

The appointed ministers (18:1–22)

Jesus Christ, it did not mean that there were to be no other prophets between Moses and Jesus' coming. The passage actually indicates that when God speaks to Israel it will be through a prophet (and not directly, v. 16), and there were many of these until he finally spoke through his Son (Hebrews 1:1–2). So guidance was also given to help the people know the difference between false and true prophets. This was necessary because there had always been 'prophets' who presumed, in the name of God, to speak words that he had not commanded them to speak (v. 20); indeed, there still are. The test given here is one of fulfilment: if the word does not come true, then whoever has spoken it has done so presumptuously and there is no need to fear him or take any notice of what he has said.

This is an extremely important passage, both about prophecy in general, showing that it frequently has a predictive element to it, and also about the ministry of Jesus Christ. He is the Word, and all he said was given to him by his Father (John 8:28). He reveals to us the Father (John 1:18) and all the Father's will for us. We must give full weight to his teaching as he fulfils his prophetic role.

Study questions
1. What applications can be made today from verses 1 to 8?
2. Which New Testament passages speak of the prophetic ministry of Christ?
3. How relevant are verses 9 to 14 to us today? In what ways may some of us be tempted to gain illicit guidance?

Chapter 22

Removing evil from the land (19:1–21)

The land the people of Israel were going to enter and settle in would be a gift from the Lord their God. It was, therefore, supremely his land, and that meant that they were to live in it in a way that acknowledged his sovereignty and gift. Evil would defile the land and would need to be either prevented or purged.

Bloodshed in the land (vv. 1–13)

The phrase 'the land the Lord your God is giving you' occurs five times in verses 1 to 14 and there is also a reference to the Lord enlarging their territory as he had sworn to do (v. 8). This indicates the importance for Israel of recognizing God's gift and living appropriately in it. As God's people in God's land, they were to live as God intended them to. Christians are God's people and the world we live in is God's, too—'The earth is the Lord's and the fulness thereof' (Psalm 24:1)—so we also must live as he intends. Our attitude to him ought to mould our attitude to what is actually his land.

We need also to keep in mind what we are told in Genesis 9:5–6: 'And for your lifeblood I will require a reckoning: from every beast I will require it and from man. From his fellow man I will require a reckoning for the life of man. Whoever sheds the blood of man, by man shall his blood be shed, for God made man in his own image.' To kill a man is an assault on someone made in the image of God. Another important passage is Genesis 4:10–11, where God says to Cain after he has killed his brother Abel, 'The voice of your brother's blood is crying to me from the ground. And now you are cursed from the ground, which has opened its mouth to receive your

Removing evil from the land (19:1–21)

brother's blood from your hand.' God's earth cried out to its Maker for justice because it had received the lifeblood of one made in that Maker's image. So it would be a terrible thing for anyone among those living in the land that was God's gift to shed the blood of one made in the image of the God who had showed such favour to them. Also underlying this chapter is the commandment 'You shall not murder' (5:17).

This passage in Deuteronomy is concerned both with preventing unnecessary bloodshed and with purging the guilt arising from the shedding of innocent blood. The need for the former arose from the practice of a family member avenging the blood of someone who had been murdered. This practice belonged to days when there was not the same social cohesion or organization as at present, with people living in a rural setting and well spread out across a region. Presumably the practice continued in Egypt, and would be likely to continue in Canaan on occasions when it was quite clear who was guilty of murder. But there was the obvious danger that the avenger would not distinguish between murder and accidental death in his 'hot anger' (v. 6) over the death of one of his relatives.

So in the land given by God there had to be clear provision for any person who had accidentally killed another—an example is given in verse 5—to escape vengeance from the dead man's family. For this purpose, initially three cities were to be set apart as cities of refuge where the person who had killed accidentally could find safety. Notice how carefully these cities were to be chosen, so that anyone could get to one easily wherever he or she lived in the land (vv. 2–3). One innocent life had already been accidentally lost, and the aim of the cities of refuge was to prevent any more innocent blood from being shed (v. 10). Later, if God enlarged their territory, three more cities were to be set apart (vv. 8–10). We see here God's concern for justice and the protection of human life, life belonging to those made in his image.

But there was always the possibility that a murderer might try to take

Chapter 22

advantage of the cities of refuge, and verses 11 to 13 deal with this. In such a case, the elders of the city were to hand the man over to the avenger of blood. The elders were involved doubtless because it would be necessary to ascertain the facts before the avenger of blood could do anything, otherwise the whole purpose of the cities of refuge would be undermined. But the main point is this: the shedding of innocent blood by murder involved guilt, and justice demanded that that guilt be purged by the death of the murderer. It is not easy to make any direct application for today, but a concern to preserve life and punish guilt is always important.

Hebrews 12:24 tells of 'the sprinkled blood that speaks a better word than the blood of Abel'. This is blood that calls not for vengeance but for forgiveness. It is blood that has been shed to make atonement for the sins of all who will avail themselves of its forgiving power. It is the blood of Jesus Christ, the 'blood of the covenant, which is poured out for many for the forgiveness of sins' (Matthew 26:28). Even murderers can find forgiveness here.

Inheritance in the land (v. 14)

The theme of the land is still pursued here, only now it is not life but property that is the concern. Once Israel had settled in the land, it was to be divided out tribe by tribe, and every family was to have its own inheritance, which was to be inalienable (see Leviticus 25:23,28; 1 Kings 21:1–19). This provision indicated the right of everyone to private property. There are at least two connections with what we have already considered. In the first place, when landmarks marking the extent of a person's property were moved or removed, it would be a sure cause of contention between neighbours, a contention which could lead to strife and even murder.

Secondly, to move a landmark meant stealing land that was used for crops and grazing animals. In a country where bad harvests caused hunger and famine, to have one's fields reduced in size could make a great difference to the ability of a family to support itself. It could make a poor

Removing evil from the land (19:1–21)

man even poorer so that he had to sell himself, and other members of his family, as a slave. But Israel lived in God's land, and the land was not given just to the whole nation, it was also shared out at God's instruction to every family. Each inheritance was God-given: it was sacrosanct; and to move the landmark was to allocate to one's own family what God had given to another. Such an act was rebellion against God and was to have no place among a people so blessed with God's gifts.

False witness in the land (vv. 15–21)

It may be that underlying this passage is a desire to prevent the shedding of innocent blood by false witness. There must always have been the possibility of someone trying to get rid of another by laying a serious accusation against him or her (consider 1 Kings 21:1–19; Matthew 26:59–62). So, as we saw earlier in the case of capital punishment, one witness to a crime was never sufficient (17:6–7): there had to be two or three. Here this law is extended to cover all crimes or wrongdoing (v. 15). If a single witness did bear testimony against someone, then the case had to be brought before the LORD, and the priests and judges. The judges would then inquire diligently into the case and presumably see if any other witnesses could be found. If it turned out that false witness had been given, the person responsible would be liable to the penalty which the accused would have received if found guilty. This would 'purge the evil from your midst' (v. 19), but would also act as a strong deterrent against laying a false accusation (v. 20).

Verse 21 teaches that the penalty was to be equivalent to the seriousness of the crime. 'Life for life' has to be understood literally as there is no other equivalence to taking away the life of another human being, but in the other cases it may be simply the principle of proportionality that is being expressed. Two further points need to be understood: this law prevented disproportionate punishment, and it applied equally to all persons, whoever they were.

Chapter 22

Verses 15 to 21 are, of course, an expansion of the ninth commandment, 'You shall not bear false witness against your neighbour' (5:20). It is important to notice that this commandment is not simply about always speaking the truth; rather it is about love for a neighbour. How can you love your neighbour as yourself if you bear a false testimony about him or her?

Study questions

1. Did Israel carry out the command to set apart cities of refuge? How many did they appoint? Where else are they mentioned?
2. Wright has written of the principle of verse 21 of 'eye for eye': 'It was a handy way of saying that the punishment must fit the crime.'[1] Can you find evidence for this elsewhere in the Old Testament?
3. How much do we think of land and property as gifts from God to us? What difference does this understanding make to our attitude and behaviour?

Note

[1] **Christopher Wright,** *Old Testament Ethics of the People of God* (Leicester: IVP, 2004), p. 310.

Chapter 23

War and peace (20:1–20)

Very shortly, Israel will be crossing the Jordan and entering the territory of the Canaanite tribes, and this will involve them in warfare. Deuteronomy 20 therefore gives instructions concerning how Israel is to wage war, both in the immediate future and in the longer term.

This chapter comes between one that is primarily concerned with preventing the shedding of innocent blood and another that begins with instructions concerning atonement for unsolved murders. It seems, therefore, to find its place under a general explication of the sixth commandment, 'You shall not murder'. This means that for Israel, while warfare, and therefore killing, is inevitable, the emphasis is on restricting killing.

Fighting in faith (vv. 1–9)

This is a remarkable passage by any standard. The LORD, Israel's covenant sovereign, is the living God, so the people of Israel need never fear when they go out to battle, for he will be with them. The passage starts with a worst-case scenario: the Israelites go out to fight and see 'horses and chariots and an army larger than your own' (v. 1). This reflects the fear felt by the people when the spies came back from viewing the land thirty-eight years earlier (1:22–33). The hearts of the people had melted just by hearing what the spies had to say, but here the men are told not to be afraid even if they see an overwhelming force confronting them. Israel, of course, has no horses or chariots, but even without them, and even if outnumbered, the LORD will be with them, and that will be enough (compare Psalm 20:7). It was he who brought them out of Egypt, demonstrating his power over Pharaoh.

Exploring Deuteronomy   **157**

Chapter 23

It is quite clear that war is seen here as part of Israel's obedience to God, as indeed it was when going into the land that God was giving them. The possibility of Israel going out to fight contrary to God's will, perhaps to enlarge its territory and for its own aggrandisement, is not envisaged at this point. It is noteworthy that most of Israel's battles following the entry into the land seem to have been defensive in their beginnings, rather than offensive and aggressive.

Before battle commenced, the priest—presumably this means the high priest—was to address the army; this was God's army and everything was to be done in his way with faith in him. The priest was to assure the ranks drawn up in battle array that there was no need to fear or panic, for the LORD their God would go with them, not only to fight for them, but also to give them the victory (vv. 3–4). It is easy for us to react to this rather glibly, but only those who have engaged in actual warfare can really appreciate the degree of faith that was being called upon for those lined up to engage a superior force in hand-to-hand fighting. There are important senses in which Christian people are called to fight—with spiritual weapons (2 Corinthians 10:4–6)—and there is a challenge here to our faith, and, indeed, to the timidity we often show.

We have to remember that at that time—and for many years subsequently—Israel had no standing army. Indeed, in those times when there were such armies, they were usually supplemented with all the available males in times of actual warfare. In those days, when a nation was threatened there was a situation such as was experienced in Britain during the First and Second World Wars: there was general conscription, when all able-bodied men were called up into the Forces, except those in essential employments.

But Israel's army was God's army that trusted in him for victory. So there were a number of males who were exempted from the general call-up. Four groups are listed in verses 5 to 9. The first consisted of those who had built a house but not yet dedicated it and moved into it. Dedicating

War and peace (20:1–20)

suggests prayer for God's blessing on those who would live in it. The second group consisted of those who had planted a vineyard but not yet enjoyed any of its fruit. The third group was of those who were engaged to be married, but who had not yet actually married. This is a different exemption from that in 24:5, which we will look at later. The final group consisted of the 'fearful and fainthearted', whose fear could easily be communicated to others.

To exempt all these from going out to battle implied a real attitude of faith on the part of Israel; there was to be no pressing into the fray every man, whatever his circumstances, out of fear of the enemy or to boost the numbers of the army as much as possible. We also see that everyday life was recognized as important and that in some circumstances it took priority even over going out to war. There is probably an implication here that warfare was not to become a way of life for any in Israel. There was a recognition, too, that some men are timid by temperament or because of some experience; these were not to be pushed into battle by compulsion or accusations of cowardice. Faith in a mighty God meant that wisdom replaced fear or thoughtlessness. The references to 'officers' (vv. 5,8,9) and the appointment of commanders (v. 9) indicates the necessary division of the troops into larger and smaller units with a chain of command. Faith in God does not mean that things need not be ordered properly.

There are a number of principles here that carry over into Christian life and church life. There is a place in God's scheme of things for ordinary, everyday life, and in some circumstances this may take priority over going into specific Christian service. Not everyone is suitable for every task, and the idea that every Christian should in faith try to do everything that others do is a mistake. Faith recognizes that we do not need everyone to try to do everything; rather, we all have our own gifts and we are to use them together in varied forms of service. Some people are shy and fearful, and we do not press them into activities of which they feel incapable, nor make them feel second-class Christians, but encourage them into service for

Chapter 23

which they are adapted. And there is always spiritual wisdom in doing things decently and in order.

The offer of peace (vv. 10–18)

The opening verse of this section is very clear about offering terms of peace to a city before beginning to fight against it. But a question arises as to whether this refers to the Canaanite cities or not. The question really is this: How do we understand verses 15 and 16? Does verse 16 mean that none of the preceding verses apply to the Canaanites, or does it simply mean that if Canaanite cities do not accept the offer of peace, then, when the cities are captured, everyone in them is to be put to death? Almost certainly it means the latter; the offer of peace was to be made to the Canaanite cities. There are at least three reasons for believing this. Firstly, it would seem strange for Moses to start as he does in verse 10 if the Canaanite cities were an exception to this rule, because Israel was on the verge of Canaan and these would be the first cities they would encounter. Secondly, verse 16 says nothing about not offering terms of peace, but only instructs that, if they fight against the city, they are to save none alive. Thirdly, Joshua 11:19, speaking about the conquest of Canaan, says, 'There was not a city that made peace with the people of Israel except the Hivites, the inhabitants of Gibeon. They took them all in battle.' This last verse seems decisive, showing that other cities could have made peace but did not.[1]

In considering this passage we have to remember the background. Warfare was usually an awful, bloody thing in those days and atrocities against women and children were commonplace. Against that background we can see how restrictions were placed upon Israel in order to preserve life; the total war that often took place had no part in Israel's strategy. We are familiar enough with appalling atrocities committed in the last century, and still in the present century, so there is no case for us to adopt a superior posture.

War and peace (20:1–20)

If a city accepted the offer of peace, the people of that city—this must mean primarily the men—would work for Israel, doing forced labour as service. This was inevitable in those days. The city would come under the jurisdiction of the captors and under their protection. This latter point is very important; we can see how it worked out in practice in the case of Gibeon in Joshua 10. In return for being spared, and because it came under the protection of the victors, such a city would owe allegiance to Israel and would have to devote a portion of its crops and merchandise to its new lord. Moreover, having to work hard for Israel meant that there would be little time or opportunity for the city to rebel and plunge them all into a war which had been averted in the first place. If Israel was true to its own Sovereign and lived by his law, it would in fact be very beneficial for a city to come under its rule.

If a city refused an offer of peace, only the males were to be killed when it was taken (v. 13). The point to remember here is that generally all the males made up the army, as already mentioned, so they were combatants. The women and children, and everything else, would belong to Israel as plunder. This meant that the women and children would actually be absorbed into Israel; there was no real way in which they could survive otherwise. The next chapter makes provision for an Israelite who wished to marry a female captive.

We have already seen that if one of the Canaanite cities refused the offer of peace, everyone in it was to be put to death. We considered this when looking at chapter 2. But we need to note again the reason given: 'that they may not teach you to do according to all their abominable practices that they have done for their gods, and so you sin against the LORD your God' (v. 18).

The provisions of these verses were enlightened by the standards of those days. There was a restriction on killing; if possible, peace was to be made. The religion of the Bible is essentially one of peace. War may prove to be a necessity, but offering peace and making peace are of the essence of godliness. The message of the gospel is one in which God offers peace to sinful people through the death of his Son (Acts 10:36; Ephesians 2:13–18). Such a message can never be promoted by force.

Preservation for the future (vv. 19–20)

These last two verses show that Israel was not to use a scorched earth policy that deprived an enemy and the future generation of necessary food. When besieging a city, fruit trees were not to be cut down. There is an interesting touch in verse 19: 'Are the trees in the field human, that they should be besieged by you?' Fruit trees were created by God and given by him to man for food (Genesis 1:29–30). It is man who makes war, and trees made by God for the good of human beings should not become the objects of human rage. Other trees could be cut down and used for siege works, but fruit trees were to be left for future generations. Because of human sin war does happen, but this chapter restricts it; its aim is to preserve life.

Study questions

1. Some Christians are pacifists, others are not. What New Testament passages can you find that help you decide which position you ought to take?

2. Do verses 5–8 give the only grounds for releasing a man from going to war, or do they give examples of the sorts of things that would exempt men?

3. May Christians make military service their career?

Note

[1] A useful book on this subject is **Peter Masters**, *Joshua's Conquest: Was it Moral?* (London: Wakeman, 2005).

Chapter 24

Protection in the land (21:1–23)

At first sight, this chapter seems to consist of unrelated instructions. But the similarity of the first section (vv. 1–9) with the last section (vv. 22–23) suggests a unity, and all the provisions here can be looked at from the perspective of protection in the land that God is giving to Israel.

Protecting the land from the guilt of innocent blood (vv. 1–9)
The opening verse shows a concern for what happens in God's land. From a Christian point of view, the world we live in is God's world, and the church is God's church. We should be concerned about what happens in God's world, and especially about what happens in God's church. Here the concern is over the discovery of a dead body. We live in a callous society, where violence and murder are taken far too casually by the general public who are not directly involved in what has happened. Even worse, Christians do not mourn as they should over evils that take place within God's church (compare 1 Corinthians 5:1–2).

In this case, if a body has been found and it is not known who killed the person, the nearest town has to take responsibility and take action so that the guilt of innocent blood being shed in God's land can be purged away. It is not possible for the people of Israel simply to shrug their shoulders and say, 'We don't know who did this, but it wasn't any of us', and just carry on as if nothing has happened. As we have already seen, to take a human life is a great evil in God's eyes, and the thought here is of averting his judgement. Here the elders of the town were to act on behalf of the citizens; being an elder was a position of responsibility rather than privilege.

Chapter 24

The procedure involved the death of a heifer, whose neck was broken in a valley with a stream of running water. Perhaps the running water symbolized guilt being washed away and removed from the area where the murder had taken place. This was to be carried out in the presence of the priests, who were God's representatives and would see what was done. The death of the heifer meant that a substitute for the murderer had died. In addition, the elders were to wash their hands over the heifer, symbolizing that the city was innocent and that the heifer bore the guilt. In this way atonement was to be made for the guilt of bloodshed. The most important words in the prayer the elders were to offer were these: 'Do not set the guilt of innocent blood in the midst of your people Israel' (v. 8). The plea was that, though innocent blood had been shed, God would not hold the innocent members of the town guilty. Atonement had been made, and presumably the real perpetrator of the crime was left to the justice of God, who sees and knows everything.

In the Old Testament we find people who identified themselves with the nation and pleaded with God on its behalf, the classic example being Daniel in his great prayer in chapter 9 of his book (see especially vv. 9–11,13,16,19 in that chapter). It is surely appropriate for Christians to pray and intercede for their own towns, their nation and the leaders of the nations of the world.

Protecting a female captive who is brought into the land (vv. 10–14)

Anyone with any knowledge of history knows that, through the centuries, women have been treated extremely badly during times of war. Invading armies have almost invariably included rape among other atrocities they have carried out. Captured women have often been taken back to their captors' country to suffer degradation and servitude. But this was not to happen when Israel went out to war against its enemies (v. 10). Captives who were brought into Israel's land (see v. 12, 'bring her home to your

Protection in the land (21:1–23)

house') were to be treated quite differently. This passage, of course, links in with the previous chapter (20:14).

If an Israelite soldier saw among the captives a beautiful woman, he was to think in terms of marriage, and this was permitted to him. But first there was to be a certain procedure. The shaving of the head, paring of the nails and change of clothing seem to signify that the woman was now in a different land from her own; she was beginning to live a new life in Israel. She was given time to adjust and to mourn the fact that she would see her father and mother no more—there is no suggestion here that this necessarily means they were dead. After a full month had passed she could become a wife, but if for any reason her husband tired of her, he could neither sell her, that is, into slavery, nor could he make her his own slave. This contrasts with what would usually have happened in those days, when the lot of women could be very difficult indeed. In fact, it was probably a great advantage if a woman was married to an Israelite, because there would be only a limited number of men available in a defeated country and some form of servitude was the likely alternative.

Protecting the firstborn's inheritance in the land (vv. 15–17)

It may be that this provision comes here because of a link with what we have just considered. A man might marry a captive in addition to his Israelite wife, or he might be dissatisfied with his foreign wife and marry an Israelite as well. In either case, the firstborn son was to have the right of inheritance, even if the husband loved the other wife more than he did the mother of the firstborn. The firstborn had a double portion, but also received the family inheritance of land, which was sacrosanct and could not be alienated. This instruction, like others, recognized that polygamy was taking place and sought to regulate it and restrict some of its worst features. Throughout this book—and the Mosaic law as a whole—we have to recognize this principle of regulating practices which were not the will of God but which were taking place and had become entrenched

Chapter 24

among the people of Israel. We might note that with most people, a second marriage was unlikely except with a captive because then no dowry would have to be paid.

Protecting parents from a rebellious son (vv. 18–21)

We can see again a connection with what has just gone before. In the words of Wright, commenting on verses 15–21: 'The next two laws balance each other. The first protects a son from an unfair father; the second protects parents from an unruly son.'[1] Clearly this is a very serious case; here is a son who simply will not listen at all to his parents and has grown up to be 'a glutton and a drunkard' (v. 20). He is not fit to receive any inheritance, and he foments rebelliousness in God's land. Note that his parents have recourse to the elders as the authority in the town. The death penalty seems very severe to us, but the point is that Israel's whole stability and continuance in the land depended on obedience, and obedience was learned first of all in the home (see 5:16). All the men were to join in stoning, showing that the whole town repudiated the spirit of stubbornness and rebellion that had been evinced in the son. Note the deterrent effect this was intended to have: 'And all Israel shall hear, and fear.' Later writers take up the language of verse 18 and apply it to Israel as a whole in its relationship with the LORD (e.g. Psalm 78:8; Jeremiah 5:23). This underlines the point: a spirit of rebelliousness may start against parents but will end against God.

Protecting the land from defilement by a dead body (vv. 22–23)

Notice how the final sentence here balances the opening sentence in the chapter with its reference to 'the land that the LORD your God is giving you'. The chapter began with the body of an innocent person defiling the land; here it is the body of a man who has suffered the death penalty. Many societies have hung up the bodies of those who have been put to death for their crimes as deterrents to others: grim visual aids. Israelites may hear

Protection in the land (21:1–23)

and fear, but not see and fear. The practice was not completely outlawed, but the body was to be buried the same day, which was a considerable limitation. Such a person was under the curse of God—the curse that issued in death—for his or her crime, so to hang up such a body was to exhibit someone under the curse of God. To make a spectacle of an accursed body defiled God's land, so the body had to be buried out of sight. Paul takes this up in Galatians 3:13–14 (see the Study questions below).

Study questions
1. Consider the relationship between verses 22–23 and Galatians 3:13–14.
2. In what ways are the provisions in this chapter in advance of pagan behaviour of the time?
3. Compare verses 18 to 21 with the parable of the prodigal son in Luke 15:11–32. What can we learn from this?

Note

[1] **Christopher Wright,** *Deuteronomy* (New International Biblical Commentary) (Peabody, MA: Hendrickson Publishers/Paternoster Press), 1996, p. 235.

Chapter 25

Laws for the good of society and laws upholding marriage (22:1–30)

The next four chapters contain a whole variety of laws. These laws were for God's people living in God's land. They not only distinguished Israel from the nations around, they were also given to show the nations how much better it is to obey God and follow his way (see 4:5–8).

The chapter title indicates that this passage has been divided into two main sections, each of which has several subsections. Laws upholding marriage were also, of course, for the good of society, but as that theme takes up the larger part of the chapter it is clearer to give it its own heading. That section applies the seventh commandment, 'You shall not commit adultery'.

Laws for the good of society (vv. 1–12)

BROTHERLY LOVE IN ACTION (VV. 1–4)

The emphasis in these verses is on the fact that in Israel, all were brothers; the word occurs five times in these four verses. Here is an outworking of the command in Leviticus 19:18, 'You shall love your neighbour as yourself', with its significant addition, 'I am the LORD.' Those who belong to the LORD recognize one another as brothers, even when they do not know one another (v. 2). Christians, too, must recognize one another as family members, brothers and sisters in Christ. But there is also an important sense in which, because God made everyone from one couple at

Laws for the good of society & laws upholding marriage (22:1–30)

the very beginning, we must recognize all neighbours as brothers and sisters.

An important word in these verses is 'ignore'. The NKJV translates this as 'hide yourself'. The idea here is that an Israelite was not to pretend that he or she did not see something that needed his or her help. If you saw an animal straying and you knew whose it was, then you were to restore it to the owner. If you did not know whose it was, you were to look after it until someone came looking for it. And you were to do the same with any lost thing you found. No 'finders keepers' here. And if you saw your brother struggling to lift up one of his animals that had fallen down, you were to help him. It is not difficult to apply this to modern life, and it is very different from the careless attitude to the property of others that so many people show today.

THREE DIVERSE LAWS (VV. 5–8)

The first of these (v. 5) condemns in strong terms the wearing of clothing of the opposite sex. This is not a condemnation of wearing clothes that are very similar; rather it prohibits transvestism, in which people dress as if they are not what they are. It may be that putting on actual clothing belonging to someone from the opposite sex is what is in mind here. Why is this prohibited and with such vehemence? There are two suggestions: firstly, because this was connected with homosexual behaviour; or, secondly, because this was something that took place in pagan religion—priests of a goddess dressing in female clothes, for example. These are not necessarily alternative suggestions, as pagan worship often included fertility rites that involved sexual misbehaviour. Both homosexual acts and idolatry are described as abominations.

Perhaps even more important is the positive message that we should live according to what we are. It is true that sometimes teenagers go through a period of confused emotions, and it is also true that some people find themselves attracted to those of the same sex, and others have a great desire

Chapter 25

to change their sexuality. There is also a very small minority of cases of physical or genetic abnormality. Leaving this last group aside, we should all recognize that we are meant to live according to the way we were made. However we feel, and no matter that some people think cross-dressing is fun and others laugh about it, a man should not be ashamed of what he is, and he should dress as a man and live as a man. And the same goes for a woman.

The second law (vv. 6–7) is concerned about resources for the future. In days when people lived in fragile agricultural economies, there would have been times when finding a bird's nest with eggs or young would be a great help in feeding hungry mouths. The temptation would be to take the bird and the eggs, but that would mean no more eggs in the future. Here is a vital principle. If you eat up all your grain, you will have nothing left to plant for next year. If you use the same piece of land year after year, it will lose all its nutritional value—therefore Israel had to leave the land fallow every seventh year. We are learning today that if we go on fishing every year, we use up the fish stocks and there will be none for the future; and the same goes for coal, and oil, and gas and so on. We are beginning to learn the hard way what the Old Testament taught centuries ago. We must conserve resources; we must think of the future; stocks have to be preserved and renewed.

The third law (v. 8) is about preventing accidents. In those days, houses had flat roofs and people would go up on to the roofs to get more of a breeze. In Israel, because God's people cared for one another, everyone was to ensure that the roof had a parapet so that no one would fall off. This is framed in a very serious way. If a house did not have a parapet and someone fell off, the owners of the house would incur blood guilt—the responsibility was theirs. In days when many people couldn't care less, God's people are to care more.

REMEMBER WHAT YOU ARE (VV. 9–12)

The instructions in verses 9 to 11 have often baffled Christians who have

Laws for the good of society & laws upholding marriage (22:1–30)

read them, and unbelievers have used them as a source of ridicule. The most likely understanding of these verses is that, by avoiding mixing things up in everyday life, the people would realize that they had to keep themselves distinct in their behaviour from the nations around. They were a holy people to God and they were to be committed to him and his law; no moral compromises and no syncretistic religion, in which elements of paganism were incorporated into the worship of the LORD. This did not mean they were to be stand-offish in their relations with people of other nations: quite the reverse. They were to show kindness to strangers and foreigners, and treat them well, remembering their own years as immigrants in Egypt (16:11–12). Christians are to be like this, following the example of Jesus himself, who was 'holy, innocent, unstained, separated from sinners' (Hebrews 7:26), yet also 'a friend of tax collectors and sinners' (Luke 7:34), whom he received and ate with (Luke 15:2).

To understand verse 12 we have to look at Numbers 15:37–41. The tassels were there for people to look at and remember the commandments of the LORD, to do them and thus 'be holy to your God'. Just as people sometimes put a knot in their handkerchief to remind them of something they have to do, so the tassels would remind the Israelites to keep God's commands. This, incidentally, tends to confirm the understanding just given of avoiding mixed seeds and so on. The people were reminded of what they were—God's holy people—and they were to live accordingly.

Laws upholding marriage (vv. 13–30)
SEXUAL IMMORALITY AND THE MARRIED WOMAN (VV. 13–22)

There are two unequal parts covered by this heading. First there is the case of a husband who hates his wife and makes a false accusation against her (though the passage also covers an accusation which is proved true). That comes in verses 13 to 21. Second is the case of a man who commits adultery

Chapter 25

with another man's wife (v. 22). We should note that, as generally in the Old Testament, this is written from a perspective which is usually called patriarchal. In Israelite society, a father had the care of his daughter up to the time of her marriage, and after marriage this responsibility fell on the husband. This means that, in general terms, the man was held responsible for any sin and the woman was responsible if she acquiesced in it. This way of looking at things did not threaten the equality of man and woman, nor the freedom of women to develop their abilities to the full (see, for example, Proverbs 31:10–31), but was based on the complementarity of man and woman in marriage, and placed responsibility and care on the man.

Among God's people, girls were to maintain their virginity until marriage, and a man who became betrothed to a young woman gave a marriage present to her father (see, for example, Exodus 22:16, where the unfortunate phrase 'bride-price' is used in the text) and expected to find her still a virgin. The point of this present was that in her home, the young woman would have given domestic service (in an agricultural society the whole family works together in various ways), and her family was being recompensed for the loss of this. Moreover, the young husband was also beginning a family life in which his bride would care for the home and children as well as help in the fields at certain times (see Ruth 1:22–2:23), so there was an economic advantage to him, and also to his wider family.

It seems that, in order to provide evidence of a young woman's virginity when she was married, a cloak or sheet (vv. 15–16) would be laid on the marriage bed and later taken into the care of the young wife's parents. In the case envisaged here, a man marries but then finds that he hates his wife and wants to get out of the marriage, so he accuses her of not being a virgin when they were married. Such an accusation would presumably be made very soon after the marriage. The upshot will be this: if the man's complaint is proved to be false, he will be punished and prevented from ever divorcing his wife; if such an accusation is true, the wife will be stoned to death.

Laws for the good of society & laws upholding marriage (22:1–30)

There are obviously aspects to this that we would like to know more about but that are not explained in the text. We might note the following points. This law was concerned to uphold the honour of a young woman who had been slandered (v. 19). The fact that the husband could not divorce his wife meant that he could not disinherit her firstborn (compare 21:15–17). It also meant that he had to provide for her for the rest of her life—a life that would have been forfeited had the accusation proved to be true. We are inclined to think that the death penalty in such a case seems excessive, but we have to realize that disobedience to a father (v. 21) undermined the whole covenant structure of Israel's life. It was in the home that obedience and faithfulness was learned, and the relationship between husband and wife mirrored the relationship between the LORD and Israel. It was not just that in this case the sexual act itself was wrong, but that this 'outrageous thing' had serious implications for Israel. The same is true for the case in verse 22 (and vv. 23–24). Adultery, of course, was consensual, and therefore both the man and the woman suffered the penalty. Here, as in verse 21 (and also v. 24) the final words are, 'So you shall purge the evil from Israel' (or 'from your midst'). Verse 22 is a repeat of the provision in Leviticus 20:10, and it is to this law that the scribes and Pharisees were appealing in John 8:3–11.

SEXUAL IMMORALITY AND THE BETROTHED VIRGIN (VV. 23–27)

We have to remember that in Israel, betrothal was a committal to marriage and any intercourse on the part of the betrothed virgin was considered adultery. This is why verse 24 speaks of violating 'his neighbour's wife'. Two cases are considered. In the case of a betrothed virgin within a city, she could cry out for help if rape was attempted. If she did not, she would be guilty of adultery. On the other hand, if she was in the open country there would be no one to rescue her (v. 27), and only the man would be punished.

Chapter 25

SEXUAL IMMORALITY AND THE UNBETROTHED VIRGIN (VV. 28–29)

In the case of a virgin who was not betrothed, if a man seized her and lay with her—in other words, raped her—he would then have to give her father a marriage present of fifty shekels of silver, a considerable sum, and marry her. Exodus 22:16–17 indicates that the father could refuse the marriage, though this would leave the girl in a very vulnerable position as other men were not likely to want to marry a girl who was not a virgin. If they were married, there was no possibility of divorce.

Although this passage presents six examples of case law, it is clear that its intention was to deter sexual immorality, and that the purpose of this was to protect marriage because of its central importance in the life of Israel as a nation and as God's people. The importance of marriage and the family is all too evident today, and can particularly be seen negatively in the results of marriage breakdown and widespread immorality. A stable society needs stable marriages and healthy family life.

A SPECIAL RESTRICTION (V. 30)

In the Hebrew Bible, this verse is actually the beginning of chapter 23, which perhaps indicates that it forms a bridge between the subjects of these chapters. This is not about not marrying one's own mother (see Leviticus 18:7–8), but not marrying a stepmother, who, of course, was not a blood relation. It is difficult to know the exact reason for this law, but the phrase 'so that he does not uncover his father's nakedness' seems to imply that it is entirely inappropriate for a son to enter into the same intimate sexual relationship that his father had occupied. The importance of this law is seen by its place in 27:20.

Study questions

1. How do John 8:1–11 and Matthew 1:18–25 affect our understanding of the application of the laws in verses 22 to 24 for today?

Laws for the good of society & laws upholding marriage (22:1–30)

2. What steps might we take to remind ourselves (v. 12) of the importance of God's commands?

3. Why is sexual purity so important?

Chapter 26

The assembly, the camp, and others (23:1–25)

This chapter deals with those who are able to meet as God's people in worship at the tabernacle, holiness in the camp, and relationships with other people. The others spoken of are slaves, Israelite daughters and sons, brothers, God himself and neighbours.

Entering the assembly of the LORD (vv. 1–8)
The 'assembly', or congregation, of the LORD refers to Israel gathered together for worship. In the Greek translation of the Old Testament the word used here was the word that is translated 'church' in the New Testament. It appears from this passage that there were some people who, while belonging fully to Israel as the covenant people of God, were not permitted to gather together when Israel came to the assembly. This would include those from other nations, the sojourners or 'resident aliens' mentioned in 10:18–19. When Israel settled in Canaan there were numbers of Canaanites who remained in the land, such as the Gibeonites (Joshua 9). So the whole question of who was eligible to come to the assembly was an important one.

While there is some uncertainty about the details of these verses, it is likely that verse 1 does not refer to those who suffered accidents but rather to those who mutilated themselves for ritual reasons, as sometimes took place within pagan religions. Similarly, verse 2 may refer to children born as a result of ritual prostitution (compare v. 17). 'To the tenth generation' probably means for ever, as also in verse 3.

Verses 3 to 6 prohibit any Ammonite or Moabite from ever entering the assembly because of their actions towards Israel as that nation approached

The assembly, the camp, and others (23:1–25)

the land of promise. In the case of the Moabites, they sought to bring a curse upon Israel, but those who curse God's people find that the curse comes upon them. Verse 6 probably means that Israel was not to enter into any treaty that would be for their welfare with such nations. Individuals like Ruth could come into the covenant people, but perhaps she would not have been able to go up to the worship.

However, the grandchildren of Edomite or Egyptian families who lived among the Israelites could enter the assembly. This is significant when we remember that a mixed multitude left Egypt with the Israelites (Exodus 12:38). After forty years there could already be Egyptians who were eligible to enter. When we remember how Israel was treated by the Egyptians for a considerable period, this is a remarkable provision, and points forward to the entry of the Gentile nations into the covenant people of God in New Testament days. Notice the striking way in which this command is framed: 'You shall not abhor an Edomite ... You shall not abhor an Egyptian'; it is the attitude towards them which is particularly stressed.

We ought not to understand these provisions in individualistic terms, as if they reflected the spiritual position of individuals before God. Rather they taught broader lessons. There was no place in the assembly of the people of the LORD for those involved in idolatrous rituals, nor for those who were antagonistic and sought the harm of God's people. But the assembly of the LORD was not exclusive to those born as Israelites; those from other nations could enter, and the Old Testament bears testimony to this. It is along these lines that we can apply these verses to the New Testament assembly of the Lord Jesus, the church.

Holiness in the camp (vv. 9–14)

The laws we have just looked at, actually beginning with 22:30, were all direct laws: 'A man shall not ...'; 'No one ... shall ...'. But at this point the instructions become case laws, the same as most of the laws in the previous three chapters: 'When ...'; 'If ...'. This section deals with the army

Chapter 26

encamped when going out against their enemies. As Israel was soon to enter Canaan, this was a situation that would arise almost immediately. The crucial verse is verse 14: 'Because the LORD your God walks in the midst of your camp, to deliver you and to give up your enemies before you, therefore your camp must be holy.' This repeats the promise of God found in 20:1, for example: 'When you go out to war against your enemies … the LORD your God is with you.'

God's presence with the army was a great encouragement, but it also brought certain obligations. What we would think of as hygiene is here viewed in terms of holiness or ritual purity. Verse 10 probably reflects the same provision as Leviticus 15:16. In a military camp, standards can easily drop, especially if battles are being fought during the day. In Israel the men were to be conscious that God was always with them. This would bring them victory, but they needed to 'keep yourself from every evil thing' (v. 9). The presence of God with us ought to have a similar effect upon us. Christians have high standards of behaviour and decency, for we serve a great and holy God.

Responsibilities towards others (vv. 15–25)

Verses 15 and 16 do not refer to an Israelite slave; verse 16 rules that out. The slave spoken of here would doubtless have run away because of ill-treatment. Israel had first-hand experience of slavery in Egypt. Israel was not to have any extradition treaty with the nations around it; this would compromise the people's allegiance to the LORD as their sovereign. The last sentence of verse 16 may simply mean, 'You shall not wrong him by sending him back', but more probably means that in Israel he was to receive no harsh treatment. Israel thus would become a haven for those seeking release from cruel bondage.

The ancient pagan religions had cult prostitutes of both sexes at their places of worship, but this was prohibited in Israel. Neither could the money received by prostitutes be brought to support the house of the

The assembly, the camp, and others (23:1–25)

Lord; such a thing would be an abomination. Because the words in verse 18 are different from those used in the previous verse, it may be that the thought is that money from prostitutes, whether cultic or not, was prohibited. Looking at this positively, it suggests that money for the work of God should be honestly earned in a reputable manner.

Once again there is an emphasis on the fact that, within Israel, all were brothers and sisters. As a result, other people were to be treated as if members of their own family. This meant that if others were in need and a loan was made, no interest was to be charged, though it was legitimate to charge interest to foreigners (vv. 19–20). We have to remember that society was ordered in a very different way from today. A loan would be required in times of need and would generally be short term. In Israel everything depended upon the blessing of God. If a person was in a position to lend, this was because of God's blessing, and God would enable the other to repay the loan.

Vows (vv. 21–23) were a part of Old Testament godliness. An example occurs in Genesis 28:20–22. It may be that not all vows began with an 'If', as Jacob's did. In some cases they would be responses to some blessing already received. The point stressed here is that there was no obligation on any Israelite to take a vow, but if a vow was made, it had to be fulfilled. In the past, Christians have sometimes taken particular vows, but this is not common these days. We must remember, however, that vows are taken in a marriage service, and baptism (or confirmation) is an implicit vow. The hymn 'O Jesus, I have promised to serve thee to the end' has the nature of a vow. Such vows are to be kept.

Finally, the way in which Israel acted as a family is underlined by a provision that is surprising to us. The word 'neighbour' in verses 24 to 25 means a person living nearby. An Israelite walking through a neighbour's vineyard, or field of grain (see Matthew 12:1–2), could eat whatever could be picked while walking along, but could not put grapes into a bag or use a sickle to obtain more grain. The land belonged to the Lord, and the fruit

Chapter 26

was an evidence of his goodness and was for the benefit of all, though this was not to be abused. So Christians, too, should be glad to share with others and help them in time of need.

Study questions

1. What evidence can you find in 1 and 2 Samuel of people who figure in the narrative but are not native-born Israelites?
2. What applications from verses 1 to 8 can reasonably be made to the church of Jesus Christ?
3. How interested is God in things that we might call hygiene or common decency?

Chapter 27

Laws and principles for a godly life (24:1–22)

There are a variety of laws in this chapter, but they illustrate how every aspect of life was to be lived before God. Not only are the laws themselves important, but the reasons given for them, and the consequences of obeying or disobeying, are vital, too.

This is a fascinating and instructive chapter. In our society there is a huge body of legislation, and the ordinary person knows only a fraction of it. In Israel there were relatively few laws and these were to be read out to the people and become part of the thinking and behaviour of everyday life. Moreover, the laws enshrined vital principles that were to be generally applied as circumstances arose. For example, there was to be justice for all (v. 17), trust in a neighbour (v. 10) and care for those in need (v. 19). Everyone in Israel was personally responsible to live according to law and principle, and to do so 'before the LORD your God' (v. 13).

Divorce, remarriage and marriage (vv. 1–5)

Verses 1 to 4 are crucial for understanding divorce in Israel and the background to Jesus' words in the New Testament. As Jesus reminded his hearers, at the beginning God made male and female and said, 'Therefore a man shall leave his father and his mother and hold fast to his wife, and the two shall become one flesh' (Matthew 19:4–5; Genesis 2:24). This is the basic pattern for marriage, the ideal, but those words were spoken before the fall into sin, and because of the hardness of people's hearts, 'Moses allowed you to divorce your wives' (Matthew 19:8).

What we have here is one long sentence and it is important to understand exactly what it says. There is a basic prohibition: if a man

Chapter 27

divorces his wife and she marries again, then, if her second husband divorces her or dies, she cannot be remarried to her first husband. To do so would be an abomination and bring sin upon the land. Why was this so? This law appears to put a limit on the toleration of divorce and remarriage. A divorced wife could remarry (and so, of course, could the husband), but to return to her first husband after that was a step too far. Wright may well be correct when he says, 'The practical effect of this rule is to protect the unfortunate woman from becoming a kind of marital football, passed back and forth between irresponsible men.'[1] There is probably also here a reason for a husband to think carefully about divorcing his wife and not act on the spur of the moment. If he divorced her, then almost certainly she would be lost to him for ever. This also meant that once divorce had taken place, both partners could put the past behind them as something that was over, and concentrate on what the future held for them.

It is also important to consider this passage further because in a number of ways it is very different from what happens in our own society. Firstly, divorce was an act of the husband; it was not the act of magistrate or judge; a third party did not have to be involved. In the Graeco-Roman world of the New Testament wives could also divorce their husbands (Mark 10:11–12; this is, of course, the background to 1 Corinthians 7). It is crucial to understand this when thinking of divorce in the Bible. In those days, a man could not simply send his wife away or go off himself; he was obliged to give her a certificate of divorce. Secondly, the Jews of subsequent days were probably quite wrong in trying to decide what the 'indecency' was (v. 1) which they thought justified divorce. The fact is that no one would divorce a wife if he was completely satisfied with her; the verse is merely saying that there would be something that caused him to divorce his wife. Thirdly, the giving of a certificate was probably to enable his wife to remarry. In those days, this would be almost a necessity, as her father would probably not want her back in his home. In view of 22:13–21, such a certificate would prove she was divorced and not simply an immoral woman.

Laws and principles for a godly life (24:1–22)

Verse 5 brings a much happier scene before us. There is a great deal of wisdom here and it shows how important marriage was considered in Israel. A new couple were to be given every chance to make a good start to their marriage, and the husband's life was not to be put in danger at the very beginning. There is a principle here that Christians would do well to apply in our own day. We must remember, too, that service in the army and public duty then was service for God's people, done in his name. In the early days of marriage, a man's duty to his wife comes first.

Life and freedom (vv. 6–9)

The first law here should be read in the light of verses 10 to 13. If a poor man borrowed money (or perhaps goods), the custom was for the lender to receive something belonging to the borrower as a pledge to be returned when the loan was repaid. But here a lender was forbidden from taking a mill or millstone from the borrower. The reason for this is that it would mean that the borrower would not be able to grind any grain to make bread. So in a literal way, to take a millstone was like taking a life in pledge. To take a millstone would leave a poor man in as bad a condition, or worse, than before he borrowed, and this was not to happen.

The second law (v. 7) concerns kidnapping, the most serious form of stealing. The purpose of kidnapping was either to enslave the person oneself or to sell him or her into slavery, which would imply the person being sold to foreigners (as in the case of Joseph), for such slavery was not permitted in Israel. This treats a person as a commodity, in effect dehumanizing and depersonalizing him or her. Perhaps this was why it attracted the death penalty. It was by capturing people and selling them that the slave trade of the eighteenth century was carried on, and this verse was used by those who opposed that terrible system.

The third law (vv. 8–9) is also about life and health. On the surface it seems a bit like advice to 'Make sure you take your medicine'! But there is

Chapter 27

more to it than that. The health, not only of a person who was infected, but also of others, depended upon careful obedience to the directions of the priest. Miriam is probably referred to because she was required to obey the command to remain outside the camp for seven days (Numbers 12; compare Leviticus 13). Just as she obeyed what the LORD commanded her, so an Israelite was to obey the priest. We ought to note also that 'as I commanded them' (v. 8) is a clear reference to the provisions of Leviticus 13.

Righteous and sinful living (vv. 10–16)

These verses first take up again the matter of loans (vv. 10–13). There are several points to notice. As mentioned in the introduction to this chapter, the lender here needed to trust the borrower to go into his house and bring out a suitable pledge; he was not to go into the house to see what the borrower had or to choose the pledge. Good relations always depend on trust. One of the evils of our day is that there is so little trust. However, trust cannot arise until one person is willing to trust another.

A second point is that if the pledge was something a man needed, like a cloak in which to sleep at night, then the lender was to give it back at sunset, presumably receiving it again in the morning. Doing this would help build good relations: 'that he may … bless you' (v. 13). Finally, acting in this way is described as 'righteousness for you before the LORD your God'. Israelites were always to seek to live in such a way, and so should Christians.

The next law (vv. 14–15) is similar in tone, particularly in its second provision. First there is a general command not to oppress a hired servant. Notice that verse 14 includes 'one of the sojourners' along with 'your brothers'. Part of not oppressing a poor hired servant included paying the wages each day (compare Matthew 20:1–16). A poor man could not wait a week or a month for his wages; his family could starve in that time. He 'count[ed] on' being paid daily (v. 15) so that he could go

Laws and principles for a godly life (24:1–22)

and buy the food that was needed. Notice that the previous command ended with the benefit of acting in accordance with the law ('he may ... bless you'; 'it shall be righteousness'), while here the consequence of disobedience is expressed: 'lest he cry against you to the LORD, and you be guilty of sin'.

The third law, in verse 16, stands rather on its own, not clearly related either to what goes before or to what comes after. However, it does emphasize personal responsibility; as Ezekiel was to express it later, 'the soul who sins shall die' (Ezekiel 18:4). It is interesting to note that, by Ezekiel's day, it is clear that this command had been forgotten. Looking at personal responsibility in a positive light, we can see how each person in Israel was to act responsibly by carrying out the laws that God had given. It is this sense of personal responsibility in the community that we need to recapture today; I am my brother's keeper.

Remembering Egypt (vv. 17–22)

The last two provisions in this chapter have the same motivation: 'You shall remember that you were a slave in Egypt and the LORD your God redeemed you from there; therefore I command you to do this' (vv. 18,22). The attitude that the Israelites were to have towards those in need, the sojourner, the fatherless and the widow, was to be based on their experience as needy sojourners in Egypt. It is the principle that Jesus gave us in Matthew 7:12: 'So whatever you wish that others would do to you, do also to them, for this is the Law and the Prophets.' The people of Israel are to remember, and to act as they would have wished the Egyptians acted towards them. If they do, they will give everyone justice, and at harvest time they will leave sufficient for the poor to glean from their fields. This section underlines these two things. The chapter is about moulding the attitudes of Israel more than looking for formal obedience to law. And, as Jesus said, this was the purpose of the law: to bring people to do to others what they would wish to be done to them.

Chapter 27

Study questions

1. Consider how the laws in this chapter are intended to help particular people.
2. What is said in this chapter about God?
3. How far should our own experience guide our behaviour?

Note

1 **Wright,** *Deuteronomy*, p. 255.

Chapter 28

Doing justly (25:1–19)

The theme of doing justly runs throughout this chapter. Judges are to act justly, and not be excessive in punishment. An ox deserves justice, as does a wife whose husband dies without leaving an heir, and wives must act justly. Those who buy and sell must be just and fair, and Amalek must receive what it deserves.

Limiting punishment (vv. 1–4)
In the ancient world, beatings were commonplace as punishment and these could be very dreadful, sometimes resulting in death. In Israel, restitution was one of the commonest punishments (see, for example, Exodus 22:1,4–15). There was no provision for imprisonment as there was in Egypt (Genesis 39:20–41:14). In this passage, corporal punishment is permitted, but limited to forty stripes (v. 3). First we should note that this was to come only after a judge made a decision that was impartial, 'acquitting the innocent and condemning the guilty' (v. 1). The number of stripes was to be proportional to the offence, and the judge was to supervise their implementation. We notice, too, that the guilty man is called a 'brother', and he was not to be beaten excessively, degrading him. His dignity was to be upheld. Although giving forty stripes was permitted, in time the Jews restricted this to thirty-nine (2 Corinthians 11:24), perhaps deciding that no one deserved the full punishment.

Verse 4 does not seem to be related either to what we have just considered or to what follows. It shows, however, that consideration was to be given to animals as well as people. Oxen were used in threshing, pulling a type of sledge over the ears of corn to separate out the grain. Just as poor people were permitted to glean in the fields (24:19–22), and everyone was allowed to eat grapes or grain when passing through fields

Chapter 28

(23:24–25), so oxen were to be able to eat the grain as they worked. This passage reinforces what we saw in considering Deuteronomy 14: that God's people are to care for animal life as well as human life. Paul comments on this verse in 1 Corinthians 9:8–10, applying its principle to those who are in gospel work receiving support and remuneration from those among whom they work. When he says, 'Is it for oxen that God is concerned?' we should understand the meaning as 'Is it *only* for oxen that God is concerned?' If God is concerned that oxen at work should be able to eat from what they are doing, as is the case, how much more is he concerned that those who labour for him in gospel preaching should be able to live from their work?

Maintaining an inheritance (vv. 5–10)

This passage sounds very strange to us and strikes us as wrong, as it involves a man having two wives. But the point is this. If a man died before there was a son and heir, it meant that his name would die out and his share of the inheritance would be lost. As the text makes clear, the brother would marry the widow in order that a son born to her might take the place and inheritance of the man who had died. The phrase 'If brothers dwell together' (v. 5) suggests that they would still be living on the family land, though not necessarily in the same house. This would normally be the case. That this was considered an important provision is seen in the treatment to be received by a brother who refused to comply with its terms. Presumably the reason for such a refusal would be the selfish one of not wanting to share the inheritance with another. But there is another factor. To follow this procedure meant that the widow was provided for (note the words of v. 5: 'perform the duty of a husband's brother to her'). If the brother refused her, presumably she would not be welcome to stay on the family land and would have to look for another husband or else return to her father's home. Instead of being immediately cared for she would face an uncertain and difficult future.

Doing justly (25:1–19)

Acting justly (vv. 11–16)

Although verses 11 and 12 have been included under this heading, there is actually a close link between them and the previous section. Those verses spoke of a man who died before an heir was born; in this passage the action of a wife could result in a man being injured in the genitals and not able to father children, possibly resulting in no heir for the inheritance. It was not just because such an act was indecent that the punishment was so severe, but also because of its potential consequences. Having a hand or other parts of the body cut off as a punishment was commonplace in the nations around Israel, but this is the only place in Old Testament law where such a punishment was prescribed. The circumstances here are unusual and it is probable that the punishment was intended as a deterrent. For a wife to intervene in that sort of way was not to be contemplated.

The next law (vv. 13–16) prohibits cheating in buying and selling. The man with two measures hoped to buy using the larger measure and sell using the smaller measure. In Israel, people were not to have two kinds of weights and measures, but 'a full and fair weight' and 'a full and fair measure'. The outcome would be that their days would be long in God's land. Cheating leads to distrust and disputes, and undermines a community. Verse 16 tells us that those who act dishonestly are 'an abomination to the LORD your God'. It is not only idolatry and sexual sin that are called abominations; dishonesty is branded in the same way.

Amalek's deserts (vv. 17–19)

This is a very serious passage and we need to discover precisely what Amalek's faults were. These verses do not refer simply to the battle with Amalek that is recorded in Exodus 17:8–16. That was a pitched battle in which Israel was given victory by the LORD; but verse 18 here refers to what led up to that battle and probably what continued to take place afterwards: 'He attacked you on the way when you were faint and weary, and cut off your tail, those who were lagging behind you.' Those who lagged behind

Chapter 28

would have been the weakest; it would have included the sick and elderly, women and little children. How easy, and how pitiless, to pick these off! It is probably this behaviour which drew the words, 'He did not fear God' (v. 18). Only utterly godless people behave in that sort of way. The Amalekites are listed along with the other Canaanite tribes in Numbers 13:29 and 14:25,43,45, so they came under the same judgement as those listed in Deuteronomy 7:1–5. They are mentioned again in 1 Samuel 15 and seem to have been a constant thorn in Israel's side (see Exodus 17:16). The sort of wicked cruelty of which Amalek was guilty, and which has constantly besmirched human history, has no excuse and will receive its proper reward at the Day of Judgement.

Study questions

1. What principles for life today can you discover from verses 5 to 10?
2. Do the types of laws in this chapter simply mitigate evils that abounded in the ancient world or can we find wisdom for ourselves from them?
3. Does the Bible help us in considering what sorts of punishments would be suitable for our society?

Chapter 29

Thanksgiving and covenant promises (26:1–19)

With this chapter, Moses brings to an end the address that began in chapter 5. It ends on a wonderful note with the thanksgiving that was to take place in the land once Israel had settled there, and with the mutual covenant promises reaffirmed by the people and the LORD on the day that Moses spoke to them.

Harvest thanksgiving (vv. 1–11)

'When you come into the land ...' (v. 1). Moses assumes that his encouragements and warnings will be heeded this time and that very soon Israel will cross the Jordan and take possession of the land. In due course, the people will be able to settle down and begin to plant crops and gain a harvest. The following instructions tell the people what to do when the first harvest comes in; it may well be that this was intended to set a precedent for harvests to come, in which case the instructions would have been carried out at the Feast of Firstfruits or Weeks (compare 16:9–12). It is not difficult to imagine the sense of gratitude and hope that would have filled the hearts of the Israelites as they put the first fruit of the ground into a basket and took it up to the place where God had put his name. You can imagine their sense of exultation as they repeated, 'I declare today to the LORD your God that I have come into the land that the LORD swore to our fathers to give us' (v. 3). God had kept his ancient promise and they were privileged to enter into its fulfilment.

As they stood before the altar, the Israelites were then to recount the mercy of God towards them, especially in preserving them in Egypt, in bringing them out with a mighty hand, and in bringing them into the land.

Exploring Deuteronomy 191

Chapter 29

A form of words like that given in verses 5 to 10 would fix in their minds the history of God's goodness. Having acknowledged that the harvest was a gift of God, they were to worship him and then rejoice in all the good that the LORD had given them. This meant eating and enjoying what God had provided, and sharing it with the Levite and the sojourner. Those who appreciate God's good gifts desire to act like him and to share with those who need their generosity. Our services of worship should often be marked by thankfulness and joy, for God has done great things for us as well.

Tithing fulfilled (vv. 12–15)

Israel was to acknowledge God's goodness not only by offering the firstfruits, but also by setting aside a tithe, and every three years this was to be shared out with the Levite, the sojourner, the fatherless and the widow. Among God's people there was to be no selfish use of God's good gifts, nor any selfish gratitude. We might note also that this sharing and rejoicing with one another would bind the people together, and would give the poor and disadvantaged a real sense of community and belonging.

When the Israelites had fulfilled their duty in tithing and sharing, they were to acknowledge this before the LORD, confessing that they had neither broken nor forgotten God's commandments. This was not intended to be an expression of pride or self-righteousness; rather it was an incentive to the people to fulfil their duty in full, and not to be satisfied with partial obedience. There would be occasions when they were tempted to use the tithe for themselves, particularly when they were shut up in their own homes (v. 14), but here they would confess that this had not been the case with them. It is not a bad thing for us from time to time to examine our lives and see whether we have obeyed God, particularly in external duties. Our inner attitudes and motives are seldom all that they should be, and we constantly need to throw ourselves upon the grace of God, but our outward acts are under our control and we should keep a watch over them.

Verse 15 is a prayer that God would look down and grant his blessing.

Thanksgiving and covenant promises (26:1–19)

This prayer is not to be understood in terms of merit: that they had obeyed God, and therefore he should bless them. It is a prayer for all Israel, not just for the man praying or for his family. It is a prayer that the God who gave great promises to their forefathers, promises which he would have kept in bringing them into the land and granting good harvests, would continue to bless them and the ground. This, however, did not mean that covenant obedience was not important. If the people knew they were guilty of covenant disobedience, their prayer would have to be one of repentance and of asking for mercy.

Covenant reaffirmation (vv. 16–19)

This occasion when Moses spoke to all the people gathered before him (5:1) fulfilled two functions. Firstly, the stipulations that the sovereign LORD laid on Israel for their obedience were given to the people; they came as commands from God, and the response that was necessary was careful obedience (v. 16). As has already been commented, many of these can be seen as the outworking of the Ten Commandments to various situations. The obedience looked for and expected, however, was not to be simply outward; they were to 'do them with all your heart and with all your soul' (v. 16). This meant not only an energetic response, but also one in which hearts were attuned to the ways of God, loved him, and saw his commands as moulding their attitudes and guiding their desires into practical living that pleased him.

Secondly, there appears to have been an overt response to what Moses said: 'You have declared today that the LORD is your God, and that you will walk in his ways, and keep his statutes and his commandments and his rules, and will obey his voice' (v. 17). In other words, the people of Israel openly affirmed their acceptance of the covenant stipulations and committed themselves to their LORD. This was then matched by the LORD declaring that Israel was his treasured possession (v. 18). This is a most tender and moving expression. God's people do not merely belong to him:

Chapter 29

God treasures them, he loves them and sets a high value on them. This is also true for his people today. We can only measure the value set by God on his people by the price he was willing to pay to redeem them: the shedding of the precious blood of his only Son.

God promised to take his people as his possession (see Exodus 19:5–6), but there is a further promise in Deuteronomy 26:19. On the one hand, God would honour them high above all nations; on the other, he would make them a people holy to himself. These go together: those who are set apart for him, who keep his commandments and walk in his ways, so living a holy life together, will always have his approval and will be honoured by him (compare 1 Samuel 2:30). The praise of God is much more important than acceptance with our peers.

Study questions

1. In what ways should we express our thanksgiving to God?
2. How do we recognize our obligation to obey God's commandments without falling into a legalistic attitude of mind?
3. Is there value in having set forms of words (such as in vv. 5–10) for prayer, confession, etc.?

Section 3:

Curses for disobedience, blessings for obedience (27:1–30:20)

In Ancient Near Eastern suzerainty treaties (made between a conquering power and what would become a vassal state), after having set out the treaty stipulations, the benefits of the treaty and the consequences of breaking the stipulations would then be set out. Deuteronomy follows this pattern. The commandments of Israel's sovereign God, the LORD, have been set down; these four chapters now promise blessings for obedience and warn of curses for disobedience.

Chapter 30

Stones, mountains and curses (27:1–26)

In this chapter, Moses commands certain steps to be taken that will be a permanent reminder to the people of God's commandments; blessings are anticipated and curses are publicly declared.

Signs of the law (vv. 1–8)
The next few chapters look forward to Israel entering and settling into the land given by God. This may be why the elders of Israel (v. 1) and then the Levitical priests (v. 9) appeared with Moses. Moses was not going into Canaan, and in future the elders, and especially the priests and Levites, would be responsible for teaching the law and reminding the people of their need to obey it. We are very familiar with the use of visual aids in Christian work among children, and here two forms of visual helps were brought before Israel: firstly, large stones and, secondly, two mountains—you can't miss seeing mountains!

The command was that, once Israel had crossed the Jordan, they should set up some large stones which would be plastered over (v. 2). On these, 'all the words of this law' were to be written (v. 3), and written 'very plainly' (v. 8). This appears to mean all the laws and instructions recorded in chapters 5 to 26, though possibly it might mean just the Ten Commandments. These stones were to be set up on Mount Ebal (v. 4). Whenever Israelites passed that way, only those who could read (which would only be a small proportion of the population) would be able to read what they said, but everyone would know that it was God's law that was written there, and they would be reminded of the importance of keeping it conscientiously. In the past, it was the tradition for the Ten Commandments to be set up in a

Stones, mountains and curses (27:1–26)

prominent place in church buildings. Even those who could not read would have known the substance of those commandments and would have been reminded of their central importance every time they visited the church.

At the same time, an altar was to be built of stones—uncut stones, as no iron tool was to be used on them. Israel would have no access to iron, having been slaves and then wanderers in the desert, and the only way of obtaining iron tools would be to get them from the Canaanites after overcoming them. But no Canaanite tool was to be used for an altar to the LORD; the associations of such implements were all pagan.

These instructions assumed that all Israel would gather to Mount Ebal; once the stones reminding people of the law were set up, sacrifices were to be offered on the altar in worship. These were to consist, firstly, of burnt offerings, offerings in which atonement was made for sins. But secondly, peace offerings, or fellowship offerings, as they are sometimes called, were also to be offered. The first were directed to God himself, but the second were shared by the worshippers; this is the significance of 'You … shall eat there, and you shall rejoice before the LORD your God.' The people ate together, and rejoiced together that their sins were covered and that the LORD was their God who had given them his holy law. Many Christians today are likely to find this inexplicable, because they think of the law only in negative terms; they think that any suggestion of law-keeping must involve legalism. But this is far from the truth. The law was given for Israel's good; it directed them into the paths of righteousness, which are paths of peace and joy. The commandments were not given for Israel to earn God's favour; they were given as the appropriate response for those who had been saved by God's grace, who had received God's promises and been brought into his land (v. 3). Keeping them was to be the response of faith, the outflow of love and faithfulness to their sovereign LORD.

Mountains that speak (vv. 9–13)

Opposite Mount Ebal, on the south side, is Mount Gerizim. Ebal is 940

Chapter 30

metres (3084 feet) high and Gerizim a little lower at 881 metres (2890 feet)—mountains that you could not possibly miss. They are very near the centre of the land of Israel, not far from Shechem. To the east there is a small fertile plain, and the mountains rise above it and are clearly visible to people travelling from south to north or vice versa. A road passed between the mountains to the Mediterranean coast. Mountains have often played a part in religion; the Canaanites had their 'high places': shrines on hills and mountains. To this day there are people who believe that certain mountain peaks possess 'spiritual' power. But these mountains bore witness to God's law, and to the promise of blessing and the warning of judgement, depending on whether that law was obeyed or not. The law was written on the stones on Ebal, and curses were proclaimed from Ebal and blessings from Gerizim. The stones and the mountains bore witness to words spoken plainly and to be received, understood and obeyed.

Verse 9 testifies to the covenant reaffirmation that we considered in looking at the end of chapter 26. It may be that the word 'become' in this verse indicates that a new generation had freely consented to the covenant. In verse 11 we are told that 'Moses charged the people', which suggests that he was giving a particularly important instruction (compare with 'commanded' in v. 1). Presumably the ritual of blessing and cursing was to take place at the same time as the sacrificial worship at the altar on Mount Ebal. The details are not completely clear, but the outline is unmistakable. Six of the tribes were to stand on Mount Gerizim to bless the people, and the other six were to stand on Mount Ebal to declare the curse. This must have been a very impressive occasion, one not easily forgotten. It is possible that it was intended to be repeated annually, though this is not stated.

'Amen' to the curses (vv. 14–26)

The Levites were to declare to all Israel a series of curses, but it appears that Moses spoke the blessings and curses recorded in the next chapter (28:1, 'that I command you today'). It is not clear how what is said here fits in

Stones, mountains and curses (27:1–26)

with half the tribes being on one mountain and the rest on the other. Certainly all Israel was to be gathered in order to hear the Levites. Perhaps the tribes were on the shoulders of the mountains lower down, rather than on the summits, with the Levites on the level ground between the two. We must not think of the curses in terms of magic. To declare a curse means that a person who disobeys a command of God will come under his judgement; such people expose themselves to the punishment that is due. The actual consequences of disobedience are spelled out in the next chapter, but in these verses there is simply a declaration of the acts which will bring people under the judgement of God. As the Levites declared these curses, all the people were to respond by saying, 'Amen'. 'Amen' was an expression of agreement; literally, it means 'surely'. 'Amen' was a liturgical response used in Israel, not only in accepting the validity of a curse, but also as a response to a blessing (see 1 Chronicles 16:36; Psalm 41:13). It is a great pity that Christian people do not respond to prayer with vocal 'Amens' and follow the pattern in Israel.

There are twelve acts set out here that attract the curse of God. In considering them as a whole we can see that, in the main, they are acts that are likely to be private and therefore not likely to be brought to the attention of the authorities. Two of them (vv. 15,24) are explicitly described as being done in secret. The point is this: God sees what is done in secret, and what might not come to the attention of others is seen and known by him, and he will judge and act. The people are being reminded of the importance of this fact; nothing can be hidden from him. Secondly, these curses deal with fundamental issues, as we shall see.

The first (v. 15) is concerned with complete faithfulness to God; faithfulness in private as well as in public worship and in appearance. When someone goes wrong here, everything else begins to go wrong. After faithfulness to God comes respect for parents (v. 16). If verse 15 reflects the first two of the Ten Commandments, verse 16 reflects the fifth. We have already seen how crucial this commandment was considered to be for the

Chapter 30

welfare of the whole family, for society as a whole and for long life in the land.

The next three are concerned with the protection of the needy and vulnerable (vv. 17–19). We have seen the importance of the landmark for those, especially the poor, who needed to provide for themselves. Misleading the blind could happen in a variety of ways; no advantage was to be taken of someone suffering such a handicap, but rather such people need help. Again, the three classes of people most at risk are referred to (v. 19). It is not charity to provide for them, but justice.

The next four are concerned with sexual behaviour (vv. 20–23). These deal mainly with incest and we are likely to find it surprising that these are the acts that are singled out for prohibition. They seem intended to uphold the integrity of family life. We have to remember that, once Israel was spread out over the land, many of the people would live in small communities, small villages and farmsteads, in which nearly everyone was related to everyone else. This posed (and in some communities and households today still poses) particular sexual pressures (this is probably why v. 21 also comes in). It could lead to serious consequences: jealousy, hatred and violence.

It is the last of these, violence, with which the next two curses are concerned: firstly, striking down a neighbour in secret; secondly, taking a bribe to kill another. The latter meant that someone who was wanting to be rid of another—perhaps a neighbour or even relative— paid someone else to do the deed, in order to avoid detection. But God would know, and retribution would follow in the end.

This review confirms that all these are issues of fundamental importance. The final curse is on anyone 'who does not confirm the words of this law by doing them'. This reminds us that the law was one; people could not pick and choose which ones they liked, and discard the others. James put it like this: 'For whoever keeps the whole law but fails in one point has become accountable for all of it. For he who said, "Do not

Stones, mountains and curses (27:1–26)

commit adultery," also said, "Do not murder." If you do not commit adultery but do murder, you have become a transgressor of the law' (James 2:10–11). It is well for us to remember that there is a sobering curse in the New Testament. 'If anyone has no love for the Lord, let him be accursed' (1 Corinthians 16:22).

Study questions
1. What signs or symbols do we find in the New Testament? Ought we to devise such things ourselves if we think that they are useful for pointing us to spiritual truth?
2. Read Psalm 119 and consider the attitude the psalmist had to God's law.
3. What general lessons can we learn for ourselves from the curses?

Chapter 31

The blessings of obedience (28:1–14)

Moses spells out the blessings which the Israelites will receive if they faithfully obey the LORD their God. The previous passage spoke of the judgement of God upon those who disobey his commands; here is set before them the prospect of unparalleled good if they obey.

Overtaken by blessings (vv. 1–2)

The words 'bless' and 'blessing' are frequently used by Christians, but what they mean by these words is not always very obvious. In these verses, the word 'blessing' means the good gifts that spring from God's grace and favour towards his obedient people. A blessing is a good gift from God; when God blesses us he grants us good gifts, and to be blessed is to receive and enjoy those gifts.

Notice in verse 1 the phrases 'if you faithfully obey' and 'being careful to do'. It is important to take note of this emphasis on diligent observance of all that God had said. At the same time, it must be stressed again that this obedience was to arise out of an already existing relationship: 'the LORD *your* God' (emphasis added). And this relationship was based on God's grace; it was not something that was, or ever could be, achieved by what Israel did. At the heart of obedience was love for God (6:5), and keeping the commandments would be the expression of that love. It is by God's grace that we become Christians and our new life of obedience springs from gratitude for his mercy and hearts set free to love him. Nor does the continuance of that relationship depend upon obedience; the relationship still continues, which is why God chastises his disobedient children

The blessings of obedience (28:1–14)

(Hebrews 12:3–11). But when we are disobedient, the relationship does suffer in terms of knowing the nearness of God and enjoying his love and receiving his blessing. The way to restore the relationship is not by trying harder to do better, but by repentance and a return in faith to Jesus Christ; that, in turn, will lead to renewed obedience.

The promise at the end of verse 1 is that God 'will set you high above all the nations of the earth'. This was not a promise which should have made the people proud; nor was it intended just for their own sake. The point is this: God would make Israel an example before all the nations. They would see that the LORD is the true God. They would see that God's commandments are wise and good. They would see that it is right and good to acknowledge the LORD as God, to submit to him, worship him and obey him. Israel would be like a light to the nations that would cause God to be praised and draw the nations to him. The nations would thus be blessed through Israel (Genesis 12:1–3; 18:18–19; Deuteronomy 4:5–8). The churches of Jesus Christ have a similar calling (Matthew 5:14–16; 1 Peter 2:12).

Verse 2 seems to picture God's blessings as active; they are pursuing God's people, they come up to them and overtake them. The imagery and the use of the plural in 'blessings' indicate that there are many good things that follow upon obedience.

Blessed in every place and in every way (vv. 3–6)

This is a picture of God's blessing coming upon every area of life. The cities prosper; the fields yield abundant crops. Children are born and grow up healthy and strong, family life is blessed. The ground bears a rich variety of fruits, vegetables and grain; the animals give birth to their young, and the flocks and herds increase. Whether buying or preparing food, whether going out at the beginning of the day or returning home in the evening, the blessing of God rests on everything. Israel would have health, wealth and prosperity!

Chapter 31

This raises a big question: Does a promise like this hold good for Christians? If we are obedient, can we too expect health, wealth and prosperity? Here are three answers to this question. Firstly, God's promise was given to a whole people that was going into the land he had told them would be flowing with milk and honey; the promise was given partly to enable them to be a witness to the nations round about, as we have seen. The circumstances of Christians today, scattered as they are throughout the world, are very different. At this point there is no real parallel between the people of Israel then and Christians today.

Nevertheless, it might be argued that if God promised to bless Israel in the way he did, we might well expect that, though our circumstances are different, yet he could still bless us in much the same way. There is a sense in which there is truth in this. We have already seen that God's commandments were for the good of Israel and that, for example, if children grew up to respect and honour their parents, it would have a beneficial effect throughout the country. It is not that God's blessings are completely detached from obedience: to a large extent they come *through* obedience. God gives commandments which actually bring blessing. So if Christians today live by what God has said, they are likely to be healthier then they would have been had they followed the way of the world; and if they work hard and well, and do not spend their money foolishly, they are likely to be better off than they would otherwise have been. In fact, this is something that is often seen: when people are converted their lives change for the better. So the second answer is that, in a restricted sense, this promise is likely to hold good for Christians.

The third answer is that, actually, all Christians are far more blessed with far greater blessings than those promised in this chapter: 'Blessed be the God and Father of our Lord Jesus Christ, who has blessed us in Christ with every spiritual blessing in the heavenly places' (Ephesians 1:3). Israel had an earthly inheritance; we have a heavenly inheritance. The blessings promised in this chapter are all this-worldly in nature, but our blessings are

The blessings of obedience (28:1–14)

spiritual blessings and they are all ours already. Good health and prosperity are good in themselves and God grants a measure of them to many of his children, but ill health and adversity have often proved to be even more beneficial, and whatever our lot as far as these things are concerned, in the things that really matter we are rich beyond measure, far beyond our present understanding. Most of us have probably only begun to enter into the experience of the spiritual blessings that are ours in Christ.

Is that all there is to say? No; but 29:29 will throw more light on both God's promises and his warnings.

The God from whom all blessings flow (vv. 7–14)

This section repeats a number of the things already commented on, but the emphasis here is this: it is the LORD God himself who grants these blessings. Seven times we read, 'The LORD will …' or 'he will …'. God is the giver of these blessings even when the blessings come through obedience. The God who gives the means—obedience—by that very act also gives the end—blessing. But there is more than that here, as we see in verse 12: 'The LORD will open to you his good treasury, the heavens, to give the rain to your land in its season and to bless all the work of your hands.' All Israel's hard work and careful obedience could not of itself bring the rain, but God could. Christian workers can remember the words of Paul: 'I planted, Apollos watered, but God gave the growth. So neither he who plants nor he who waters is anything, but only God who gives the growth' (1 Corinthians 3:6–7). As Hudson Taylor is reputed to have said, 'God's work, done in God's way, will never lack God's blessing.'

Verse 9 contains this promise: 'The LORD will establish you as a people holy to himself …' Israel will not only be a people separated to God by his choice and deliverance, they will also be seen to be separated to him by the holiness of their lives, by their love for him and obedience to him. They will be established as God's people, reflecting something of his holiness and glory. This is something we should long for and pray for: that God's people

Chapter 31

today will really look like God's people! The next verse continues: 'And all the peoples of the earth shall see that you are called by the name of the Lord, and they shall be afraid of you.' 'Afraid of you' cannot mean afraid that Israel will attack them or deal falsely with them, for that would not be in keeping with God's commandments. Rather it means afraid to attack Israel (v. 7), afraid to deal unjustly with the Israelites or to speak ill of them or of their God. They would respect Israel and would feel a restraint on their own attitudes and actions. It is true that godly people earn respect (compare Acts 2:47; 5:13; 6:10), and that faithful and caring churches gain a good name in a community and further afield (1 Thessalonians 1:8–10). There will, of course, always be some who speak against the gospel and vilify Christian people, but we are supposed to live down the false accusations and the reports such people give (1 Peter 2:12).

Study questions
1. Make a list of some of the spiritual blessings that belong to believers in Christ.
2. What encouragements can you find here for Christian life and work?
3. Consider further the promises of prosperity in this chapter. To what extent may we expect material blessing, and in what respect do we need to exercise care in this matter?

Chapter 32

The consequences of disobedience (28:15–68)

If there are blessings, there are also curses for disobedience. Moses, as a wise leader who cares deeply for the people, utters an extended warning of the consequences that disobedience to God will entail.

This is a very long passage with not a little repetition, and one that moves to a tragic conclusion. It is not possible or necessary to look at each section in detail, so several themes will be identified and considered. Notice that verses 15 to 19 are the opposite of the opening verses of the chapter, verses 1 to 6.

A serious warning

Imagine parents whose son or daughter is going to leave home for the first time, perhaps to go abroad on a school trip, perhaps on a holiday with friends, perhaps for education or work. It is likely that most parents would have some words of advice and warning to give. The people of Israel would shortly be facing a new situation, going into the land that God was giving them. Moses had a deep concern for them, arising out of his call by God (Exodus 3:10) and expressed especially in his prayers for them (e.g. Exodus 32:30–34). So we find him warning the people and explaining to them the consequences of disobedience. He had been brought up in a pagan environment in Egypt; he knew the temptations and dangers which would confront them (Hebrews 11:24–26).

But behind the warnings of Moses lie the warnings of God himself. We must not deduce from a passage like this that God is a God of threats and curses. God had already shown his love for Israel; he was about to keep his promise to them as they went into a land flowing with milk and honey, a

Chapter 32

good land where he would provide for them. But God is a God of justice, and sin is always wrong and does not go unpunished. God's own people are chastised when they walk in disobedience to him (Hebrews 12:5–17). So it is due to his mercy that the Bible has the warnings that it does, as in this passage. For this reason, all faithful teachers and preachers of God's Word issue warnings also: 'Be sure your sin will find you out' (Numbers 32:23). Temptation is very real, and the temptations of a Canaan are very different from those of an Egypt. Indwelling sin and the subtlety of Satan mean that there is always a need for serious warning to believers as well as to unbelievers.

The nature of the curses

These verses speak of a whole variety of evils which will come upon the people of Israel if they are disobedient to God and his commandments. Many of these were experiences that were common in those days: illness, drought and famine, invasion by enemies, frustration at the way things turned out—they are still common in the world today. Just as the natural outcome of keeping God's commands would mean a good measure of prosperity, so the natural outcome of disobedience would be bound to mean that that measure of prosperity would be forfeited. But, of course, there is more than that here. Nor is it merely that God will withdraw the blessing that obedience would have brought; rather God will actively bring calamity upon the people ('The LORD will make the rain of your land powder … The LORD will bring on you and your offspring extraordinary afflictions, afflictions severe and lasting, and sicknesses grievous and lasting', vv. 24,59). It is a terrible thing to turn God against us.

Part of the consequences of disobedience would be that their best efforts would come to nothing: 'You shall carry much seed into the field and shall gather in little … You shall plant vineyards … but you shall neither drink of the wine nor gather the grapes … You shall have olive trees … but you

The consequences of disobedience (28:15–68)

shall not anoint yourself with the oil' (vv. 38–40); 'The LORD will send on you ... frustration in all that you undertake to do' (v. 20). There is a sense of deterioration running through the passage. In the first part of the chapter things seemed to get better and better under the blessing of God; here it is the opposite. There is a downward spiral, which sadly was to become reality in Israel's history.

Just as God's blessing on the people would be a witness to the nations, so would be the consequences of their disobedience: 'And you shall be a horror to all the kingdoms of the earth' (v. 25); 'And you shall become a horror, a proverb, and a byword among all the peoples where the LORD will lead you away' (v. 37). There are perhaps two thoughts here. Firstly, Israel would be known as the people of the LORD; his reputation was bound up with theirs. If, therefore, they disobeyed him, and lived in ways that were unholy and unrighteous, he would be dishonoured. Chastising them would be giving visible evidence of his displeasure and upholding his own honour. Secondly, if they were wise, the nations around might learn from this. If God would not tolerate evil in his own people, how would they fare if they continued in idolatry, immorality and violence (compare 1 Peter 4:17–18)?

The reasons for judgement

In considering why God gave such strong warnings, and why he would act as he threatened if Israel disobeyed, we need to pick out two sentences in these verses. The first begins in verse 47: 'Because you did not serve the LORD your God with joyfulness and gladness of heart, because of the abundance of all things, therefore you shall serve your enemies ...' At first sight this might seem surprising, but a moment's thought shows us how important it is. The problem identified here is ingratitude. God would be putting them into a land which had all they needed and in which they would find rich provision (8:7–10). Their hearts ought to overflow with thanksgiving to him and be full of joy in all that they had. Years later, God was to speak to them through Jeremiah in this way: 'And I brought you into a plentiful land to enjoy its fruits and its good things. But when you came in, you defiled my land and made my heritage an abomination' (Jeremiah 2:7). How important it is that we who have been blessed with all spiritual blessings in Christ should appreciate God's goodness, and that this should express itself in thankfulness and joyful worship!

The second sentence to note begins in verse 58: 'If you are not careful to do all the words of this law that are written in this book, that you may fear this glorious and awesome name, the LORD your God …' Carelessness in attending to God's law and putting it into practice indicates a failure to grasp just what God is like, how great he is, how glorious his character. God is awesome; he deserves the deep respect and reverence of all men and women. Israel had had proof of God's greatness when he sent the plagues upon Egypt, in the way he brought them through the Red Sea, in his provision of manna and water, and in the way their clothes did not wear out and their sandals remained intact. They had seen his greatness and glory when they had trembled at the foot of Mount Sinai; how foolish and blind of them to think they could play fast and loose with God! How foolish of us, also!

The danger of apostasy

As this passage draws towards its conclusion the picture grows darker and we see the possibility of Israel breaking covenant with the LORD altogether. This would result in God plucking them off the land altogether (v. 63). They would then be scattered across the world, dwelling among pagan peoples and finding not a resting place but 'a trembling heart and failing eyes and a languishing soul' (v. 65). Life would become utterly burdensome for them (vv. 66–67), and the LORD would do the unthinkable—send them back to Egypt, breaking his promise to them never to do that. Even worse, they would offer themselves as slaves, but no one would want them; they would find themselves rejected by God and man.

The consequences of disobedience (28:15–68)

These are solemn words indeed. We do not necessarily have to understand the return to Egypt literally; after all, they wouldn't need to go back there in ships. But spiritually, as far as their relationship to the LORD was concerned, they would be back in bondage once again. In thinking of this we need to remember that by no means did everyone in Israel truly believe in the LORD, even though they belonged to the chosen nation in an outward sense (Romans 2:28–29). Moreover, even though Israel did go into exile, God in his grace brought them to their own land again. There was always a remnant chosen and saved by grace (Romans 11:1–6). So the possibility of turning right away from God entirely—apostasy—was real, but some would always be preserved and would enter into God's promise, even if they might suffer with the rest for a time and also be chastised for their own sins.

The New Testament shows us that the possibility of apostasy is still real; think of Judas Iscariot. There are those who come under the sound of the gospel and make what appears to be a genuine profession of faith, yet in the end turn finally away from God, showing that they were never true believers (1 John 2:19). There are clear warnings against this. Hebrews 10:26–27 says, 'For if we go on sinning deliberately after receiving the knowledge of the truth, there no longer remains a sacrifice for sins, but a fearful expectation of judgement, and a fury of fire that will consume the adversaries' (it is worth reading on to the end of the chapter). Those two verses seem to fit Deuteronomy 28:66–68 very well. This does not mean that Christ does not keep those who are his—he does; or that we cannot have assurance of our salvation—we can. It does mean, however, that we must avoid sin and resist temptation: 'Therefore let anyone who thinks that he stands take heed lest he fall. No temptation has overtaken you that is not common to man. God is faithful, and he will not let you be tempted beyond your ability, but with the temptation he will also provide the way of escape, that you may be able to endure it' (1 Corinthians 10:12–13).

Chapter 32

Study questions

1. Is it right to think of God judging churches because of their sin? What about nations today?
2. What should a church do if it seems that all its efforts always come to nothing?
3. How can we tell the difference between the troubles that come to all, believer and unbeliever alike, and chastisements from our Father?

Chapter 33

Covenant renewal in Moab (29:1–29)

Forty years earlier, Israel had solemnly entered into covenant with the LORD at Mount Sinai (Exodus 19:1–9). There is now a new generation of Israelites and they are in the plain of Moab ready to cross the Jordan and go into the land promised to them. Moses has set before them all the commandments and instructions that the LORD has given to him, and now he calls upon all gathered before him to enter into sworn covenant with the LORD their God.

The LORD has led thus far (vv. 1–9)

The end of chapter 26 speaks of the people affirming their intention to acknowledge the LORD as their God, to walk in his ways, keep his commandments and obey his voice (26:17). It seems that, in chapter 29, this general declaration is made into a formal renewal of the covenant, just like the original covenant made at Sinai (or Horeb, v.1). We have to remember that all the generation that had stood before God at Sinai had passed away (apart from Joshua and Caleb, and Moses, who would not be permitted to enter Canaan). This was a time, then, for the new generation formally to acknowledge their response of allegiance to the LORD who had graciously entered into covenant with Abraham and their fathers.

To start with, Moses reminds them of the way in which the Lord has led them and provided for them during the years in the desert. When he says 'You have seen all that the LORD did before your eyes in the land of Egypt', he is referring to the fact that many of them were children at that time. They were present when their fathers refused to enter the land of Canaan, but were not responsible for that decision. Indeed, God said that the

Chapter 33

children would enter the land while the older generation would not (Numbers 14:31–32). We might wonder why Moses found it necessary to keep reminding the people of all that God had done for them. For us, we simply have the record of God's mighty acts in Egypt and of his provision through the forty years and the capture of Gilead, and we can read it all in a matter of an hour or two. But it was a very different thing for the Israelites trudging day after day through a barren landscape, staying near some oasis for periods which they knew could only be temporary before resuming their travels, until forty long years had passed—that's more than half a lifetime for most of us. In those circumstances, it was easy to focus on the hardships they endured and to take for granted the manna and the fact that their clothes did not need to be replenished. They knew in the backs of their minds all that the LORD had done, but they did not have a heart to understand it all (v. 4). Such is the human heart that it needs the LORD to grant eyes to see and ears to hear and a heart to understand.

The LORD is here today (vv. 10–15)

These verses describe a very vivid scene. Notice that the word 'today' occurs five times in these verses and again significantly in verse 18. This is obviously a special occasion; all the people are standing before the LORD in order to renew the covenant. The word 'standing' suggests a sense of formality; we might almost paraphrase it, 'You are on parade today before the LORD your God.' Their great Sovereign and Commander-in-Chief had come to hear his people avow their allegiance to him and their readiness to live by his word. Verses 10 and 11 pick out all the groups of people who were present. All the leaders, all the men, their wives and little ones, all the sojourners, down to those who performed the most menial of tasks—all were there, all were included in the covenant, and all were to swear their agreement to it.

Notice that it was the LORD who was making the covenant with them (v. 12). This was not a covenant between equals, nor was it one initiated by

Covenant renewal in Moab (29:1–29)

Israel; it was a sovereign act of God himself. He had sworn to Abraham, Isaac and Jacob, and the promise he gave to them and their descendants had been repeated at Sinai, and now was to be ratified with the present generation. The covenant was one in which the people responded to the gracious act of God. The essence of it was that they would be his people and he would be their God (v. 13). These simple words embraced wonderful truth and privilege. They would be God's special people, his treasured possession, a kingdom of priests and a holy nation (Exodus 19:5–6). The LORD would be their protector, the one who supplied their need, who was going to lead them into the land he had promised, a land of abundance where they could know his rich blessings (Deuteronomy 28:1–14).

This renewal of covenant was not made at that time simply because this was a new generation. It was a significant moment because they were poised to cross the Jordan and embark on the conquest of Canaan. As they anticipated warfare, they would need the help and strengthening of the LORD. As they looked forward to a new opportunity opening up before them—nationhood in their own land—it was entirely appropriate that God should call them to renew the covenant. He was committed to them and they were to signal their commitment to him. Then they could go forward into the new experience that awaited them across the Jordan. And there was more to it than that: they were to think of the generations to come—'and with whoever is not here with us today' (v. 15). To secure the future for their children and for the succeeding generations, they needed to be committed and faithful to the LORD in their own lifetime.

There is a great deal here that is applicable to believers in Jesus Christ. We, too, by God's grace, have been called into covenant with God through Jesus Christ, a commitment on our part signified by baptism. It is entirely appropriate that, from time to time, perhaps at the Lord's Supper at particularly important milestones in our lives, we should recommit ourselves to our God. 'High heaven, that heard the solemn vow, That vow renewed shall daily hear.'[1] Yes, there is also a sense in which we are daily to renew our trust and hope in God.

The LORD is Lord of the future (vv. 16–28)

Moses now turns to consider the future. For forty years Israel has been united, dependent on one another and on the LORD. Yet the older ones remember what it was like in Egypt, surrounded by idolatry, with its temptations and attractions, which led to the worship of the golden calf (Exodus 32). And all of them have had contact with Moabites (Numbers 25), and with Edomites, Canaanites, Amorites and Midianites. So Moses gives a serious warning (v. 18): even on this occasion, 'today', it is possible that there is someone whose heart is turning from the LORD, someone who will take part in the covenant renewal ceremony but say in his heart, 'I shall be safe, though I walk in the stubbornness of my heart' (v. 19).

God's judgement will fall on any person of whom this is true (v. 20). It is hypocrisy, deception and wilful rebellion of a most heinous nature. When Moses says, 'The LORD will not be willing to forgive him', it does not mean that there will be no forgiveness if there is true repentance, but rather suggests that true repentance in such a case is very unlikely. The main point to notice is that saying in the secrecy of one's heart, 'I shall be safe', is utter folly. Nothing could be further from the truth. The last phrase of verse 19, 'This will lead to the sweeping away of moist and dry alike', seems to mean that both the righteous and the unrighteous will be caught up in the consequences of disobedience. This is often true; but verses 20 and 21 indicate that there is personal responsibility: 'The LORD will single him out from all the tribes of Israel for calamity' (v. 21).

The rest of the passage, however, indicates a deeper problem here. Such a thing will be like 'a root bearing poisonous and bitter fruit' (v. 18). An attitude like this in time begins to spread. Out of sight the roots are spreading out; the poison infiltrates the lifeblood of the people until it breaks out in compromise and adaptations of Israel's religion to pagan

Covenant renewal in Moab (29:1–29)

practices, and eventually to open defiance of the LORD and his ways. And this, in turn, will bring the judgement of the LORD, so that a future generation of Israelites will find the land of promise turned into a scorched desert (v. 23). They will say, and all the nations with them, 'Why has the LORD done thus to this land? What caused the heat of this great anger?' And the answer will be, 'It is because they abandoned the covenant of the LORD, the God of their fathers …' (vv. 22–25).

Hypocrisy, deceit and secret reservations are by no means things of the past. It is right for us all to examine our hearts from time to time and to cry out to God, 'Keep back your servant … from presumptuous sins' and 'Unite my heart to fear your name' (Psalm 19:13; 86:11).

The LORD both hides and reveals (v. 29)

At first sight this verse seems to stand on its own, unrelated to what has gone before or to what comes after, but this is not the case. The verses that come before are particularly vivid, so much so that it looks as if these things are definitely going to happen. Is such apostasy inevitable? Or, on the other hand, do God's promises inevitably mean that once Israel has settled in the land, the people can look forward with assurance to entering in to all the blessings set out at the beginning of chapter 28? This verse answers questions like this and those that other passages (28:3–6, for example) have raised. What the future holds is a secret known only to God; our business is with 'the things that are revealed … that we may do all the words of this law'.

In reading through Deuteronomy, one becomes conscious of a tension between the ideal and the real. The law is set out and its blessings promised, but will Israel ever really live in the way the law prescribes? The answer clearly is 'No'. Such a thing is not possible and the fact that the sacrificial system was part of the law indicates that there would always be the need for repentance and forgiveness. But is the alternative simply disobedience and curses? Again the answer has to be 'No'. Life for God's

Chapter 33

people was, and is, much more complicated than that. God understands it all perfectly; we don't, but we are to put into practice what he has revealed, and that means confession and repentance, keeping short accounts with him, trusting his grace and renewing our obedience after falls and failures.

Men and women have always been curious about the future, and pagan religions often used various magical practices to try to find out what was going to happen. But the Israelites—and we too—are not to try to pry into the future. Of course, on occasions, God did reveal things that he had planned, through prophecy—although even that was not always clear-cut, especially when it came to indicating when the prophecy would be fulfilled. Christians are to live by faith, not by sight (2 Corinthians 5:7). Abraham went out not knowing where he was going, but trusting God to lead him, and much of the Christian life is like that. We have to beware of looking for God to guide us in the way desired by those who read what astrologers say or go to fortune tellers.

This verse inculcates humility. There are many things that we are incapable of knowing or understanding at present. There are things that God does not intend us to know now. Jesus once said, 'What I am doing you do not understand now, but afterward you will understand' (John 13:7). There are probably also things that we will never be capable of knowing or understanding; even in glory we will still be creatures, and God is the great Creator. Our business is with the things that are revealed. They have been revealed for our good; they have been revealed for our obedience; and it is much better to spend our time ensuring we receive and do those things, rather than speculating about things which are above and beyond us, and about which we will never have certainty in this world.

Study questions

1. Consider again and make a note of God's goodness to Israel since the time they were in Egypt.
2. Read verses 22 to 28 again. What effect should God's action in

Covenant renewal in Moab (29:1–29)

judgement have on the generation of Israel that sees it, and on the nations around?

3. Why might someone appear to profess allegiance to the Lord while having secret reservations?

Note

1 **Philip Doddridge,** 'O happy day, that fixed my choice.'

Chapter 34

A matter of life or death (30:1–20)

Moses now brings this section of his address to the people to a great climax. Even if they do sin and the LORD judges and scatters them, yet if they truly return to him, he will restore them. There is life for those who listen to the LORD and respond to him, but death for those who persist in disobedience.

Repentance and restoration (vv. 1–5)

The last verse of the previous chapter, verse 29, looks forward to what is said here as well as coming as a suitable conclusion to that chapter. If the people of Israel do disobey the LORD and he 'uproot[s] them from their land in anger and fury and great wrath, and cast[s] them into another land' (29:28), is that the end? No; there is no point in trying to second guess what is going to happen in the future or how things will ultimately turn out. That is God's province. What is revealed is this: even if the Israelites disobey God and they are cast far away into exile, if they turn back to him with all their heart and all their soul, he will restore their fortunes and they will know his blessing once again.

This wonderful promise became one that was repeated throughout Israel's history and brought great encouragement to those who believed it. We find it again in Jeremiah 29:12–14, for example, where it takes its place in a letter written by Jeremiah to those who were already in exile in Babylon. We can see traces of it in Daniel's great prayer in chapter 9 of his book. It forms the basis of his conclusion: 'For we do not present our pleas before you because of our righteousness, but because of your great mercy. O Lord, hear; O Lord, forgive. O Lord, pay attention and act. Delay not,

A matter of life or death (30:1–20)

for your own sake, O my God, because your city and your people are called by your name' (vv. 18–19).

The promise is a very wide and gracious one: 'If your outcasts are in the uttermost parts of heaven, from there the LORD your God will gather you … And he will make you more prosperous and numerous than your fathers' (vv. 4–5). The promise is given to true repentance: heart and soul repentance, a determination to return to the LORD and to obey his voice in all that he commands (v. 2). It is a promise that is still true and still relevant, and the call to repent and return to God is one that needs to be heard loud and clear today. Currid points out that 'outcasts' (v. 4) is actually in the singular. He comments: 'Perhaps this signifies that God's mercy and compassion will extend to each and every person who repents, no matter where he or she lives.'[1]

Loving God and God delighting (vv. 6–10)

At the heart of a real relationship with God is a recognition of our helplessness apart from his working within us: our problem is not merely disobedience in behaviour but sinfulness in the heart. So God promises that he will deal with this problem (v. 6). What God desired—and still desires—was the love of the hearts of his people. Obedience was to be the outflow of that love, not, as some people misunderstand it, a rigorous external obedience to law in order to gain the favour of a reluctant God. Those who truly turn to God do so in faith that he will hear, honour his promise and work within their hearts, and this is what he promises to do. As a result, Israel would again 'obey the voice of the LORD' (v. 8).

In turn, the LORD would make the people 'abundantly prosperous' (v. 9) and would grant renewed blessings (compare 28:1–6). And more than this: just as the LORD took delight in their fathers, so he would take delight in prospering them. The picture is one of great joy: God delighting over his people, granting them his choice blessings, and his people loving him with

Chapter 34

all their hearts and doing what he says. This is the same prospect that the New Testament sets before all Christians.

Life and good, death and evil (vv. 11–15)

At this point Moses turns to application. We might look at this passage as the climax of the whole book. It brings to a conclusion all that he has been saying to Israel so far, clearly showing them that he has set before them both life and good, and death and evil, and urging them to choose life.

First, however, he tells them that the message he has for them is not too difficult for them. It is not above them, as if someone had to ascend to heaven and bring it down to them; nor is it far away, as though someone had to make a long journey to bring it to them. It is plain and straightforward, near at hand, in their mouth and in their heart. In essence it is simply this: it is a call to love the LORD their God, to obey his voice and hold fast to him (v. 20). But the heart of it is to love the LORD (6:4–5). Loving God is the only proper, and therefore acceptable, response to his love: 'We love because he first loved us' (1 John 4:19). To respond to him in love and obedience means life and good. To reject his love, and to turn from him and his ways, means death and evil. Nothing could be more straightforward than this.

The apostle Paul takes up Moses' words in Romans 10:

Brothers, my heart's desire and prayer to God for them [the Jews] is that they may be saved. For I bear them witness that they have a zeal for God, but not according to knowledge. For, being ignorant of the righteousness that comes from God, and seeking to establish their own, they did not submit to God's righteousness. For Christ is the end of the law for righteousness to everyone who believes.

[v. 5]For Moses writes about the righteousness that is based on the law, that the person who does the commandments shall live by them. But the righteousness based on faith says, 'Do not say in your heart, "Who will ascend into heaven?"' (that is, to bring Christ

A matter of life or death (30:1–20)

down) or '"Who will descend into the abyss?"' (that is, to bring Christ up from the dead). But what does it say? 'The word is near you, in your mouth and in your heart' (that is, the word of faith that we proclaim); because, if you confess with your mouth that Jesus is Lord and believe in your heart that God raised him from the dead, you will be saved. For with the heart one believes and is justified, and with the mouth one confesses and is saved. For the Scripture says, 'Everyone who believes in him will not be put to shame.' For there is no distinction between Jew and Greek; for the same Lord is Lord of all, bestowing his riches on all who call on him. For 'everyone who calls on the name of the Lord will be saved' (vv. 1–13).

What is remarkable here is that in verse 5 Paul quotes from Leviticus 18:5, the whole verse reading: 'You shall therefore keep my statutes and my rules; if a person does them he shall live by them: I am the LORD.' He uses this to show how Moses described the righteousness that is based on the law, which is what the Israel of Paul's own day is trying to achieve, establishing their own righteousness (Romans 10:3). But then in verse 6 Paul quotes from Deuteronomy 30:12–14 in order to demonstrate 'the righteousness based on faith'. It is the same Moses who wrote both passages and both refer to the same 'commandments, statutes and rules' (Deuteronomy 30:16). Yet one is used to illustrate 'the righteousness that is based on the law', and the other, 'the righteousness based on faith'. How are we to understand this?

At first sight we might be tempted to think that Paul is simply using Moses' words from Deuteronomy and taking them out of their context so that he can apply them to Christ, but it is very doubtful that he would do this. The answer is much more likely to be along the following lines. In Deuteronomy, and explicitly in verses 10 to 15, Moses is laying the emphasis on love for God. But love for God arises from faith; from that faith which itself arises from seeing all that God has done in his love and the promises that are attached to his gracious acts. Moses, then, is calling for a response of faith and love. This is what Paul is speaking about, too; but he

Chapter 34

naturally bases his call on the fullest expression of God's love as seen in the gift, death and resurrection of Jesus Christ.

Abraham 'believed the LORD, and he counted it to him as righteousness' (Genesis 15:6), but that didn't mean that Abraham did not need to obey God in the future. Quite the reverse, for later God said to him, 'Walk before me, and be blameless' (Genesis 17:1) and of him, 'I have chosen him, that he may command his children and his household after him to keep the way of the LORD by doing righteousness and justice' (Genesis 18:19). So, as Moses makes clear in this passage in Deuteronomy, faith that issues in love will also issue in 'walking in [God's] ways' and 'keeping his commandments' (v. 16). There is all the difference in the world between trying to make oneself righteous before God by keeping the law, and, having been accounted righteous by faith, walking in the righteous way that the law prescribes out of love for God and thankfulness for his mercy.

The continuing choice (vv. 16–20)

So Moses has set before the people life and good, death and evil. There is a way of life, which starts with the response of faith and love, and leads to obedience and good—all the blessings God has for his people. And there is a way of death, the way that turns from God and what he has said, a way of evil that leads to disaster. Although Moses urges the people to 'choose life' (v. 19), there is no long-drawn-out appeal, no extended pressure put either on the emotions or on the will. Rather he relies on a clear, straightforward setting-out of the options. Once he has done that, the way Israel should choose is obvious. This is a valuable model for evangelism: a clear exposure of the options facing people so that they are in no doubt about what the Word of God says to them. This should not be done coldly, without a heartfelt plea to make the right choice, but it is the setting-out of the truth that makes the right choice obvious.

We might note that all these people were second-generation Israelites; all the older generation had died on the journey. So they had grown up as

A matter of life or death (30:1–20)

God's people and they took it for granted that they belonged to the LORD. Here, however, was an opportunity, a challenge even, for them to affirm from the heart their commitment to love him. Children brought up in a Christian home, or in a generally 'Christian' society, are in an analogous position and need to hear the same call to definite commitment. Moreover, there is an important sense in which this was a continuing choice that would always confront the people. There were going into Canaan. New temptations would arise, new challenges to their faith and obedience to the LORD. Would they remain faithful? If they put their hand to the plough, would there be no looking back (Luke 9:62)? The same questions arise for all Christians.

Study questions

1. Is the explanation given of Paul's use of verses 11 to 14 correct? Ought it to be modified? Can it be enlarged upon?
2. What can this chapter teach us about evangelistic preaching?
3. What do we learn about God from this chapter?

Note

1 **Currid,** *Deuteronomy,* p. 467.

Section 4:

Moses succeeded by Joshua (31:1–34:12)

At this point the book begins its conclusion with the appointment of Joshua to succeed Moses. This leads to Moses' song of warning, his final blessing and then his death.

Chapter 35

Moses looks to the future (31:1–29)

It is likely that all that is recorded from 5:1 onwards took place on the same day, with all Israel gathered before Moses. But now Moses has finished giving the law and setting blessings and curses before the people. He knows that his leadership is almost over, so he prepares to hand over to Joshua and to give his final warning and advice.

This chapter is not easy to divide up as there are several themes in it that are repeated in different places. For this reason, instead of looking at sections in the chapter, we shall look at the themes; this will mean looking at verses from different parts of the chapter together, and sometimes looking at verses more than once.

The LORD the real leader (vv. 1–8)

While it is true that the LORD called Moses to lead the people out of Egypt (Exodus 3:7–12), it is also true that the LORD himself was always the real leader, and Moses was simply his servant, doing his will and teaching what he gave to him. So, although Moses is going to tell the people that, when they cross the Jordan, 'Joshua will go over at your head' (v. 3), he is careful to begin by saying, 'The LORD your God himself will go over before you' (v. 3). Note the emphasis: 'The LORD your God *himself*'; and note the words 'before you'. He goes to prepare the way; the LORD goes first and the people follow where he leads. That way there is security, and the people can be sure they are going the right way.

But that is not all. Not only will the LORD go before, he will also grant his help and give victory, just as he has already done (vv. 4–5). This 'going before', however, does not mean that the LORD is not actually with them,

Exploring Deuteronomy **227**

dwelling among them, and going with them: 'It is the LORD your God who goes with you' (v. 6). And along with this goes one of the fundamental promises that God gives to his people: 'He will not leave you or forsake you' (v. 6). This promise is given also to Joshua (v. 8) and repeated by God himself in Joshua 1:5; it can be traced through the Bible and comes to explicit expression again in Hebrews 13:5, after which the author draws the following conclusion for all God's people: 'So we can confidently say, "The Lord is my helper; I will not fear; what can man do to me?"' (Hebrews 13:6), bringing together Psalm 118:6–7 and Psalm 56:4,11.

Moses began by saying, 'I am 120 years old today. I am no longer able to go out and come in.' Moses had been wonderfully—miraculously—strengthened by God (34:7), but it is not surprising that he was feeling his years and the burden of leading Israel, something which had often taxed his resources over the years (see, for example, Numbers 11:10–15). All God's human servants reach the point where they have to look to God to send someone else to take over and fulfil their ministry, or, at least, to enable the ministry to be fulfilled in other ways. It is not always easy to know when to retire, and some find it difficult to hand over responsibility to others, but God knows how to provide for his people; just as we serve in faith, so there are also times when we have to step back or step down in faith. Under-shepherds ought to know that the real Shepherd and Overseer of souls is the Lord Jesus Christ himself (1 Peter 2:25).

Joshua the human leader (vv. 7,8,14–15,23)

Having spoken to the people, Moses now calls Joshua to him and, 'in the sight of all Israel', appoints him to go with them 'into the land that the LORD has sworn … to give them, and … put them in possession of it' (v. 7). In this he was carrying out the words of the LORD in 3:28. Such a public appointment made it quite clear that Moses knew who would succeed him

Moses looks to the future (31:1–29)

and that, when the time came, as soon it would, Joshua would not be usurping the leader's place. Joshua, of course, had already proved himself as a military leader (Exodus 17:8–16); such a man would be needed as battles lay ahead. Moses encouraged Joshua by calling on him to be strong and courageous, qualities he would certainly need as he led the people to capture the land that God was giving them. And Moses repeated the promises of the LORD's presence that he had already given to the people as a whole: 'Do not fear or be dismayed' (v. 8).

But Joshua was also to have an explicit divine commissioning (vv. 14–15,23). At this point we cannot be sure of the chronology, and what is recorded here may have taken place on another occasion, although certainly not much later. Moses and Joshua were called to present themselves to the tent of meeting: an awe-inspiring event when the LORD appeared in a pillar of cloud. This would have been seen by all the people, who would then have recognized that what Moses had told them was actually of God's choosing: Joshua was the new leader. The actual commissioning by the LORD comes in verse 23: 'Be strong and courageous, for you shall bring the people of Israel into the land that I swore to give them. I will be with you.' So the LORD repeated words that Moses himself had used, and he would do so again in Joshua 1. It is interesting to note that, while Moses was very reluctant to respond to God's call (Exodus 3:11), no such thing is noted of Joshua. Moses was called unexpectedly to the task while a shepherd; Joshua served an apprenticeship with Moses (Exodus 24:13).

The law the practical leader (vv. 9–13,24–29)

If the LORD was the real leader, the One who was over his people, and Moses and Joshua served as human leaders under him, it was the law that served to guide the Israelites in their daily lives and worship. In practice they were governed by the law, and both Moses and Joshua were also under the law and committed to governing by it. To transpose this into

Chapter 35

New Testament terms, it is true that there are pastors and teachers in the churches, but they are all under Christ our Head, and they lead and guide the churches according to his Word. Jesus Christ rules as Lord in his churches by his Word and his Spirit: both together, and neither without the other.

Verse 9 tells us that Moses wrote 'this law'. This is probably a reference to the book of Deuteronomy, but it could be a reference to the whole of the Pentateuch, the first five books of the Old Testament. All these books follow on, one from the other, and the likelihood is that Moses wrote them at this time when the Israelites were camped in the plain of Moab. We do not know precisely how long they stayed there, but it must have been for some months while Gilead was being settled. It would seem unlikely that he could have written these books on the march, although he may well have kept notes as they travelled (see Numbers 33:2). Moreover, he would not have been in a position to write Genesis until after the Exodus, because his main upbringing was in the Egyptian court and he then spent forty years with Jethro, priest of Midian.

Having written the law, Moses was concerned to ensure that it was preserved and read to the people. So he entrusted it into the hands of the priests and all the elders of Israel. It looks as if in verse 9 the word 'priests' is being used in a wider sense to include all the Levites, for it was not the Aaronic priests who carried the ark (see Numbers 3:1–39). The law was to be read every seven years in the year of release (see 15:1–11; compare 15:12–18) at the Feast of Booths. This context is very important. It was the time when the people were showing kindness to the poor and needy in view of God's mercy to them when they were poor and enslaved, and when they also rejoiced in the harvest provision that the LORD had given to them (16:13–15). It was also one of the occasions when all Israel was to gather to the place where God had put his name. In this case, everyone was to be there, as they were before Moses on the plains of Moab: men, women, children, and the sojourner from every town.

Moses looks to the future (31:1–29)

The law was to be read before everyone, but it was especially important that it should be heard by the children who would be growing up in the land (v. 13). We do not know how many copies of the law there were. Certainly one copy was to be kept alongside the ark of the covenant (v. 26), and it might possibly be this one that would be read before the people. Fathers would remember parts of the law which would then be taught to their children, and the Levites would be responsible for teaching the law in the towns where they lived (Malachi 2:4–9), though we cannot assume either that every Levite or priest could read, or that there were copies of the law available for them all. In the time of Josiah, the Book of the Law seemed to have been unknown until Hilkiah discovered a copy in the temple (2 Kings 22:8–11). The purpose of all this was that everyone, including each rising generation, might 'hear and learn to fear the LORD your God, and be careful to do all the words of this law ... as long as you live in the land that you are going over Jordan to possess' (vv. 12–13). It is a tragedy that somewhere in Israel's history, and quite early on, it appears, this first became a mere formality and later was discontinued altogether.

The fatal inclination (vv. 16–22,24–29)

The tragedy was that Israel was always prone to rebelliousness. So the LORD said to Moses, 'I know what they are inclined to do even today, before I have brought them into the land that I swore to give' (v. 21). And Moses said to the Levites, though he had all Israel in mind, 'Behold, even today while I am yet alive with you, you have been rebellious against the LORD. How much more after my death!' (v. 27). Note the repetition in these verses of 'even today'. There was a fatal inclination on Israel's part to turn away from the LORD, and Moses had experienced their tendency to apostasy all too often. Such a tendency is in us all (Psalm 14:2–3; Isaiah 53:6a), and it is only regenerating grace that turns us to God and enables us to persevere. Even so, believers often pass through periods of backsliding

Chapter 35

and have many falls on the road to heaven, and we need to take care over our hearts and our attitudes.

In view of this, the LORD told Moses to write a song and teach it to the people of Israel. At one level we must look upon this as a strong warning to them, but at another level it would act as a witness against them when they had actually turned away (vv. 19–21). The reason why it would act like this is because songs, once learnt and sung, are not easily forgotten. So it had to be a song, one put into their mouths (v. 19), for then it would remain unforgotten even in the mouths of the children who would also learn it (vv. 21–22). We often underestimate the influence that songs have upon us, and we do not always appreciate the great value of teaching children good, Bible-based songs and hymns. Putting the Book of the Law alongside the ark of the covenant was also to serve as a witness against Israel (v. 26), so there would be two witnesses: the song and the law (compare 17:6). (Note that a third witness appears in verse 28.) The law functioned as a witness in the days of Josiah. There alongside the ark it was a permanent record of God's will for the people that would either guide them into right paths or condemn them. God's word always has that dual function. The ministry of the prophets was based firmly on the law. It was against its background that the prophets rebuked Israel, recalled them to repentance and pronounced judgement upon them.

Does what is said here in verses 16–18 and 26–29 mean that Israel was certain to turn away from God in days that were to come? Yes, it meant that they would, but exactly when they would do this was another matter (though God knew when, of course). All that Moses said, and the song he taught, might have helped restrain the next two generations from any great apostasy (see Judges 2:7–10). Do not forget 29:29. God's foreknowledge does not compel any to act sinfully; what he foreknows is the sin that people freely commit.

Moses looks to the future (31:1–29)

Study questions

1. What place should reading the Word of God have in Christian instruction and worship?
2. How can we help prevent a new generation turning away from the Lord?
3. What can older leaders and aspiring leaders learn from this passage?

Chapter 36

The song of Moses (31:30–32:52)

This chapter of Deuteronomy contains the song that God told Moses to write and teach to the people of Israel (31:19–22). As the instructions concerning the song are closely connected to those regarding the reading of the law every seven years (31:9–13), it is likely that the Song was intended to be sung at the same time as the law was read. In this way it would become a living memory to every generation. This song is written from the general perspective of what will take place in the future. However, it is not so much about what will happen, and certainly not about when any event will take place; rather it is about God, his judgement, grace and sovereignty. So it functions as a warning (vv. 46–47), and, if this is not heeded, as a witness against the people (31:19,21).

This song can be divided into a number of stanzas. A stanza is a unit similar to a paragraph in prose, one which has a completeness of thought, even though it will be related to what has gone before and what comes afterwards. We cannot use the word 'verse' for obvious reasons. It is not possible to be absolutely sure about where each division should come and I do not follow the ESV divisions in every detail. The song has echoes throughout the rest of Scripture, and it is the first place where God is described as a Rock (no fewer than six times) and also as the 'father' of his people (v. 6). It is very moving in its description of the relationship between the LORD and Israel, and it ends on a great note of promise and hope.

A good beginning (vv. 1–4)

Notice verse 2. The teaching of this song will be like rain: it refreshes, it

The song of Moses (31:30–32:52)

promotes growth and fruitfulness. It begins with God; his greatness and goodness (vv. 3–4). There is a tragic contrast between the character of God in verse 4 and that of the people in verse 5.

A sad accusation (vv. 5–9)

The form of the song follows the ancient pattern of covenant accusation, where a king would bring an accusation of rebellion against a vassal nation. Verse 6 is important. What had the LORD done for Israel that they should repay him by corrupt dealing? The last phrase of verse 5, 'a crooked and twisted generation', resurfaces in the New Testament (Matthew 17:17; Philippians 2:15). But there is not just accusation; there is also a call to remember what God had done for Israel in the past.

A wonderful settlement (vv. 10–14)

This stanza, following on from verse 9, explains God's tender goodness to Israel and the way in which he settled the people in a land that provided abundantly for every need. 'Desert land' may refer to the wilderness or even Egypt; Craigie points out that being in Egypt was also a desert experience for Israel.[1] The point is the gracious way in which the LORD preserved Israel and brought the people out of such dire circumstances and into the bounty described in verses 13 and 14. Note the tender imagery of verses 10 and 11, and also the emphasis of verse 12: the LORD alone did everything, and this should have elicited thankfulness and faithfulness.

A terrible response (vv. 15–18)

Instead, Jeshurun (this is a pet name, the special name by which parents might refer to their child) grew fat and kicked, like an unappreciative, rebellious teenager. He took God's good gifts, gorged himself on them and kicked God out of his life. Note the awful contrasts: 'he forsook *God who made him*'; he 'scoffed at *the Rock of his salvation*' (v. 15,

Chapter 36

emphasis added). In turning to 'strange gods' (v. 16), the Israelites 'sacrificed to demons' (v. 17), a point which Paul takes up in 1 Corinthians 10:20. The accusation of verse 18 is tragic and unanswerable.

A jealous reaction (vv. 19–22)

The word 'jealous' (v. 21) is often used in a bad sense, but it can refer to a proper reaction when someone in a relationship of love is provoked by the undeserved unfaithfulness and treachery of the other. God determines to hide himself from his people and show his favour to another people, a foolish nation that has not had the benefit of revelation and understanding. This is to provoke Israel, and ultimately lead to its return to him (see Romans 10:19; 11:11).

A severe chastisement (vv. 23–27)

Because of their sins, God will bring disasters upon the people. As we have seen already, while in one sense it is true that God does this, in another sense, those who turn from God bring disaster upon themselves. One of the tragic things is that, when enemies attack, or famine or epidemic strikes, everyone is involved (v. 25). However, God will not utterly destroy the people, not because they do not deserve this, but because if he allows their enemies to overwhelm them completely, those enemies will say, 'Our hand is triumphant, it was not the LORD who did all this' (v. 27).

A perceptive assessment (vv. 28–33)

What is so sad is that all this is quite unnecessary and would never have taken place if only Israel had had the sense to see what was happening. In the NIV, verse 29 begins with 'If only …', while the NKJV has 'Oh, that they were wise …'. In the past, God had granted them great victories: when they were few they overcame their enemies (see Numbers 21:24–25,31–35),

The song of Moses (31:30–32:52)

but now it is quite the reverse. Are they so blind that they can't see that the reason is that the Lord has given them up (v. 30)? Their enemies have no real Rock to protect them or give them victory; indeed, they belong to the same tribes and have the same resources as Sodom and Gomorrah, whom the Lord had overthrown centuries before. It is perhaps salutary for Christian people today to ask why it is we seem to be powerless and defeated so often when we have the God we have.

A merciful intervention (vv. 34–38)

Although God has to chastise his people, the day will come when he will deal with their enemies. He will have compassion on his people, but first he will allow them to reach the point when they have no power (v. 36). Then he will bring home to them the folly they have shown in turning to other gods who have not been able to do anything to help them (vv. 37,38). The first clause in verse 35 is quoted in Romans 12:19, and this and the first clause in verse 36 are quoted in Hebrews 10:30. They both contain principles that can be applied to God's people and also to those who are not. The Greek version of verse 36 used the word 'judge' and this is followed in Hebrews, but judging can have one of two outcomes, vindication or condemnation, and 'vindicate' is appropriate here because God is having 'compassion on his servants'.

The fundamental principle (vv. 39–43)

The fundamental principle comes in the opening verse: 'I, even I, am he, and there is no god beside me.' The previous section shows that God will act in a way that brings Israel to realize this fundamental truth that is set before them in this final stanza. It is striking that 'kill and … make alive' comes before 'wound and … heal'. Even when it looks as if the Lord has finished with his people, there is still hope that he will make alive if they return in true repentance. He is sovereign, and there is no hope in any other.

Chapter 36

Verses 41 and 42 use very vivid imagery taken from the battlefield. When God judges his enemies in human history, he generally uses the warlike nature of human beings to carry out his judgements. He did this with Israel when they entered Canaan and also when, for example, the Medes and Persians overthrew the Babylonian empire. Sin and violence is thus punished by sin and violence, God giving people up to the sinful instincts of their fallen natures.

The final verse of the song has a number of difficulties about it which are too technical to find a place here. This exposition follows the NIV translation: 'Rejoice, O nations, with his people, for he will avenge the blood of his servants; he will take vengeance on his enemies and make atonement for his land and people.' Paul quotes the beginning of this verse in Romans 15:10 to show that, through Israel, the Gentile nations would be blessed, a reality that began to come about largely through his ministry as the apostle to the nations. In the NIV translation of Deuteronomy 32:43, 'enemies' are distinguished from 'nations'. Enemies are all those who refuse to bow to King Jesus, not a particular nation or race or class. God avenges his servants (see Revelation 6:10; 19:2), and has indeed made atonement for his land and people; in this, all nations can have a share and rejoice with believing Israel.

Take to heart these words (vv. 44–47)

Moses and Joshua recited this song to Israel and Moses followed it up with a final warning, bringing to a close, in effect, everything that he had been saying to Israel in this book: 'It is no empty word for you, but your very life, and by this word you shall live long in the land that you are going over the Jordan to possess' (v. 47). Once more we have a tension between what the future appears to hold for the Israelites and the appeal to heed what has been said so that they might live long in the land. The people are accountable before God for the way in which they respond to what has been urged upon them.

The song of Moses (31:30–32:52)

Moses' death anticipated (vv. 48–52)

On that very day the LORD spoke to Moses. He was to go up on to Mount Nebo and view the land. He would see the land that God would give to Israel in accordance with his promise, but he would not enter himself: he was going to die there on the mountain. What an example this would be to Israel; what an incentive for them to be faithful to the LORD who had so graciously taken them into covenant with himself (see v. 51)!

Study questions

1. The song is poetry and therefore uses imagery extensively. Note down the images that seem to be most striking, and consider how they are used and what they signify.
2. God is God (v. 39). What different aspects of his character are brought before us in this song?
3. What are the most relevant lessons for us today from this song?

Note

1 **Peter Craigie,** *The Book of Deuteronomy* (New International Commentary on the Old Testament; Grand Rapids: Eerdmans, 1976), p. 380.

Chapter 37

The last words of Moses (33:1–29)

The last words of Moses are neither the law that he gave nor the song with its strong note of warning; rather he blesses the tribes of Israel. In doing so he follows the example of Jacob (also called Israel—Genesis 32:28), who blessed his sons from whom the tribes sprang (Genesis 49); thus Moses acts as a second father to the people (see Numbers 11:11–12).

The LORD the king (vv. 1–5)

Moses is called 'the man of God' in verse 1 not simply because he was a prophet who mediated revelation from God, but because he was a godly man: a God-centred man, a servant of God. He had cared for Israel for forty years, bearing with the people's faults and grumbles even when they turned on him. Now, before he dies and they turn to the daunting task of crossing the Jordan to take the land of promise, he blesses them, encouraging them and turning their thoughts to their great and gracious God.

There are some translational difficulties in this blessing (as there were in the song), but the main thrust of its opening is quite clear. Moses is setting before the people the majesty of the LORD who revealed his greatness and power at Sinai and entered into a covenant of love with them, becoming their sovereign LORD, their king (v. 5). We have to remember here, and throughout this blessing, what the people were immediately facing: there was warfare ahead and they needed an assurance of God's ability to help. We might wish there was no warfare, but sadly it is a constant in a fallen world, and if God cannot help in time of war, we are in a bad case. This

The last words of Moses (33:1–29)

does not mean that we can simply transfer God's promises to Israel to Britain or the Western world today: we certainly must not. But it does mean we have a God who is bigger than any earthly power, who is a refuge for all who trust him in times of bloodshed and violence, and who works out his purposes through and in spite of the evils and terrors of war. More importantly, Christians are in a war with spiritual powers of evil, with temptation and sin, and also for the hearts and minds of unconverted people; this is where our battle lies, one for which we need a vision of the almightiness of our God and King.

The blessing for Reuben and Judah (vv. 6–7)

Reuben comes first because he was the eldest son of Jacob. His blessing is basically a prayer for his preservation. Other translations give an opposite rendering to the second half of the verse (the NIV has 'nor his men be few'), which in the context seems more likely. It is probable that Judah comes next because this was the tribe that went in front when Israel was on the march (Numbers 10:14). They would be in the vanguard when it came to battle. Again, the blessing is a prayer: that God would hear the voice of the people of Judah as they cried for help when going out against the enemies that confronted them.

The blessing for Levi (vv. 8–11)

This blessing is much longer than most of the others—only that for Joseph matches it—because of the crucial function of this tribe in Israel. It was a tribe that, in the persons of Moses and Aaron, had been tested and reproached by the rest of the people (v. 8b), and one that had put zeal for God before natural ties when the people fell into idolatry at the time of the golden calf (Exodus 32:26–29).

It was through the Urim and Thummim that God gave guidance, so the first part of the blessing is a prayer for continued guidance through Levi. At the end of verse 9, Levi is set before the people as an example of covenant obedience. Verse 10 begins by speaking of the role of the Levites in teaching the law, and then that of the priests in offering sacrifices for the sins of the people. This shows that it was through the Levites that God would bless Israel, so a blessing upon Levi and all that his people did as a tribe would mean blessing for everyone. If the work of Levi was acceptable to God (v. 11), it would be good for Israel. The enemies of Levi were really enemies of the people—even if they were from Israel itself—hence the prayer that such opposition would be brought to nothing (v. 11b).

The blessing for Benjamin and Joseph (vv. 12–17)

Benjamin was particularly loved by his father, Jacob (Genesis 44:20), and the tribe was 'beloved of the LORD', though this should not be understood as being preferred to the other tribes but rather as an example of the love of the LORD for his people. All the beloved of the LORD dwell in safety; God surrounds them with his protection, his arms are around them and they rest on him.

Moses calls down a blessing on Joseph in the land to which Israel is going. This has been described already in glowing terms (8:7–10), and here comes another anticipation of the rich provision that the land of promise will give. Along with this goes 'the favour of him who dwells in the bush' (v. 16), a description of the LORD that Moses carried with him ever since that momentous day recounted in Exodus 3. It was when God revealed himself in the burning bush that the promise of deliverance from Egypt and entry into the land was given and Moses was called to lead the people. The last clause in verse 16 obviously refers to Joseph as a prince in Egypt. He brought deliverance to the family, and now that it has grown into a nation, his tribe will enter into the richness that God has for his people.

The picture of the majestic bull (v. 17) refers to the tribe entering the land and driving all its enemies before it. Of course, Joseph had two sons who formed two of the tribes of Israel, and they are mentioned at the end of the verse.

The last words of Moses (33:1–29)

The blessing for Zebulun, Issachar and Gad (vv. 18–21)

The first two of these tribes are mentioned together in verse 18. There is probably no special significance in the fact that Zebulun is to rejoice in his going out, and Issachar in his tents. Both are going to settle in the land and will have an abundance of what they need. Their blessing is that of rejoicing in God's goodness to them—as is ours, too.

Gad is pictured as a lion, again a reference to prowess in the war ahead. The end of verse 21 seems to mean that Gad executed justice upon the Canaanite tribes along with the rest of Israel.

The blessing for Dan, Naphtali and Asher (vv. 22–25)

Dan is also pictured as a lion, but a young lion. Naphtali will be greatly blessed of the LORD. The reference to 'the lake and the south' (v. 23) is not easy to understand. The lake would mean the Sea of Galilee, for Naphtali's portion of the land after the conquest was on the west side of that lake and extended northwards alongside the territory of Asher.

Asher means 'blessed' or 'happy', so this blessing is a play on words. 'Oil' (v. 24) refers to the general fruitfulness of the land; olive trees were found in abundance there. 'Bars [of] iron and bronze' means that in future days Asher would live securely in fortified towns, and the people would live out their days strengthened by the LORD. The last promise is often taken to mean that believers will be given the strength to fulfil all that God wants them to do. This is true, but strength isn't promised for us to do all that we want to do!

There is none like the God of Israel (vv. 26–29)

The blessing concludes with another great description of the LORD God. This, of course, is particularly relevant to Israel as they go into the land, and the very last sentence of this section speaks of Israel's enemies coming before them in submission. But we can look at this as a revelation of all that God is to all his people down to, and including, our own day. God is our

Chapter 37

helper, the One who comes winging his way through the sky to our aid. As the eternal God, he is always the dwelling place of those who trust him (Psalm 90:1); his strong arms are always there to bear us up.

As far as Israel was concerned, it was he who would thrust out the enemy so his people could live in safety, enjoying all the provision of a fruitful land. How happy would Israel be: saved by the LORD, their shield and sword! Yet, sadly, Israel would turn from him and lose the joy of those early days. All those who are in covenant with God, who know him and love him, are truly happy (Psalm 144:15). In our Christian pilgrimage, in our struggles and service, this God is 'our God forever and ever' (Psalm 48:14).

Study questions

1. Which parts of the blessings are prayers? Which parts are prophetic?
2. Why were Levi's duties so crucial for the spiritual health of Israel?
3. What promises here may we apply directly to ourselves?

Chapter 38

The death of Moses (34:1–12)

This is a sad, realistic but encouraging chapter. It is sad because it speaks of Moses' death and thereby reminds us of his sin. It is realistic: all God's servants die and are replaced by others in due time. It is encouraging: God is always the same; his people, and those who lead and serve them, are always in his hands.

This chapter must have been added after Moses' death. It is likely that verses 10 to 12 were either added or expanded quite some time afterwards, when Israel had been in the land for a good period.

Moses views the land (vv. 1–4)

Moses went up to Mount Nebo and the LORD showed him all the land, as he had said he would (3:23–27). This was because of Moses' sin at Meribah (Numbers 20:2–13). It is worth remembering that this incident took place very near the end of his life and ministry. It has to be 'Watch and pray' right up to the end. As a leader, he failed to hallow the LORD before the people. This was a tragic failure, for if he did not reverence God, how could he expect the people to do so? It is all too easy for Christian leaders to undermine their own ministries by ungodly attitudes, actions or words. His sin, of course, was pardoned, but it had consequences that he had to bear (3:23–25).

But now, with sight undimmed (v. 7), he was able to see all the land set out before him. He could survey its length and breadth. Moses might have failed, but God was going to keep his promise: there was the good land stretching out into the distance. It is good to survey the promises of God, the blessings he has already granted us and the hope he has set before us. Yes, God is good, in spite of our failures and unworthiness, and it is right to count our blessings and give thanks for his mercies.

Chapter 38

Moses dies in Moab (vv. 5–8)

From one point of view it does not matter where we die, but Moses felt very deeply the fact that he was not going to die in, nor would be buried in, the land of promise, but the land of Moab. The words 'Moses the servant of the LORD' give an added poignancy to this, though at the same time they are a recognition of his submission to God and the great task he performed in bringing Israel out of Egypt, serving the LORD and the people faithfully for forty years. It was the LORD who buried Moses, and he is the only one to know exactly where this was. Perhaps if Moses' burial site had been known, the people would have turned it into a shrine, which could have hindered their allegiance to Joshua and, in time, meant that they focused more on Moses than on the LORD as the one who had brought them out of Egypt.

Moses was given an exceptionally long life and also experienced the fulfilment of 33:25: 'As your days, so shall your strength be.' This is a reminder also of Philippians 4:13: 'I can do all things through him who strengthens me.' Even Moses, however, had to learn the importance of not taking on more than he could bear and of delegating responsibility to others (Exodus 18:13–27). Not every servant of God is given such exceptional vigour. Normally, as we get older we can expect our bodily powers to wane (Ecclesiastes 12:1–8). This is not a sign of lack of faith. We must remember that what we are is much more important than what we do. The greatest commandment is to love God, and even when memory has gone and a Christian is weak in body and mind, he or she is still in the hands of a loving God (Deuteronomy 33:27a).

The tears of the people for Moses (v. 8) were no doubt genuine. It is a sad fact of experience that it is often not until someone dies that his or her real worth is appreciated, and many would be astonished if they heard the tributes paid to them. The people of Israel often grumbled about Moses, but when he died they realized how great their loss was. Thirty days of mourning seems excessive to us, but it is a mark of the respect felt for

The death of Moses (34:1–12)

Moses and all that he did for Israel. Our mourning often seems unnecessarily perfunctory.

Moses succeeded by Joshua (vv. 9–12)

Moses had already prepared the way for his successor, so Joshua became the leader, acknowledged by everyone. Joshua was prepared for leadership in another way as well: he was 'full of the spirit of wisdom' (v. 9), a quality he would certainly need. This, of course, was what Solomon asked the LORD to give him on becoming king (1 Kings 3:5–9). There is no doubt that Christian wisdom is something very much needed in the churches today (see also 1 Chronicles 12:32). Joshua's wisdom came through Moses laying his hands on him. The gift of wisdom came from God, but the laying-on of hands signified it.

The last few verses form a brief obituary for Moses. The comment in verse 10, 'There has not arisen a prophet since in Israel like Moses', is a reflection on 18:15. We will take this up below, but first we can note how Moses' uniqueness is emphasized in these last verses. He was unique as a prophet, especially in the intimacy he knew with the LORD (v. 10b), experienced particularly during his time on Mount Sinai (see Exodus 34:29–35). In Numbers 12:8 God says of Moses, 'With him I speak mouth to mouth, clearly, and not in riddles, and he beholds the form of the LORD.' This intimacy with the LORD included a measure of sight, and also a direct form of prophecy, 'mouth to mouth', speaking precisely and clearly what God had given him to say. The law of Moses is really the law of God.

And there was 'none like him for all the signs and the wonders that the LORD sent him to do' (v. 11), both in Egypt and for Israel. God's great act of redemption was marked by special miracles, just as the greater act of redemption by Jesus Christ would be. Throughout the whole of the Old Testament era, although there were some miracles, particularly during the ministries of Elijah and Elisha and at the time of the exile, there was nothing on the scale of the great acts of God through Moses.

Chapter 38

So Moses' life had come to an end. Israel had to face Canaan with a new leader. The future contained a new challenge, but there was still the challenge of faithfulness to the covenant. If they were faithful in the latter, they could face the former with confidence.

But now there has arisen a prophet like Moses, only even greater: One who was always face to face with God (John 1:1) and who spoke the word of God in truth; One who also died, but who rose again and lives for ever. How we face the challenge of the future depends on our faithfulness to him, Jesus Christ our Lord.

Study questions
1. What can we learn from the life of Moses?
2. In what ways was Joshua prepared for taking over from Moses?
3. In what ways does Moses point us to the Lord Jesus Christ?

Select bibliography

The most useful and straightforward books for the general reader are listed first and the more technical and specialized later. I have found the two books marked with an asterisk particularly helpful.

***Wright, Christopher,** *Deuteronomy* (New International Biblical Commentary; Peabody, MA: Hendrickson Publishers/Paternoster Press, 1996)
Harman, Allan, *Deuteronomy* (Focus on the Bible; Tain: Christian Focus Publications, 2001)
Currid, John, *Deuteronomy* (Darlington: Evangelical Press, 2006)
Merrill, Eugene, *Deuteronomy* (The New American Commentary; Nashville, TN: Broadman and Holman Publishers, 1994)
***Craigie, Peter,** *The Book of Deuteronomy* (New International Commentary on the Old Testament; Grand Rapids, MI: Eerdmans, 1976)
Millar, J. Gary, *Now Choose Life: Theology and Ethics in Deuteronomy* (New Studies in Biblical Theology; Leicester: Apollos, 1998)

About Day One:

Day One's threefold commitment:

- To be faithful to the Bible, God's inerrant, infallible Word;
- To be relevant to our modern generation;
- To be excellent in our publication standards.

I continue to be thankful for the publications of Day One. They are biblical; they have sound theology; and they are relative to the issues at hand. The material is condensed and manageable while, at the same time, being complete—a challenging balance to find. We are happy in our ministry to make use of these excellent publications.

JOHN MACARTHUR, PASTOR-TEACHER, GRACE COMMUNITY CHURCH, CALIFORNIA

It is a great encouragement to see Day One making such excellent progress. Their publications are always biblical, accessible and attractively produced, with no compromise on quality. Long may their progress continue and increase!

JOHN BLANCHARD, AUTHOR, EVANGELIST AND APOLOGIST

Visit our website for more information and to request a free catalogue of our books.

www.dayone.co.uk

Other books from Day One

Exploring Joshua

COLIN N PECKHAM

PAPERBACK, 240 PAGES

ISBN 978-1-846250-93-4

Joshua—what a book! It is a necessary bridge between the Law of Moses and the rest of Israel's history. It magnifies the faithfulness and power of God. It runs from the epic crossing of the Jordan to the final conquest of the land, this being seen as a vivid and graphic picture of claiming our rich inheritance in Christ. It shows that they could only get into the land of victory and fullness through crossing Jordan, the 'river of death', this being a picture of our dying with Christ and rising with him to a new and abundant resurrection life. It reveals the reasons for their failures and shows obedience and faith to be the basis for their victories.

Joshua is a very important book in the canon of Scripture and this devotional commentary merits your attention. It will challenge you with penetrating insights into Scripture and into your own heart. That in essence is its objective—to confront men and women with the necessity of integrity, purity and victory through obedience and faith.

Rev. Dr Colin Neil Peckham was born in South Africa where he had ten years of evangelistic ministry and youth work before entering Bible College in Cape Town. He then emigrated to Great Britain and was principal of the Faith Mission Bible College. As principal emeritus he now has an extensive preaching ministry in Britain and abroad and has authored several books.

If you are looking for a fast moving, down-to-earth and challenging insight into Joshua, then this is it. Colin Peckham presents a grasp of the book that is easy to take in, particularly the long historical chapters, and manages at the same time to show how the book's message is just as vital for today as it has always been. Buy it, study it and act upon it.
—*Rev. Dr A M Roger, Principal, The Faith Mission Bible College, Edinburgh*

Other books from Day One

Exploring Nahum and Obadiah

TIM SHENTON

PAPERBACK, 112 PAGES

ISBN 978-1-846250-87-3

Nahum: Approximately one hundred years after Jonah preached to the citizens of Nineveh to turn 'from their evil ways' and escape imminent judgement, God commissioned Nahum to prophesy the city's complete destruction. At the time of his 'burden', the Assyrian Empire was both strong and wealthy, yet Nahum prophesied that soon the entire kingdom would be crushed forever under the power of God's wrath.

Obadiah: Obadiah's prophecy unveils God's sovereignty over all nations and events, and gives an example of his direct intervention in the political and military affairs of human history. The Sovereign LORD does as he pleases with the powers of heaven and the peoples of the earth. No one can hold back his hand or say to him: 'What have you done?'

Both prophecies are a revelation of God's character and his moral government of the world—a revelation that contains a message of hope, comfort and encouragement for every Christian: 'THE LORD REIGNS FOR EVER'! It matters not how many nations oppose his rule or oppress his people; it makes no difference how many spiritual forces of evil ally themselves for his dethronement, for the Lord's purposes will prevail. All that he has promised will be fulfilled. He is in control. His dominion is an eternal dominion.

Tim Shenton takes us to the most neglected of the Old Testament prophecies, Nahum and Obadiah, and gives us a clear verse-by-verse explanation. Better yet, he consistently shows these little prophecies to have ongoing significance. ... This is a book that provides both understanding of difficult books and comfort for difficult times—and that certainly makes it well worth reading!
ROGER ELLSWORTH

Other books from Day One

Exploring Habakkuk

TIM SHENTON

96PP, PAPERBACK

ISBN 978-1-84625-055-2

Why does a righteous and sovereign God tolerate wrongdoing? How are the divine attributes reconciled with the triumph of the godless? Why do the wicked prosper and rule over the righteous? Why does God raise up 'ruthless and impetuous' nations to execute judgement on his own people? These are some of the questions that perplexed Habakkuk, challenged his faith and caused him to question God's government of the world. These are some of the questions that still perplex Christians today. Tim Shenton helpfully addresses these points in a clear and substantial exposition of the text of Habakkuk.

Tim Shenton is the Head Teacher of St Martin's School and an elder at Lansdowne Baptist Church, Bournemouth. He has written a number of other books, including daily readings for younger readers, a study on revival and is engaged in several writing projects. He and his wife, Pauline, have two daughters.

Habakkuk is the record of a perplexed prophet, unable to comprehend the depth of divine purpose in his day. Written as a dialogue between himself and God, and concluding with a profound expression of worship, this brief book is of great relevance to thoughtful Christians today. We contemplate it and understand the seer's perplexity. Now, to make the book even more accessible to the modern reader, Tim Shenton has provided us with a very helpful commentary on the writings of this man of God. Careful and clear, it is an excellent aid for every believer who would know and love the Lord. Take it and read. And then, bow before the Lord in worship.

—*JAMES RENIHAN, DEAN, PROFESSOR OF HISTORICAL THEOLOGY AT WESTMINSTER SEMINARY, INSTITUTE OF REFORMED BAPTIST STUDIES, ESCONDIDO, CALIFORNIA*

Other books from Day One

Exploring Haggai

TIM SHENTON

PAPERBACK, 80 PAGES

ISBN 978-1-846250-86-6

A selfish disregard for the purpose of God is all too common among Christian people who live in 'panelled houses' while God's house 'remains a ruin'. As in the days of Haggai, excuses for apathy are shamelessly voiced, blind eyes are turned to the judgements of God, and defiled hearts sink into unfaithfulness. And yet the LORD Almighty remains faithful to his people and true to his word. Through repeated trials he calls the backslider to repentance, with timely encouragements and gracious promises he strengthens the downhearted, and for his own glory he transforms the sins of neglect and ignorance into the servants of his purpose.

With urgency the prophet condemns the wickedness of waiting for the 'right' time when duty calls today, and of lamenting the past—desiring an experience today similar to that of yesterday. And he warns of the grave peril of expecting immediate material results. It is a message that must be taken seriously by the twenty-first century church.

The book of Haggai presents a powerful challenge and provides great encouragement for the church in the twenty-first century. Tim Shenton's lucid exposition of this dynamic book gets to the heart of the prophet's message by carefully explaining and skilfully applying the text. Although this is a short commentary, the author's meticulous research had enabled him to enlighten us with invaluable background information which will sharpen our understanding of its urgency and passion.

SIMON J ROBINSON, SENIOR PASTOR, WALTON EVANGELICAL CHURCH, CHESTERFIELD, ENGLAND